CAUCASIAN PRAYER RUGS

Published 1998 by Laurence King
Publishing in association with
Hali Publications Limited

Laurence King Publishing is an imprint
of Calmann & King Ltd
71 Great Russell Street
London WC1B 3BN

Hali Publications are the publishers
of HALI, *The International Magazine
of Antique Carpet and Textile Art*
St Giles House
50 Poland Street
London W1V 4AX

Text copyright © 1998 Ralph Kaffel
Appendix essay on Design and
Symbolism copyright © 1998
Jim Dixon

A catalogue record for this book is
available from the British Library.

ISBN 1 85699 117 9

Designed by Mark Vernon-Jones
Edited by Christine Davis
Special photography by Don Tuttle
Dixon essay edited by Sacha Trone
Line drawings by Mike Wilson
Map artwork by Maureen Verity
Digital cartography by James Anderson
Index by Vicki Robinson

Printed in Belgium

HALI

Laurence King in association with HALI

CAUCASIAN

PRAYER

RALPH KAFFEL # RUGS

CONTENTS

Caucasian Prayer Rugs is the first in a planned series of oriental carpet and textile art books produced by Laurence King Publishing in association with the publishers of *Hali: The International Magazine of Antique Carpet and Textile Art*. These include John Wertime's *Sumak Bags of Northwest Persia and Transcaucasia*, published in tandem with this title in 1998, as well as proposed works on Bijar, Afshar and Beshir rugs.

I use the term 'series' with some reservations, as it can imply rigid uniformity. The shared aim of all the volumes is to offer the reader the best and most beautiful of collectable antique oriental weaving in a manner that is at the same time useful and informative for those with an established interest in the field, and accessible and inspirational to newcomers. The expert authors – who include professional scholars, knowledgeable amateurs, private collectors and commercial dealers – will, inevitably and desirably, employ a great diversity of individual approaches to their subjects. The books are illustrated with textile art of the utmost quality, much of which has been specially photographed to the highest professional standards.

Caucasian prayer rugs of the nineteenth century, as indeed all good quality weavings of the period from the villages of Transcaucasia, are widely collected. Their charm lies in the immediate 'eye' appeal of their boldly colourful designs, in their size and format (they can easily be used as mural hangings), and not least in the indefinable mystique of art objects that were initially intended, if not always used, for prayer. Although the best of them can command very high prices, most are not prohibitively expensive and fall within the financial compass of 'ordinary' collectors.

Ralph Kaffel is a collector of village and tribal rugs from the most significant weaving areas of the Orient. As an author he is unquestionably an amateur in the best sense of the word – one who loves his subject with passion and commitment, an individual for whom oriental carpets are an enthusiastically pursued, even all-consuming, hobby, but not a livelihood. He brings to his subject the benefits of a varied and interesting background, an extremely successful career in another field, and, above all, good taste in this fascinating area of the decorative arts.

Ralph and his wife Linda have been collecting oriental rugs since 1979. Linda is a full partner in this activity. Their 'hobby' began in a way that is almost a cliché in the rug world – buying rugs at auction to furnish the house. But after a couple of bad experiences, they determined to learn much more about what they were doing, so in a typically clear-headed manner, Ralph's picture 'index' or 'database' was begun to track the types in which they were most likely to be interested. The index now includes over 10,000 entries and is the basis for most of the comparative 'statistical' information which lies at the heart of Ralph's approach as the author of *Caucasian Prayer Rugs*. The 'Kaffel Index' is also invaluable in his largely unacknowledged role as one of the main contributors to *Hali*'s popular and authoritative bi-monthly analysis of the oriental rug market at auction, 'Auction Price Guide'.

The Caucasian prayer rugs in this book come from top private collections in Europe and North America. Many are unpublished; just one is from a museum, the Victoria & Albert Museum in London. The Kaffels' own collection is broadly focused. Ralph and Linda buy what appeals to them, viewing rugs as 'art', rather than following the 'postage stamp' method – one of every known type – in the cultural regions to which their taste inclines. They have a wide variety of Turkish and Caucasian village rugs; northwest Persian sumakh bags; and south Persian, Baluch and Turkmen tribal and village rugs and trappings.

I still look forward to the day when I will be able to see the collection in its entirety, but judged by those pieces of all types that I know from elsewhere, and those Caucasian prayer rugs in this book, it surely ranks among the finest of the present generation. As collectors of oriental rugs, the Kaffels must take their place among the best informed, least dogmatic and most level-headed of their peers. I trust that readers will find that all these qualities, plus the critical element of abundant good taste, are reflected here.

Daniel Shaffer, Editor, *Hali*

FOREWORD

The eighteenth-century philosopher David Hume wrote that 'beauty in things exists in the mind that contemplates them' (essay, 'Of the Standard of Taste', 1757). In 1878, Margaret Wolfe Hungerford paraphrased the quotation as 'beauty is in the eye of the beholder'. Their sentiments are particularly apposite for oriental rugs. While all of us in the 'rug world' would agree that antique oriental rugs and textiles surely rank among humankind's most beautiful creations, there exists a wide and healthy divergence of opinion about which particular weavings are the most attractive, important and worthwhile. This difference of opinion is a major element in making rug collecting and rug studies such a fascinating exercise in exploration, investigation and rediscovery.

As far as scholarship is concerned, the study of rugs is a relatively young discipline. The first rug book was published in 1877.[1] Of the 52 rug books published between 1877 and 1926, only 12 were considered 'important' by eminent rug scholars Walter Denny and Daniel Walker, writing as recently as 1988.[2] Even today, with hundreds of rug books in print, rug studies amount to an amalgamation of historical fact, theory, guesswork, myth, statistics and deductive reasoning. No expert is immune from error. By way of example, the latest *Hali* magazine (at the time of writing) reports on major errors in the classification and dating of 'Salting' carpets, committed by no less than Kurt Erdmann, May Beattie and Charles Grant Ellis.[3] At the Eighth International Conference on Oriental Carpets (ICOC) in Philadelphia (November 1996), James Allen and Craig Carriere proposed a revolutionary revision in the dating of Turkoman weavings. Just a few years ago, antique Kaitag embroideries were unknown in the West, and pre-1800 Caucasian village rugs were routinely attributed to Anatolia. In such a context, I would not be at all surprised if new discoveries might cause a reassessment of our ideas about Caucasian prayer rugs in the not too distant future.

Early travel and other literature contains many references to the production of wool, dyes, carpets and other weavings in the Caucasus.[4] Actual examples of early Caucasian pile weaving begin with the fabled 'Dragon' carpets, which were produced from the sixteenth to the eighteenth centuries in Armenia, Karabagh and Azerbaijan during the Persian occupation. These carpets, incorporating Persian and Chinese motifs, were commissioned pieces made in commercial workshops. They were exported to mosques, palaces and the homes of the khans, and benefited from the patronage of the Persian ruler, Shah Abbas. Production and export of these pieces, as well as the later 'Blossom' and 'Shield' carpets, continued in the eighteenth century during the Turkish occupation of parts of the Caucasus. A disproportionate number of Dragon rugs have survived in Turkish mosques and museums, their longevity due in part to their unique structural characteristics and because many were stored rather than used.

But what of village pieces? Pre-1800 village weavings from the Caucasus are extremely scarce, rarer even than their prized Anatolian counterparts. While they were probably produced in great numbers, they were woven solely for personal use and most have disappeared due to the ravages of use over time. The Caucasus also suffered from repressive trade policies and high inventory taxes during the Russian governance early in the nineteenth century, and consequently Caucasian woven products could not compete as export items with Persian or Turkish production. In fact, it was not until very late in the nineteenth century that Europe 'discovered' Caucasian rugs.

Prayer rugs are mentioned in various Persian and Turkish writings as early as the ninth century. A thirteenth-century Seljuk prayer rug is at the Museum of Turkish and Islamic Art in Istanbul. There are known examples of fifteenth- and sixteenth-century Turkish prayer rugs as well as a relatively large number of seventeenth- and eighteenth-century pieces. But there are almost no documented early (pre-1800) Caucasian prayer rugs. Some writers have suggested that they are a nineteenth-century phenomenon, but that speculation lacks credibility. Surely, such a diverse variety of pieces could not have been created spontaneously and simultaneously throughout the region, without the benefit of a systematic process of design evolution? (Empirical evidence in support of either argument, however, is scarce.) Prayer rugs were woven for a specific purpose; they had to be

PREFACE

small, personal and portable, and were subjected to intense use, as Muslims pray five times daily. Under such circumstances, survival of 200-year-old pieces would have been highly unlikely. Although pre-1950 publications have tended to assign improbably early dates to Caucasian prayer rugs, contemporary literature has been much more conservative.

As a matter of personal taste and preference, I consider antique Caucasian prayer rugs to be among the most beautiful of all oriental carpets. As special-purpose weavings that were intended to be important items of social and religious significance, great care was lavished on their creation. The best examples possess an unrivalled grace, dignity and quiet beauty. Many of these were specially commissioned pieces woven by master weavers using the best available materials, with quality being a priority over cost.

This book illustrates in colour and comments on 97 superb examples from all of the rug-weaving areas of the Caucasus. Some pieces, from private collections, are published for the first time. Other pieces, previously published, are included herein on the basis of merit, uniqueness, rarity and importance. My pictorial database of over 2,000 Caucasian prayer rugs has been a key element in the selection process. Specific rug types from each weaving area are described, and their design and structural characteristics analysed. The relative rarity of the various types is also discussed.

Caucasian prayer rugs have now been recognized as great works of art, and are steadily gaining popularity in the rug collecting community. It is hoped that this book will assist in the continuation of this process and in the promotion and appreciation of this unique art form.

A number of friends and fellow collectors have been of great help to me during this project. Special thanks are due to Alan Marcuson for suggesting the concept and to Danny Shaffer of *Hali* magazine and Mary Scott of Laurence King Publishing for seeing this project to its conclusion; to Jim Dixon, for allowing 17 of his prayer rugs to be included and for his valuable contribution of the essay on design and symbolism (Appendix A), which greatly enhances our understanding of rug design. To Herbert Exner, for his unfailing cooperation and for permission to include 12 of his rugs. To Berdj Achdjian, for his pieces and for his considerable help and wisdom. To Peter Bausback, Jim Blackmon, Jim Burns, Jackie Coulter (Sotheby's London), Gil and Hillary Dumas, John Eskenazi, the Hali Archive, Eberhart Herrmann, Wells Klein, Jo Kris (Skinner's), Hans-Jürgen Krausse, Alberto Levi, Detlef and Christa Maltzahn (Rippon & Boswell), Al Mazzie, Richard Mull, Mary Jo Otsea (Sotheby's New York), Michael Rothberg, Rosalie and Mitchell Rudnick, Judy Smith, Raoul Tschebull, the Victoria and Albert Museum, Ignazio Vok and Ross Winter, all of whose images enrich this book. To Don Tuttle, Herbert Exner and all of the photographers. To Michael Craycraft, who placed his vast library of antique and rare travel books at my disposal. To Peter Stone for permission to reprint excerpts from his book, *Rugs of the Caucasus: Structure and Design*. To Ron O'Callaghan for images from the *Oriental Rug Review* archives. To Christine Davis, my editor extraordinaire. To Professor George Hewitt and Robert Chenciner for their valuable advice and suggestions, and to Jennifer Wearden for editing the technical analyses of the plates. To Mark Vernon-Jones for his excellent book design. To the Fantasy Records art department, especially Gilles Margerin for his computer drawings and to Steve Maruta for photography. To Tara Lochen, Rikka Arnold, Peggy Van Steenhuyse and Fredrica Drotos of the Fantasy production and legal departments for typing the manuscript and learning a whole new language in the process. And finally a great big thanks to Linda Kaffel, my wife and fellow collector, for all her help, patience and forbearance, and for sharing with me a love for rugs and an enthusiasm for this project.

I

HISTORY OF THE REGION The Caucasus (Caucasia, or Kavkaz in Russian) has been called the cradle of mankind. In ancient times it was known as the end of the world,[1] and early Arab writers called it Yubel-al-Suni ('Mountain of Languages').[2] Isolated by its geography and topography, it has from prehistoric times been a refuge and home to many diverse, wandering tribes, seeking freedom and independence. Herodotus, the so-called father of history, wrote in the fifth century BC of the 'many and every sort of nation the Caucasus contains within itself, most of them living from the fruit of wild trees.' (He goes on to describe how people dyed their woollen clothes and paint them with 'figures of animals' that 'grow old with the wool'.[3])

Few places on earth have had a history as turbulent as the Caucasus. It has been invaded, colonized and occupied by Scythians, Greeks, Romans, Byzantines, Huns, Khazars, Seljuks, Arabs, Mongols, Tartars, Turkomans, Persians, Turks and Russians. An ancient region, formed some 1,300 million years ago, it occupies the area between the Black Sea and the Caspian Sea. The Caucasus mountain range runs from the northwest to the southeast, diagonally dividing the region. These mountains are loftier than the Alps, the highest peak being Mount Elbrus at 5,642 metres (18,481 feet). Russia is to the north, Turkey and Iran to the south. (The area stretching from the Turkish and Iranian border to the Greater Caucasus mountains is often referred to as Transcaucasia.)

A wealth of myths and legends surround the region. In Greek mythology, Jason and the Argonauts sailed to Colchis (on the eastern shore of the Black Sea) in search of the Golden Fleece. Part of Colchis was later known as Mingrelia, which today is a part of Georgia. (Mingrelian sheep are still known as Colchian sheep.[4]) The capital of Mingrelia was Zugdidi, and further east the capital of the west Georgian province of Imereti is Kutais (Kutaisi); some Caucasian rugs were called Kutais rugs well into this century (see caption to plate 86). According to another Greek legend, Prometheus, one of the Titans, was chained to a rock in the Caucasus as punishment for stealing fire. The Abkhasians

BACKGROUND

(Abkhazians), the world's 'longest living people',[5] claim they are descended from him.[6] Armenians and Georgians, meanwhile, claim descent from Noah's great-grandchildren, Haik and Karthlos. They are the only Caucasian peoples with a written history, and a proud history it is too. In the ninth century BC, the ancient kingdom of Urartu (roughly corresponding to historical Greater Armenia) rivalled Assyria as the most powerful state in the Middle East.

The Greeks were the first colonizers of the Caucasus, settling on the eastern shore of the Black Sea in the seventh century BC. The Persians conquered Armenia in 521 BC and held sway there for almost a century. It was during this time that the Pazyryk, the world's oldest known pile carpet, would have been made. Carbon-dated to 500 BC, the Pazyryk was discovered in 1949 in a Scythian tomb in Siberia, still in a good state of preservation.[7] In the fourth century BC Alexander the Great's all-conquering army found its way to Armenia and Georgia and for 800 years the region was ruled by Rome and Byzantium. In about AD 500 the Khazars from Central Asia invaded, conquering northern Caucasia. They were supplanted in the seventh century by Arab invaders; Islam was soon widely adopted, except in the Christian enclaves of Georgia and Armenia. In the tenth century the Khazars reconquered the northeast Caucasus. Predominantly of Turkic origin, the Khazars had converted to Judaism in AD 740 and the Khazar empire became the largest ever Jewish state. At the peak of its power, Khazaria encompassed large tracts of the Caucasus, stretching from Kiev in the northwest to Sarkel and Astrakhan in the northeast, Crimea in the southwest, and Derbent in the southeast. There are today Mountain Jews (Tats) in Daghestan. The eleventh century saw a Seljuk invasion of the Caucasus. Georgia was nevertheless a dominant regional military power during the reign of Queen Tamar (Tamara) (1184–1213),[8] occupying Azerbaijan and launching successful military forays into Persia.

In 1226 the Mongols and other Tartar tribes first appeared in the Caucasus and eventually conquered Azerbaijan, Armenia and Georgia. Baku, Kuba, Shirvan and Genje became independent khanates at this time. In the late fourteenth century the entire Caucasus region was ruled by Timur-i-Lang (Tamerlane), a Mongol chieftain from Samarkand whose empire, at its height, stretched from India to Asia Minor including Persia and Turkey.[9] After the death of Timur in 1405, Georgia was on its knees and split into a number of kingdoms and principalities. From the early sixteenth century influence over the Caucasus passed back and forth between Turkey and Persia, eventually causing Christian Georgia to look to Holy Russia for protection.

The Russian invasion started in 1722, when Peter the Great captured Derbent and Baku from Persia. Central and eastern Georgia were annexed by Russia in 1801, and the southern and southeastern khanates were ceded to Russia by Persia by the Treaty of Tiflis in 1814. The Russians fought intermittently with Turkey and Persia and the various tribes of the northern Caucasus for 140 years.

The Daghestani tribes were first led by Kazi Mullah, an Avar religious leader killed fighting the Russians in 1832. His place was taken by Hamza Bek, and, after his assassination in 1834, by another Avar, Shamyl, known as the 'Lion of Daghestan', who led a relentless *jihad* (holy war) against the Russians until he was defeated and captured in 1859.[10] This defeat led to a concentration of efforts by the northwestern Caucasian resistance, the collapse of which in 1864 caused an exodus of several hundred thousand Circassians and other tribes from the Caucasus to Ottoman lands. Chechenia, in the centre of the northern Caucasus and where Shamyl had found strong support, remained – albeit turbulently – under Russian control until the break-up of the Soviet Union in 1991.

The history of the Caucasus, with its wars, expulsions, invasions and migrations, has created a population that is very ethnically diverse. The main groups can be identified as follows:[11] The Armenians, who are Christian (Armenian Gregorian), are concentrated in the south-central region, west of Lake Sevan (roughly between the village of Fachralo and the city of Erivan) and in south Karabagh. The Azeri Turks or Azerbaijanis, who are mostly Shia Muslims, occupy almost the entire eastern Caucasus, from Derbent to Lenkoran along the Caspian Sea and inland as far as Genje and Nakhichevan (administratively part of Azerbaijan). A large part of Azerbaijani territory lies in northern Iran. The mountaineers of Northern Caucasia include the numerous tribes of Daghestan inland

1 The south side of Mount Elbrus, the highest mountain in the Caucasus, with the Asan glacier in the foreground. (Published in *Asia* by Augustus H. Keane, London 1882.)
II Mount Ararat, the 'Grand or Sublime Mountain' to the Armenians, the 'Steep Mountain' to the Turks and 'Noah's Mount' to the Persians. (Published in *Asia* by Augustus H. Keane.)

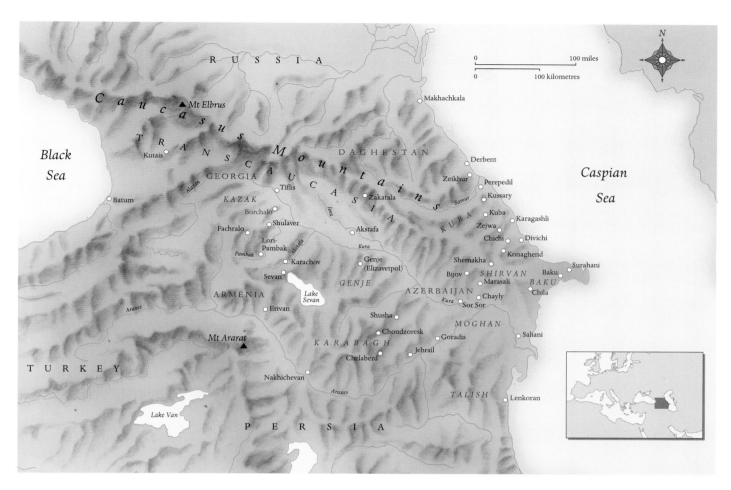

A map of the Caucasus in the nineteenth century, showing the approximate rug-weaving areas.

III Queen Tamar (Tamara), the last in a long line of Georgian rulers. Georgia's power reached its peak during her reign, but the 'golden age' ended with the Mongol invasion soon after Tamar's death in 1213. (Published in *From Constantinople to the Home of Omar Khayyam* by A.V. Williams-Jackson, New York 1911.)

IV Circassian or Cherkess. Once the most warlike of all Caucasian tribes, the Circassians undertook a mass exodus to Turkey after the Russian conquest in 1864. (Published in *Asia* by Augustus H. Keane.)

III

IV

v

VI

from the Caspian (Avars, Lesghians, Dargins, Tabassarans, Laks, etc.), the north-central Caucasian Chechens, Ingush and Bats (predominantly Sunni Muslims), plus the north west Caucasian Circassians, Abazinians and, in Transcaucasia, the Abkhazians. For northwestern Caucasians still living in the Caucasus, religion is of less importance than elsewhere. Both Muslims and, especially in Abkhazia, Christians are found. The Georgians (Orthodox Christians) live in the west-central region of the Caucasus, capital Tblisi, formerly Tiflis. To their north are the Ossetes/Ossetians, a group who are mostly Orthodox Christians. The Kurds, as usual, are divided among the Transcaucasian republics. The Talish, who are Shia Muslims, live in the southernmost region of the Caucasus along the Caspian Sea. (See Appendix B for the Russian census in 1897, giving a detailed ethnic breakdown.)

RUGS AND TRADE   Art collecting is inextricably linked to trade and commerce, while trade is itself affected by geographic and political factors. There is no doubt that for many centuries Turkey and Persia gave a high priority to trade relations with the West, while the Caucasus – with its wars, strife and internal turmoil – was not a player in the international trade arena. In evaluating the many and varied theories about the extreme and disproportionate scarcity of early (pre-1800) Caucasian tribal weavings, proper weight must be given to the impact of the trade practices and export conditions of the times.

In ancient times, the Caucasus had been a major trade route from East to West – one of the reasons why the region was such a prize for its invaders. Pliny (AD 23–79) describes how merchandise would be sent from Greece and on to the Caspian Sea.[12] From the fifteenth century, however, trade in the region became restricted. The Black Sea, a major trade route, was under Turkish control for 300 years after the destruction of the Genoese colonies in Crimea. It was thus closed to the West. Even when the Turks lost control, trade was inhibited through high local taxes. In 1817 Odessa became a free port, but only remained so for five years; in 1822 a new law was passed that made it necessary to pay duties on all unsold warehouse inventories. The Transcaucasian provinces enjoyed commercial freedom for only a short period – from 1821 to 1832. The gateway port was the Mingrelian city of Redout-kalé, from where goods were shipped to Tiflis and Erivan. The trading freedom ended when Tiflis (a major carpet trade centre) was made the centre for customs administration. All merchandise was forced to pass through the city, and duty had to be paid.

After 1832 the Transcaucasian provinces were closed to the West as Russia waged a trade war with France, Germany and England, and transit trade was forbidden. Russia was insular in trade matters, particularly exports, and was outdone and outsold by the more worldly merchants of Persia and Turkey. The volatile situation in the Caucasus in the eighteenth and nineteenth centuries made trade a low priority, as testified by many historians and travel writers from the era. Russia inhibited trade by a draconian system of high taxes, tariffs and duties, including an inventory tax on warehoused goods, imposed in 1822. All of this had a detrimental effect on the export of local products, including rugs and carpets. Early travellers' accounts contain many specific references to the prohibitive trade situations of the times, including problems with transport, travel and banditry. Back in 1753, Jonas Hanway, a British merchant, wrote:

Shamakee [Shemakha], the capital of Shirvan, was the residence of Russian merchants where they drove a considerable trade … But the Lesgees having invaded Persia and plundered Shamakee in 1712, Yevreinoff, a Russian merchant, lost near 200,000 crowns. This accident discouraged the Russian traders, that they almost quitted the field to the Armenians, who were more enterprising in commerce …

Despite this turbulent situation, foreign trade evidently did take place. Hanway was interested in procuring silk and wool and his account mentions that silk was exported by the Russians from Shirvan via the Caspian Sea.[13]

In the 1820s another Briton, Major George Keppel, visited a number of Caucasian provinces. He found the country in turmoil, and in many areas he could only make his way from one military post

v Types of Georgians. (Published in *From Batum to Baghdad via Tiflis, Tabriz and Persian Kurdistan* by Walter B. Harris, London 1846.)
vi Types of the Caucasus. (Published in *From Batum to Baghdad via Tiflis, Tabriz and Persian Kurdistan*, by Walter B. Harris.)
viii–x Costumes of the Caucasus. (Published in *La Russie, tome deuxième* by M. Chopin, Paris 1838.)
vii, xi–xiii Vignettes of life in nineteenth-century Caucasia provided ample subject-matter for Russia's sculptors. vii Bronze by Samonov depicting a camel with his turbaned

driver. (©1989 Sotheby's Inc.) xi Bronze group by Lanceray depicting a goatherd in pursuit of a goat. (©1986 Sotheby's Inc.) xii Bronze group by Evgene Lanceray depicting a victorious Caucasian warrior astride his horse. (©1985 Sotheby's Inc.)
xiii Bronze group by Vasili Gratchev depicting a warrior and his bride travelling in the Caucasian mountains. (Kaffel Collection).
xiv Tiflis (Tblisi), the nineteenth-century capital of Georgia and centre of the rug trade. (Published in *From Batum to Baghdad via Tiflis, Tabriz and Persian Kurdistan* by Walter B. Harris.)

VII

VIII

IX

X

XI

XII

XIII

XIV

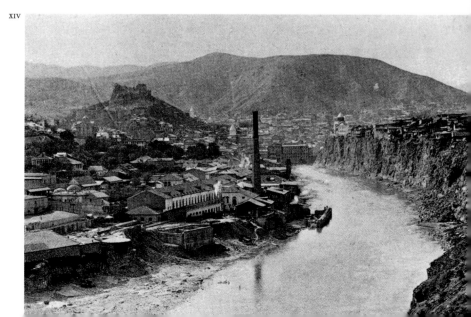

Background   17

xv

to another.[14] Xavier Hommaire De Hell, a French civil engineer, had similar first-hand experience. The account of his travels, published in 1847, describes the increasingly grasping nature of Russia's trade practices, and contrasts these practices with those of Persia and Turkey.[15] (See Appendix C.)

It is highly probable that the only Caucasian rugs exported to the West prior to the second half of the nineteenth century were the 'Dragon' and 'Kuba' workshop carpets. These rugs were large and sturdily constructed pieces, featuring all-over floral and/or animal patterns incorporating Persian and Chinese motifs. Charles Grant Ellis surmises that a small number of these may have reached the west via Anatolia: '... from the seventeenth century on they have made their way over the trade routes across Anatolia ... There seems little reason to think that except for an occasional stray, they entered the European trade before the end of the nineteenth century.'[16]

By the last quarter of the nineteenth century, Russian subjugation of the Caucasus was total and complete. Export trade became a priority as a means of raising hard currency, and Caucasian rugs began arriving in the West.

The concept of what early Caucasian tribal rugs might have looked like depends on which of the many existing theories one subscribes to. Jean Lefevre, the London auctioneer who played a vital role in the improvement of rug cataloguing during the 1970s and early 1980s, declares that 'the early tribal carpets of the Caucasus are unknown and may have disappeared completely' and that none reached Europe in time to appear in paintings.[17] But Ian Bennett suggests that some of the carpets depicted in European paintings of the fifteenth century could have come from Anatolia or the Caucasus,[18] while Liatif Kerimov states unequivocally that some carpets in the paintings by Crivelli, Van Eyck and Holbein were without doubt from Azerbaijan.[19] Şerare Yetkin, a leading Turkish authority on oriental carpets, added 'Amico di Sandro', Hans Memling and Filippo Lippi to the list.[20] It has also been speculated that two famous fifteenth-century rugs – the Berlin Dragon and Phoenix rug and the Marby rug – were both Caucasian (rather than Anatolian as is generally assumed).[21]

The lack of information about early (fifteenth- to seventeenth-century) Caucasian village weavings makes it almost impossible to chart a clear pattern of design evolution, as can be done with Turkish and Persian pieces. Furthermore, the region's various occupiers have left their indelible marks on tribal designs, leading to further confusion in provenance. Caucasian village rugs adapted many of the earlier Turkic, Persian and even Central Asian elements. The so-called Lesghi star, for example, is a possible derivative of the Turkoman gul, as are Moghan octagons. Turkish village rugs have exerted an unmistakable and considerable influence on Kazak rugs, and many early Caucasian tribal products have been erroneously classified as Turkish.[22] East Caucasian animal carpets follow models from the Safavid era, while palmette designs from Shirvan and Daghestan derive from early Persian 'Vase' carpets, among other sources. The Avshan and Harshang patterns are related to designs on earlier rugs from east and northwest Persia, and the curled-leaf borders found on many Caucasian 'Shield' carpets are identical to those seen in certain Tekke asmalyks from Central Asia.

Throughout the Caucasus and beyond, people from various tribes moved back and forth, bringing with them traditions which influenced their art. Indigenous sources were also used; some pile weavings from the late eighteenth and nineteenth centuries evolved from earlier (seventeenth- and eighteenth-century) silk and cotton embroideries from Azerbaijan, Karabagh and Daghestan. (These had themselves evolved from Safavid brocaded silks.) References to sericulture in the region are many. In 1832 Major Keppel wrote about the 'Laurijaumee tribe ... near Karabagh ... winding raw silk,'[23] and there were references to silk production in Hanway's account of his travels 80 years earlier.[24]

By the third quarter of the nineteenth century, Caucasian village rugs were becoming known in the West. Herbert Coxon journeyed from Newcastle to the Caucasus in the 1880s in search of Caucasian rugs; his travels were chronicled in his book of 1884 entitled *Oriental Carpets – How They Are Made and Conveyed to Europe*. A Caucasian prayer carpet (similar to plate 81) was depicted in an 1877 painting by Henri Fantin-Latour (fig. XVI),[25] and French poster artists of the nineteenth century, such as Eugène Grasset and René Péan (figs XX–XXII), included Caucasian tribal rugs in their works. Rugs also made their way to North America, where they were highly prized despite so little being known about them.

xv Karabagh prayer rug, published in the July 1906 issue of *Country Life in America* and inscribed AH 1223 (1808)
XVI *La Lecture*, 1877, by Henri Fantin-Latour (1836–1904), depicting a Caucasian prayer rug similar to plate 81. (Musée des Beaux-Arts de Lyon; Studio Basset-69300 Calvire.)

Caucasian Prayer Rugs

XVI

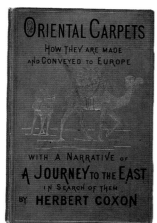

Country Life in America, in July 1906, published a Karabagh prayer rug dated 1808, 'worth $325', and 'a rare Guenje, at least 200 years old, valued at $550'.[26] (A 1907 Cadillac would have cost around $850.)

Some scholars – predominantly Soviet – see the nineteenth century as the 'golden age' of Caucasian village rugs. David Tsitsishvili claims that from the fifteenth century until the Russian conquest in the mid-nineteenth century, constant warfare and conflict reduced the population to poverty and led to a decline in the arts and crafts.[27] This view was probably influenced by Soviet dogma, although it is true that with peace and tranquillity came a corresponding expansion of weaving activity and prosperity for the population.

We have seen how commerce expanded from the mid-nineteenth century, through increased prosperity and relaxed trade barriers. But it is important to note that rugs continued to be woven for various local purposes: as luxury goods for the rich, for princes and their courts, for mosques and churches, for gifts or simply for the home.

Rugs for 'everyday' purposes would be woven at home by the women of the village, following more or less predefined patterns, while teams of master artisans would be commissioned for the more prestigious pieces. Berdj Achdjian, a rug dealer and author from Paris, has witnessed this division at first hand during visits to his native Armenia. Through his conversations with old women from rug-weaving families, he learnt how cartoons for domestic rugs would be passed down through the generations.[28]

Achdjian was also told how the work of 'master weavers' would be instantly recognized by all in the community – their distinctive work was like a signature. Most rug-weaving villages would have their own master weavers, master dyers and master designers (*nakkash*) who would make special pieces; some villages, however, would need to import some of these masters. 'Master' weavers were in fact mostly women, while master designers were mostly men. These masters were in great demand and moved around from place to place.

Most of the 'masterpieces' would be commissioned by royalty, the aristocracy or upper echelons of the military. Some patrons ordered them to be donated to a church or mosque, thus elevating their own status in society, while other rugs were used as gifts or bribes. The creation of such pieces involved very high costs of materials and craftsmanship, and they are understandably rare.

Achdjian suggests that these specially commissioned pieces should properly be divided into three distinct time periods. Up to around 1800 (the beginning of the period of Russian influence), these weavings would have been created for three types of patron: the court (there were 50 or more local fiefdoms in the Caucasus, and rugs would have been required for castles and fortresses across the land); religious authorities (for use in mosques, churches and synagogues); and the merchant class (including dealers, traders, bankers and caravaneers). Special pieces would also have been commissioned by the local rulers. From around 1800 to around 1870 we should add weavings made for the Russian aristocracy, military and clergy, as well as for export to Russia. And from 1870/80 to around 1915 another category should be added: weaving for European and American markets, and for the Russian administration in the Caucasus.

EARLY PRAYER RUGS Prayer rugs hold a special significance for collectors, for devout Muslims and for the weavers themselves. Special care and attention were taken in their creation. That they are often more finely woven than others from the same area is an indication of that attention.[29]

Essentially, prayer rugs are generally small weavings with a directional motif perhaps intended to orient the faithful towards Mecca. The motif can take the form of a niche or 'mihrab', or a gabled arch. (In Anatolian rugs, this is often supported by architectural elements such as columns.) Various objects of significance to the act of prayer may be included in the rug's iconography, such as the hanging mosque lamp and the requisite objects of cleanliness and purity, the ewer, comb and scissors. A small square or rectangle may represent the Kerbala stone, a small holy ornament made of clay from the cities of Kerbala or Meshed.[30] The square could also refer to the Ka'ba in Mecca, the most venerated stone in Islam. A representation of hands, most often seen in Caucasian or Baluch prayer rugs, has

XVII Cover of Herbert Coxon's *Oriental Carpets – How They Are Made and Conveyed to Europe*. This was one of the first 'carpet books' in English, published in 1884.
XVIII An unusual, inscribed Genje prayer rug published in the July 1906 issue of *Country Life in America*.
XIX Coxon negotiating the purchase of prayer rugs in Daghestan. (Published in *Oriental Carpets – How They Are Made and Conveyed to Europe* by Herbert Coxon.)

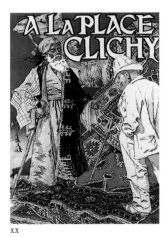

been the subject of various interpretations: they may be Allah's hands, poised to avert evil; they may call for Allah's help; they could be the hands of the martyr Hussein; or the four fingers and thumb could represent either Allah and the four archangels or Mohammed and the first four caliphs. The most popular interpretation is that they symbolize the Prophet Mohammed's family: Mohammed, Fatima, Ali, Hassan and Hussein.[31] The prayer rug itself may also represent the hereafter or 'the gateway to paradise.'[32] (For further discussion of the symbolism of prayer rugs see Appendix A.)

There are surprisingly few books that deal exclusively with the subject of prayer rugs, especially when compared to the hundreds of general rug books, and books on specific geographical areas, that exist. The first book dedicated to the subject was probably Dr Mohamed Mostafa's *Turkish Prayer Rugs* (1953), which illustrates the prayer rugs from the collection of the Museum of Islamic Arts in Cairo. This was followed in 1961 by R.E.G. Macey's *Oriental Prayer Rugs*. Macey photographed some 2,000 rugs for the London dealer House of Perez, and all of his 65 black and white plates are taken from that source.

As rug scholarship and collecting expanded simultaneously in the 1970s, many more books on the subject were published. In 1973, the Renaissance Society at the University of Chicago published the catalogue of their exhibition on *Islamic Prayer Rugs*. In 1974 the Textile Museum in Washington, DC, issued *Prayer Rugs*, chronicling their exhibition of September–December 1974, as well as the pamphlet *Prayer Rugs from Private Collections* (a catalogue of a concurrent exhibition). Collector Christian Roll, writing in *Arts in Asia* (July / August 1974), illustrated 21 prayer rugs in his article 'Prayer Rugs of the East'. The Palo Alto Cultural Center in California mounted an exhibition of prayer rugs from Bay Area collectors in 1975, which was accompanied by a now-scarce catalogue, *Oriental Rugs, An Introduction: Prayer Rugs* (with an essay by Cathryn Cootner). In the same year the Association Libanaise des Amateurs du Tapis Ancien held an exhibition of prayer rugs in Beirut.

Károly Gombos of the Museum of Applied Arts in Budapest organized Hungary's first prayer rug exhibition in 1976. (He also wrote several publications on the subject from the late 1970s to the mid-1980s.) Californian rug dealer Michael Craycraft published *Belouch Prayer Rugs* in 1983,[33] and the New England dealer Steven King published the catalogue of his *Prayer Rugs* exhibition in 1983.

Little is known about when prayer rugs first became commonplace, and there has been much discussion about their history and how they were used. One theory is that initially the prayer rug was a decorative rather than a religious article, and would have been a symbol of status and wealth for those who could afford to acquire them. As Dr Sohbi El Saleh points out in his introduction to the Beirut catalogue cited above: 'There is no law in Islamic religion stipulating that the believer should put down a rug every time he wants to pray. Islam has indeed dispensed with a fixed spot for a place of worship. This is why the Prophet said in one of his teachings: "The ground was made for me as a pure place to pray on."'[34]

For the earliest evidence of prayer rugs and their use we have to turn to texts. Patricia Fiske of the Textile Museum in Washington, DC, asserts that prayer rugs were recorded in texts as early as the eighth century,[35] and Lucy Der Manuelian, the expert on Armenian art, has cited a mention by an anonymous Persian geographer in 982 of prayer rugs woven in Azerbaijan. Manuelian also points out that according to the Arab historian Beha ed-Din (1137–1193), a prayer rug was provided for Saladin by an Armenian.[36] Gombos, however, has found no mention of prayer rugs earlier than the ninth century, when stones were said to have been used for prayers. He proposes that the prayer rug originated in the ninth century as mosque architecture developed and ornate mihrabs, mimbars and lamps – all design elements of prayer rugs – became more commonplace. He declares that Mohammed used a 'fabric' and Caliph Muáviya, the first caliph of the Umayyad dynasty (AD 661–680), used a 'mat'.[37]

Gombos has a fascinating theory about prayer rugs, suggesting that they may have been introduced by Sufi monks. These ascetics, who wore woollen, hooded cloaks, were obliged to sit on prayer rugs and turn their faces toward Mecca.[38]

Two of the earliest published prayer rugs are the thirteenth-century red-ground Seljuk rug in the Konya Museum (Central Anatolia),[39] and a thirteenth-century multiple-niche Seljuk prayer rug in

xx Poster by Eugène Grasset for the Paris dry goods store, A la Place Clichy, c.1891. Other versions of this poster proclaim the store to be 'number one in the world for its oriental imports'. (Kaffel Collection.)

xxi A different and quite rare poster by Grasset for the same store, depicting a Lori-Pambak Kazak rug and an armchair upholstered with various rug fragments, including part of a Caucasian border. (Kaffel Collection.)

xxi

the Museum of Turkish and Islamic Art in Istanbul.[40] The Israeli collector Benjamin Sofer, in *Hali* 44, 'Letters', cites a thirteenth-century mention of a prayer mat (*sag-ada*) by Rabbi Asher Ben Yechiel (1250–1327) of Toledo. (*Sejjadeh*, the name for a prayer rug, comes from the Arabic *sujûd* or *sajd*, which means 'the act of kneeling and bowing in reverence'.)

We can also gather evidence from the visual arts. The carpet scholar John Mills supposes that on the basis of their appearance in paintings, the earliest prayer rugs date from the late fifteenth century.[41] Murray Eiland, however, cites their earlier (fourteenth-century) depiction in miniatures.[42] According to Maurice S. Dimand, the former head of the Islamic department at the Metropolitan Museum of Art, New York, 'the earliest representation of a Persian prayer rug appears in a Timurid miniature of 1436 in the Bibliothèque Nationale, Paris'. (He also asserts that the 'prayer rugs of the Safavid period follow the decorations of sixteenth- and seventeenth-century rugs in general.'[43]) A fifteenth-century Anatolian 're-entrant' prayer rug is in the Topkapí Collection in Istanbul, and a very similar rug appears in a painting of around 1470 by Gentile Bellini. The Museum for Islamic Art in Berlin has an apparently unique Mamluk prayer rug, dating from the fifteenth century.[44] A sixteenth-century prayer rug with a realistic depiction of the Ka'ba is in Istanbul's Museum of Turkish and Islamic Art.[45]

Some of the earliest surviving prayer rugs were woven as 'saffs', multiple-niche or family prayer rugs. A sixteenth- or seventeenth-century fragment from central Anatolia is published as plate VII in Ettinghausen et al., *Prayer Rugs*, where it is described as 'probably the oldest surviving Anatolian saff in western collections'. Other antique examples have been illustrated and discussed by Walter B. Denny in his article 'Saff and Sejjadeh: Origins and Meaning of the Prayer Rug'.[46] These include a twelfth-century fragment from Egypt with representations of a mosque in the collection of the Kuwait National Museum;[47] a fourteenth- or fifteenth-century saff from Central Anatolia in the Museum of Turkish and Islamic Art in Istanbul,[48] and a fifteenth- or sixteenth-century saff from west or central Anatolia in the same museum.[49]

We have so far discussed the prayer rug design only in terms of Islam. However, rugs with the design of arches or niches are not exclusively an Islamic concept; indeed, the idea pre-dates Islam by many centuries. Volkmar Gantzhorn, in *The Christian Oriental Carpet*, suggests that the 'idea of the arch-form carpet originated in Palestine'.[50] He proposes that it developed into the 'use of Torah-shrine curtains, and of curtains intended to cover the entrance to the temple, the holy of holies' in the 'Jewish cult'.[51] Ottoman prayer rugs with Hebrew inscriptions specifically for use as Torah curtains or wall carpets were woven in the sixteenth and seventeenth centuries in Cairo. The inscription on a prayer rug from a Sephardi synagogue, now in the Wolfson Museum in Jerusalem, reads, 'This is the gate of the Lord the righteous shall enter'. An identical inscription appears on a similar rug illustrated as plate XXX in Ernst Kühnel, *Cairene Rugs and Others Technically Related*.[52] A fourteenth-century Spanish carpet with representations of arched Torah shrines is in the collection of the Berlin Museum.[53]

Certain arched prayer rug designs woven by Armenians were without doubt intended for church use, as altar or wall carpets. Some depicted church arches or representations of floor plans of churches.[54] Gantzhorn points to the importance of the arched and columned 'Gorzi carpet' (dated 1651) because its inscription provides information concerning not only dating but also the original use of the carpet. Here we learn that it was used as a 'door curtain to the Temple of the Holy of Holies in Saint Hrispime [in Armenia]'.[55]

The arch is the characteristic element of any so-called prayer rug, and it is essential to attempt to trace its history. Possibly its earliest surviving depiction is in a sixth-century pile textile from Egypt, which contains representations of arches supported by columns.[56] Gantzhorn also illustrates a reconstruction of a sixth-century Coptic curtain which features an arch.[57] In Christianity and Judaism, as in Islam, the columned arch symbolized a gate. (In Islam and Christianity this stands for the gates to paradise; in Judaism it is more likely to represent the door to the synagogue or to the Torah arch.) Arch-form carpets have been used as burial carpets, and elaborately embroidered cloths have been used as burial objects.[58]

XXII Poster by René Péan for the Paris oriental carpets store, Aux Trois Quartiers, 1899. The merchant sits in front of an eastern Caucasian boteh rug. (Kaffel Collection.)

2

OVERVIEW Although there is documentary evidence tracing the evolution and development of Anatolian prayer rugs from the twelfth century, there is precious little about their Caucasian counterparts from before 1800. Differences of opinion exist among scholars and experts as to how far back Caucasian rugs go, and some scholars have even suggested that Caucasian prayer rugs are a late development created in the nineteenth century to satisfy European demand. Whereas the German rug collector and expert Martin Volkmann has pointed to the long tradition of prayer rugs in the Caucasus,[1] Cathryn Cootner, former curator of textiles at the De Young Museum in San Francisco, conjectures that 'as no Caucasian prayer rugs have been discovered that pre-date the nineteenth century, this style of weaving could represent a late development'.[2]

It is, however, difficult to accept such a premise. Surely the great sophistication and variety in nineteenth-century prayer pieces could only have developed through design evolution over time. There was virtually no demand for or awareness of Caucasian rugs in Europe until late in the nineteenth century. I find more credible the theory of Seattle collector and author James D. Burns. In his book *The Caucasus: Traditions in Weaving* he argues that early pieces, which were made for personal purposes, were never exported, received heavy use and just wore out. Burns estimates that the average lifespan of a village rug was about 30 years.[3] He also cites harsh climatic conditions in the Caucasus as a contributing factor to the deterioration of these rugs. The nineteenth century saw uncommonly heavy rains and huge snowfalls in the area, producing excess moisture which destroyed the rugs' foundation. Ian Bennett makes an important point in the introduction to his book *Oriental Rugs: Volume 1, Caucasian*:

When looking at the main body of illustrations, it is important to realize that they represent only the end of a long tradition and not the tradition itself; the many types of surviving eighteenth-, seventeenth- and possibly even sixteenth-century Caucasian carpets testify to the brilliance of the tradition.[4]

CAUCASIAN PRAYER RUGS

These ideas apply equally well to the rugs illustrated in this book, although we can only imagine what very early Caucasian prayer rugs may have looked like.

The dating of rugs is an inexact science. Earlier books on the subject pursued a somewhat adventurous dating criteria and a number of Caucasian prayer examples were dated as pre-1800. Rug dating became more conservative in the latter half of this century, however, and most of these early datings would be revised today. There are very few Caucasian prayer rugs in contemporary literature that can be accurately dated to the eighteenth century. Ulrich Schürmann, in his book *Caucasian Rugs*, illustrates two. The first (plate 7) is a silk-pile Kazak with an inscribed date of AH 1210 (1796), but I find the early date difficult to believe, having seen this rug at the 1993 ICOC dealers' fair in Hamburg. The multiple border system (the rug has six borders) and the design elements in both arch and borders are typical of weavings from the second half of the nineteenth century. On the other hand, the superb Kuba rug he illustrates as plate 97 is quite probably an eighteenth-century example, as he suggests. This rug belongs to an interesting, exclusive and early sub-group of Kubas that have a blue/black version of the 'Kufic' border and feature flowers within the latticed field that have leaves on only one side of the stem. (Plate 43 below is such an example.[5])

A gold-ground Shirvan rug published by Peter Bausback is another early piece. Dated AH 1210 (1796), it is not a classic prayer design, but rather a directional animal design with two large horses with riders facing each other so as to form a niche. This could be an example of an attempt at dual-purpose weaving (a rug for religious and secular use).[6] An obviously early Daghestan was published as plate 24 in the 1979 Achdjian & Fils exhibition catalogue, *Tapis d'orient anciens*. Although Berdj Achdjian doubts the accuracy of the 1644 date woven into this rug (in Armenian numerals), it is quite conceivable that it is a late eighteenth-century example.

According to Kurt Erdmann, the earliest dated Caucasian prayer rug is the black Marasali donated by James Ballard to the Metropolitan Museum of Art, New York, in 1922.[7] It is dated AH 1223 (1808/9) and is from a small rare group of early Marasalis with curved, rather than angular, arches. (This group also includes plates 89, 90 and 91 below.) The Kazak rug illustrated as plate 19 below (belonging to Burns) pre-dates Ballard's by one year, being dated AH 1221 (1806/7), and the collector Jim Dixon believes that his undated Avshan Kuba prayer rug (plate 44 below) is an eighteenth-century example. In addition, a small group of rugs, attributed variously to Kazak and Karabagh, bear very early dates ranging from 1776 to 1815 (see caption to plate 31). If the dates are credible, this group would be among the oldest Caucasian prayer rugs that survive.

The Victoria and Albert Museum in London started acquiring Caucasian carpets during the last quarter of the nineteenth century, purchasing almost exclusively from London dealers. All eight of their Caucasian prayer rugs were acquired as part of a collection purchased in 1880 from Vincent Robinson of Wigmore Street, at prices ranging from £5 to £9.10s. The rare Karagashli prayer rug with two niches illustrated as plate 52 below was one of the purchased pieces. At the time of acquisition, these carpets were classified as Persian.[8]

The relative scarcity of early (pre-1800) Caucasian prayer rugs can be illustrated by comparing the numbers of Anatolian and Caucasian prayer rugs published by dealers over a period of time. I have compared the catalogues of two of Europe's leading antique rug dealers, Eberhart Herrmann (formerly of Munich, now operating from Switzerland) and Peter Bausback of Mannheim, Germany; the findings are published as Appendix D. Between them, Herrmann and Bausback published 182 prayer rugs – 86 Anatolian and 96 Caucasian. Thirty-eight Anatolians were dated to before 1800, yet all 96 Caucasians were assigned to the nineteenth century.

STYLES AND REGIONS   The Caucasus region has always been something of a stylistic melting-pot. At different periods, various Persian rulers controlled different parts of the eastern Caucasus, and many Caucasian rugs, including prayer rugs, were influenced by the floral motifs of Persian carpets. Those of the mountainous southwest region, meanwhile, were influenced by earlier Anatolian carpets, and prayer rugs from this area display the architectural motifs, free-floating mihrabs and large areas of solid colour that characterize their ancestors. As seen earlier, the origin of many Caucasian motifs can be traced to neighbouring regions and ethnic groups.

There are no steadfast rules regarding the classification of Caucasian rugs. Various groupings and terms have been employed over the years, and I am here adopting what I believe to be the most popular and widely accepted system today. Caucasian rugs fall into two basic groups: the southwestern group (sometimes known as the Kazak/Karabagh/Genje group) from the the southwestern highlands, and the eastern Caucasian group from along the Caspian Sea. The southwestern rugs, from colder climes, are heavier and have longer pile; eastern Caucasian pieces are thinner and finer.

The 'types' within each group are based on design; this in turn generally reflects geographic origin (although the structure of the rug is a surer indicator). Weavers move from region to region, however, bringing their traditional designs with them, and the situation can become somewhat confusing. Plate 22, for instance, shows a Shirvan-design rug woven in a Kazak area with a Kazak structure.

In the survey of rug types that follows I have drawn substantially on my own pictorial database. This index of over 10,000 rugs (including over 2,000 Caucasian prayer rugs) has been compiled over a number of years from rug books, magazines and catalogues, and also includes unpublished pieces that I have had the opportunity to photograph. Although it is not completely comprehensive, it does include every Caucasian prayer rug that I have seen over the last 18 or so years. I therefore believe it to be a very useful way of identifying stylistic similarities. I have drawn on the database for many of my conclusions regarding the most common designs in a particular area. The results are summarized in the text that follows, and tabulated in Appendix E. The table below is a summary of the individual types within the two main rug groups in the Caucasus. The figures refer to my index, and give the number of pieces of each type in the database and the percentage of the total this represents.

THE KAFFEL DATABASE

regional group	rug type	rugs in database	percentage of total
Southwestern Caucasian	Borchalo	149	7.3
	Fachralo	252	12.3
	Kazak	169	8.2
	Karabagh	142	6.9
	Genje	73	3.5
	Talish/Lenkoran	21	1.02
	Moghan	23	1.1
	SUBTOTAL	829	40.5
Eastern Caucasian	Baku	26	1.3
	Kuba	42	2.04
	Konaghend	18	0.88
	Perepedil	28	1.4
	Chichi	66	3.2
	Karagashli	5	0.25
	Zeikhur	10	0.5
	Daghestan	332	16.3
	Lesghi	19	0.9
	Shirvan	357	17.5
	Bijov	12	0.6
	Akstafa	69	3.4
	Marasali	232	11.3
	SUBTOTAL	1,216	59.5
	TOTAL	2,045	100

BORCHALO Borchalo (Borjalou, Bordjalou, Borchaly) rugs come from the northernmost rug-weaving area of the Lesser Caucasus, in Georgia. Of all Caucasian prayer rugs, Borchalos are the least Islamic in appearance, containing many symbols related to the cross. Red grounds predominate with green or blue diamond-shaped medallions (fig. 1) flanked by hexagons. Borders are usually of reciprocal trefoil or 'running dog' design (figs 2 and 3) in brown and ivory. The database, which lists 149 rugs assigned to Borchalo, shows a preponderance of double-diamond field designs.

Borchalo prayer rugs differ so radically in colour and design from their secular counterparts that one marvels that they come from the same rug-weaving area. Prayer rugs with the zigzag latchhook designs typical of secular Borchalo rugs are unknown. Instead, animals and birds often appear, as do ewers or water pitchers (*ibrik*) as a symbol of cleanliness. (The other typical ornaments of religious significance, such as the comb, lamp, scissors or hands, do not feature however.) Humans are often depicted; there is even one example in which a large female figure in a horizontally striped skirt dominates the field.[9]

Borchalo 'crosses' have been variously interpreted. Wilfred Stanzer sees them as magic symbols that might suggest a former cult use (perhaps as an altar cover or in an animal cult).[10] They may alternatively derive from tamgas, the branding marks used for cattle (fig. 4). It has also been pointed out that the design is very similar to the crosses carved on many medieval Armenian churches, and it may well have evolved from this tradition.[11]

FACHRALO The Fachralo (Fakhralo, Fakhrali, Fekhraly, Fekkarly, Fakkarlo) weaving area lies southwest of Borchalo, directly west of the village of Shulaver. The village of Fachralo is the westernmost weaving village in the Kazak area. Fachralo rugs are all wool, relatively loosely woven, with ivory or brown warps and red or pink wefts. Red fields predominate in prayer rugs, with green or blue mihrabs.

The database considers 252 Fachralos, making this the largest single group among the Kazaks. In contrast to Borchalos, Fachralo prayer rugs very much resemble their secular counterparts. Their dominant feature is the signature star-like medallion (fig. 5) which has its origins in much older Anatolian carpets. Richard Ettinghausen referred to the famous sixteenth-century 'Munich' carpet in the Bavarian National Museum as an antecedent of the medallion.[12]

Heraldic motifs, such as a variant of the 'waterbug' palmette (fig. 6), appear in many Fachralo rugs. A beetle-like design, named 'chafer' by Ulrich Schürmann,[13] often appears in the field or as a secondary border motif (fig. 7). The majority of rugs in the study feature mihrabs with re-entrant motifs, and a 'confronting dragons' design within the re-entrant niche is a frequently occurring element (fig. 8; plates 8, 12, 14). This motif is also used as field decoration in other types, including secular Fachralos[14] and Karachov Kazaks.[15] The 'leaf-and-calyx', 'serrated leaf' or 'meandering vine and leaf' border is the most common (fig. 9), followed by various zigzag designs (fig. 10 shows a typical example.) A complex leaf and branch border (fig. 11) also appears in a number of pieces. Fachralo rugs have been among the most highly prized prayer rugs of the Kazak district, as the auction prices reached for a red-ground rug with a blue mihrab (Phillips, London, 1990),[16] and a red-ground rug with a green mihrab (Rippon Boswell & Co., Wiesbaden, 1990) indicate.[17]

KAZAK Kazak (Kasak, Kazakh, Gazakh) is a collective term for a group of rugs from the Kazak weaving area not assigned a specific geographical or design name. The area is in the south Caucasus between Tiflis to the north and Erivan to the south. Although there are no doubts regarding the Kazak weaving area itself, there is much ambiguity about whether or not there is a corresponding place-name. Some rug maps show the village of Kazak, and Eiland suggests that the name derived from a large town on the road between Genje and Tiflis. He also mentions a Kazak khanate appearing in some seventeenth- and eighteenth-century maps.[18] But Stone declares that 'there is neither a Kazak province nor a Kazak people in the Caucasus'.[19]

1 Radiating diamond motif, a common element in Borchalo prayer rugs.
2 Reciprocal trefoil border design.
3 'Running dog' or wave border design.
4 'Tamga' sign (a cattle brand); the motif is sometimes interpreted as a rudimentary Tree of Life.
5 'Fachralo' central medallion.
6 'Waterbug' palmette.
7 'Chafer' or scarab palmette.

Among rug aficionados the name 'Kazak' evokes images of colourful, heavy, densely piled and 'meaty' rugs. Kazaks were woven in the coldest of the rug-weaving areas and were made to provide warmth, as well as for other utilitarian or decorative purposes, much like Anatolian bed rugs or 'yataks'. As Lefevre has pointed out:

As these types of Kazak are made in very similar size and proportion and have approximately the knot count of symmetrical knots found in certain Anatolian weavings, the relationship is apparent. In fact, some known examples have been assigned to the Caucasus by certain experts and to Asia Minor by others.[20]

Structurally, virtually all Kazaks have wool warps and wefts. Of the 297 Kazaks with warp fibre indicated tabulated by Stone in *Rugs of the Caucasus, Structure and Design*, all but one had woollen warps, and of the 262 Kazaks with weft fibre indicated, 253 had woollen wefts. The weft colour is usually red or pink.

The Kazak weaving area comprises many different types that have been variously classified. Some groupings are based on geographical area, and others on design type. Liatif Kerimov, the first to attempt a systematic classification of Caucasian rugs, defines 13 types for the Kazak area.[21] Ulrich Schürmann, who used Kerimov's designations as a basis for his own, shorter nomenclature, lists six categories in the Kazak group, namely: Kazak, Lambalo, Karaklis, Idjevan, Karachov and Shulaver. (Karaklis and Idjevan are terms not used today.) Sevan (Sewan) Kazaks should be added to the above, an appellation which designates rugs from an area around Lake Sevan in Armenia. In addition, a number of Kazaks are known by their design type rather than place of origin. These include Swastika or Pinwheel Kazaks, Star Kazaks, Memling Kazaks, Medallion Kazaks and Tree Kazaks. (The 'Eagle' Kazak is in the Karabagh group.)

Many of the quintessential Kazak types or designs, which are highly prized by collectors, are quite rare in prayer formats. There are no known Star Kazak prayer rugs, for instance; only three known Pinwheel or Swastika prayer rugs;[22] only three with the distinctive 'Lori-Pambak' medallions;[23] and few 'Memling' gul prayer rugs. (The Karachov double-niche so-called prayer rugs use arches as a purely decorative device and it is doubtful that they were ever meant for prayer. Their larger format also argues against their intended use as prayer rugs.)

A small group of prayer rugs (represented by plate 31 below), all bearing early dates and previously thought to be Kazaks, are now attributed to Karabagh. They are almost certainly the antecedents of a larger group of Kazak prayer rugs which borrow major elements of that design but are more coarsely woven and drawn with somewhat less refinement (fig. 12 is a representation of the type of medallion which appears in these rugs). The border is almost always an arrowhead design (fig. 13), but sometimes a scrolled 's'. There are at least 45 published examples.[24] Plate 21 below is a member of that group. Four earlier versions of the design, all with angular cartouche borders, are known.[25] The well-known prayer rug published as plate 8 in Denny and Walker, *The Markarian Album,* is another variant of this group, strongly influenced by Fachralo designs.[26]

Kazak prayer rugs also feature keyhole or garden designs, mostly of large size, but, in contrast with Karachovs, these are clearly directional.[27] These rugs invariably feature open hands (palm up) in the spandrels (possibly symbolizing the five most important religious figures in Islam or the hands of Fatima) and ewers, symbolizing cleanliness. There is also a fairly large group of Kazak prayer rugs that feature linked medallions and diamond forms; an example is shown in plate 23 below.[28]

A total of 570 Kazak area prayer rugs formed the basis for this study. Borchalo and Fachralo Kazaks accounted for 76 percent of the total, with the rest being 'generic' Kazak types. It should be noted that although 'generic' Kazak rugs do not generally compete price-wise with Fachralo prayer rugs, there are exceptions. Secular carpets from the Kazak group, however, have been among the most highly prized of all eighteenth- and nineteenth-century Caucasians, setting many recent records on the international auction circuit.[29]

8 'Confronting dragons' motif.
9 'Leaf-and-calyx' border design, also called 'meandering vine and leaf'.
10 Meandering vine or zigzag border design.
11 Leaf and branch border design.
12 Karabagh central medallion.
13 Arrowhead border design, common in Kazak and Karabagh rugs.

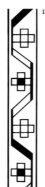

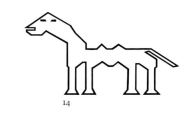

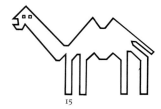

KARABAGH The Karabagh district is the southernmost of the central Caucasian weaving areas, with Shusha its principal city. (According to some experts, Dragon carpets were woven here from the sixteenth to the eighteenth centuries.) Karabagh weavings reflect the diversity of its population of Armenians, Azeri Turks and Kurds. 'Karabagh' means 'black garden'; its Iranian neighbour to the south is 'Karadagh', which means 'black mountain'. Because of the geographical proximity of the two regions, many typical northwest Persian designs, such as Herati and Mina Khani, are also used in Karabagh weavings, and it is often rather difficult to discern if a particular piece comes from the Caucasian or Iranian side of the border.

Major design types of Karabagh rugs include Chondzoresk or 'cloud-band', Chelaberd or 'Eagle Kazak', Kasim-Usag, Goradis, Chan-Karabagh and Lampa-Karabagh. Most of the prayer rugs from the district are not design- or appellation-specific, however, and are simply called Karabagh. They draw on numerous Caucasian designs such as linked medallions, 'crab' floral fields, latchhooked diamonds and so forth, and are characterized more by their bold execution than by any specific motif. Structurally, Karabaghs are similar to Kazaks (indeed, the two are often confused, unintentionally or on purpose), with wool warps and wefts, but cotton weft is sometimes used and the weft colour is brown, beige or ivory. Although madder is the source of red in most Caucasian rugs, cochineal is used in the oldest Karabaghs.[30]

Some prayer rugs feature depictions of horses and camels, with or without riders, that cover the entire field (figs 14 and 15). The oldest published example of this type appears to be plate 25 in Erdmann et al., *Kaukasische Teppiche* (a catalogue of the 1962 Frankfurt exhibition). These rugs usually feature a gabled prayer arch surmounting a compartmented rectangular reserve (fig. 16). Schürmann designated a group of boteh-field prayer rugs as Chan-Karabagh ('Chan' being a corruption of 'Khan'),[31] a designation subsequently also applied to rugs with a floral 'crab' field (see plate 32). Both types generally employ the prayer arch design depicted in figure 17, which is typical of Karabagh.

Another group of Karabagh prayer rugs features fields of narrow vertical stripes or bands, upon which two or three rhomboid medallions are superimposed.[32] The New England dealer Steven King sees a Persian influence in this design, and finds it suggestive of mosque architecture (see plate 28 for a Karabagh prayer rug depicting a mosque). A further, rare type adopts the designs usually found on the ikat-printed silks and velvets of Central Asia and Persia. Two such rugs are illustrated here (plates 25 and 26), and another was the subject of a *Hali* 'Connoisseur's Choice'.[33]

Prayer rugs from Karabagh account for 142 (6.8 percent) of the Caucasian prayer rugs in the database. Of these, 122 are assigned to a specific design type. The remaining 20 are rather more difficult to classify as they combine various designs. The various classifications, based on field design, are tabulated in Appendix E.

Karabagh prayer rugs employ such a wide variety of borders that it is difficult to isolate 'typical' examples and match them to field designs. Some of the most commonly used border motifs are: the 'arrowhead' design, used on various types (fig. 13); the 'latchhooks and triangles' border, usually used with 'crab' motif rugs (figs 19 and 20); the 'dragon' border, used on various types and throughout the Caucasus (fig. 32); and the 'crab' motif border (fig. 21), usually on Chelaberd palmette (fig. 18) rugs.

GENJE The Genje (Gendje, Ganja, Gyandzha, Gyanja) district lies between the Kazak and Karabagh weaving areas. The population is comprised primarily of Azeri Turks and Armenians. The name of the capital city, Genje, was changed to Elizavetpol by the imperial Russians and to Kirovabad by the Soviets. Prior to the Russian conquest in 1804, Genje was a Persian khanate and a centre of Islam in the Caucasus. Structurally, Genje weavings are almost indistinguishable from Kazak. Both use woollen warps and wefts almost exclusively, although Genje rugs occasionally use cotton wefts. Kerimov placed both types into a single group he called 'Gianja-Kazakh' with three sub-groups of Genje rugs.[34]

Genje rugs acquired an (undeserved) reputation for inferior quality among early writers, as evidenced by this passage by John Kimberly Mumford, written in 1900:

14 Horse, as depicted in Karabagh prayer rugs.
15 Camel, as depicted in Karabagh prayer rugs.
16 Typical Karabagh gabled prayer arch.
17 Typical Karabagh prayer arch.
18 Waterbug palmette, typically found in Chelaberd prayer rugs.
19 Latchhooks and triangles border design.

20

In Constantinople, as in the American market, miscellaneous bales of rugs, all measuring between three and five feet in width, and six and eight feet in length, are jobbed under the name of Ghenghis, or, as the bills of lading have it, 'Guendje'. They are made up of the odds and ends of Shirvans, Karabaghs, Mosul and other secondary fabrics of the Caucasian class which usually come from Elizavetpol, the old Armeno-Persian name for which was Gandja.[35]

According to Schürmann, 'there are no rugs in the Caucasus the quality of which varies so greatly than in Gendje.'[36] Having such an unenviable reputation, it is no wonder that many Genje rugs have been attributed by dealers to other districts such as Kazak, Karabagh or even Shirvan. Although this goes for all Genje rugs, prayer examples do have certain characteristic design features that identify them as Genje products. Whereas many Karabagh prayer rugs feature vertical stripes or bands, Genje prayer rugs often have diagonal stripes containing small 's' forms. The unusual triple-linked medallion with a 'head and shoulder' motif is another typical Genje prayer rug design.[37]

The database contains 73 prayer rugs identified as Genje, accounting for 3.5 percent of rugs tabulated. Diagonal stripes are the most common field design (27 percent), followed by boteh and then floral designs (see Appendix E for database summary). The borders in Genje rugs are similar to those of Kazak, Karabagh and the eastern Caucasus. The most commonly used is the linked arrowhead (fig. 13), the leaf-and-calyx (fig. 9), latchhooks and triangles (fig. 19), diagonal stripes (fig. 25), 'dragon' border (fig. 32), scrolled 's' variant (fig. 22) and variations of linked hexagons (fig. 23). The scrolled 's' border is arguably the most characteristic of Genje weavings.

TALISH/LENKORAN/MOGHAN There is a strong opinion among collectors that these three types of Caucasian rugs should constitute a separate group rather than be allied with either the southwestern Caucasian Kazak/Karabagh/Genje group or with the eastern Caucasian group of Baku/Kuba/Daghestan/Shirvan. Geographically, the region is rather isolated from the other major weaving areas (the eastern end of the Lesser Caucasus lies between the Moghan steppe and eastern Karabagh). The Moghan steppe is south of the Araxes river and borders Iran. Lenkoran and Talish, situated on the western shore of the Caspian Sea, are the southernmost areas of the Caucasus. The region's inhabitants are mainly Azeris, along with Talish people (speaking their own distinct language) who live in the southernmost part of the region around Lenkoran.

Some of the most sought-after, distinctive and beautiful Caucasian rugs were woven in this area. Secular Talish rugs are easily recognized by their *met-hane* (plain) fields, typical rosette and box-flower borders, and medachyl and box-flower guard borders. Indigo fields are the most frequently encountered, with red and green fields much more rare. Striped and patterned Talish rugs are also known. Lenkoran rugs are distinguished by their characteristic medallions, which are geometric abstractions of dragon forms. Both types are generally long and narrow. Moghan rugs, woven west and northwest of Talish are, according to Peter Stone's survey, the rarest of all Caucasians.[38] Typical designs are 'Memling' guls in an all-over pattern and a design that Bennett describes as a 'medallion with bar appendages'.[39] All three types are finely woven, with a higher incidence of cotton wefting than in southwestern weaving.

The region's prayer rugs are another story, however; their designs appear to be totally different to those of secular rugs from this area. Very few were produced, and only 44 prayer-format rugs in the database (2.1 percent of the total) have been tentatively ascribed to the region. Talish prayer rugs can be very similar to Genje or Kazak designs, and are often given this attribution.[40] Lenkoran prayer rugs are usually coarser than their secular counterparts and are a late development. The Lenkoran medallion did not lend itself favourably to the smaller dimensions of a prayer rug and the result tended to be cramped and unappealing.[41]

Moghan prayer rugs feature fields of lattice design, vertically linked latchhooked diamonds, or rows of octagons on ivory fields. The latter type, shown in plate 37, was catalogued as Moghan by Jean Lefevre although similar examples have been attributed to Shirvan.[42]

20 'Crab' floral border design or field motif.

21 'Crab' variant or linked star border design.

22 Scrolled 's' variant border design.

23 Linked hexagon border design.

21

22

23

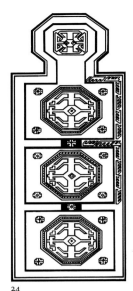

24

BAKU Baku is the principal city of the desert landscape of the Aspheron peninsula, and has been the capital of Azerbaijan since 1920. 'Azerbaijan' means 'garden of fire', from the burning natural gas that spurts from the ground in and around Baku.[43] The cult of Zoroastrianism, characterized by fire worship, had flourished in the region since ancient times, and the oil industry developed there in the 1880s. The carpet dealer Herbert Coxon wrote in 1884 that 'until last year one of the priests of the creed still tended the sacred fire, a few miles from Baku'. He adds that 'Baku is not a very pleasant place to live in. The dust is abominable. An attempt is made to settle the dust in the streets by drenching it with oil.'[44]

Baku has been described as being founded by Alexander the Great as a penal colony, which brought in people from all over the vast Macedonian empire.[45] Over 50 languages are still spoken there, with Azeri Turks forming the vast majority of the population. In the 1880s Baku was a centre for carpet trade, and many rugs came to be known as Baku simply because they were sold there. Older carpet literature contains a diversity of opinion regarding Baku rugs. While Walter Hawley, for instance, declared in 1921 that 'no other rugs in the Caucasus have greater individuality of colour and design than Bakus',[46] Wolfe and Wolfe's *How to Identify Oriental Rugs* of 1927 describes the characteristic hue of a Baku as 'a dim, soft version of a Daghestan'.[47]

Schürmann divided the Baku group into four types, based on area of origin: Baku, Chila (subdivided into Boteh-Chila and Avshan-Chila, according to design), Surahani and Saliani.[48]

Boteh designs are typical of secular Baku rugs, indeed earlier this century rugs with boteh designs were almost automatically classified as Baku. Wolfe and Wolfe wrote that 'while the fabrics of Baku and Shirvan are very much alike', Bakus could be distinguished by 'their fondness for angular cone shapes in the field'.[49] As knowledge about Caucasian rugs grew it was acknowledged that 'boteh' rugs were also woven in many other parts of the Caucasus and that the design was not limited to Baku rugs.

Paradoxically, there are no known boteh-design Baku prayer rugs. Indeed very few prayer rugs from the area exist (only 26 are thus identified in the database). The main designs are 'head and shoulders' (fig. 24) with octagons (plate 39), often featuring a diagonally slanted 'barber pole' (fig. 25);[50] Avshan design (plate 38); Memling guls; 'cemetery design';[51] and all-over stepped polygons (fig. 26). (See Appendix E for database summary.) Structurally, Baku rugs use mostly wool warp, and cotton is used as often as wool for wefting.

KUBA The khanate of Kuba belonged to Persia until 1806, when it was captured by Russia. The population, as in Baku, is mostly Azeri Turks, Lesghis and Mountain Jews. Seventeenth-century Kuba carpets fascinated George Hewritt Myers, founder of the Textile Museum in Washington, DC, and he eagerly collected them. The oldest known Caucasian rugs, the Dragon and Blossom carpets, were at one time attributed to Kuba. Some of them still are, but since the publication of Charles Grant Ellis's book *Early Caucasian Rugs* in 1975, most have been attributed to Karabagh (Shusha) and Shirvan. Ellis suggested that the 'Kuba' carpets were made in the workshops established by Shah Abbas in Karabagh and Shirvan early in the seventeenth century.[52] The latest (1995) theory proposes that these carpets may have been woven in the workshops around Tabriz on the grounds of structural similarity.[53]

In the nineteenth century, Kuba and its environs were the largest production centres for rugs in the Caucasus.[54] Some of the oldest known Caucasian prayer rugs are Kubas. They have little in common structurally or design-wise with the early workshop carpets. Along with Shirvans, they are the most finely knotted of all Caucasians. The warp is almost always wool and most have wool wefts, although cotton is sometimes used. The selvedges are often blue, and the ends are often bundled in a macrame-like fashion.

The oldest Kuba prayer rugs have latticed fields and elaborately executed geometric arabesque scrolled borders, most often in blue-black (plates 41–43, fig. 27). Arguably, the oldest known rug of this type is published as plate 97 in Schürmann's *Caucasian Rugs*, dated to the eighteenth century. A northwest Persian version of this border is published by Yetkin in *Early Caucasian Carpets in Turkey*, vol. 2, ill. 224, p. 96.

XXIII

XXIV

24 'Keyhole' or 'head and shoulders' prayer niche.
25 'Barber pole' diagonal border design.
26 Stepped polygon.
27 Arabesque border design.
28 'Kuba' flower motif.
29 'Kuba' flower motif.
30 Bar and rosette border design.
31 Typical Chichi prayer arch.

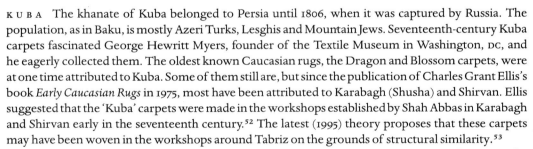

25

26

XXV

Some Kuba lattice prayer rugs are distinguished by two very unusual depictions of flower motifs, with leaves attached to only one side of the stem (fig. 28) or with a red tripartite blossom (fig. 29).

There are 42 Kuba prayer rugs in the database, The most common field design is lattice, and 12 of these have the arabesque border.[55] Floral palmettes are another common design feature.[56] (See Appendix E for database summary.)

KONAGHEND Konaghend is a village directly south of Kuba, and the southernmost weaving area of the Kuba district. Konaghend rugs are quite distinctive, easily recognizable by their unique field design of complex vine-like tracery,[57] usually worked in ivory on blue (and more rarely green) fields in secular rugs and some prayer rugs, and in blue on red fields in most prayer rugs. Konaghend prayer rugs are rare (see plates 45 and 46), with only 18 in the database, accounting for less than one percent of the total. Of these examples, eight have red fields, 14 have 'Kufic' borders and 17 have the tracery motif.[58] This design is characteristic of, but not exclusive to, Konaghend, being rarely used in other northeastern Caucasian weaving areas.[59] As in other Kuba types, wool warps are used exclusively and most are wool wefted (cotton wefts are occasionally used).

27

PEREPEDIL Perepedil (Perpedil) rugs are woven in an area north of the town of Kuba. Many of them have the sombre tonality of Chichis and Konaghends, except for a group of white-ground and (very rarely) yellow-ground rugs. Structurally the three types are similar. Christine Klose points out that the earlier Perepedils are wool wefted, while the later ones are cotton wefted.[60] The typical Perepedil 'ram's horn' field design (*wurma*) has been variously interpreted as a floral or animal motif. Klose traces the design back to what she claims to be its earliest origins: seventeenth- and eighteenth-century Caucasian silk embroideries and later northwest Persian carpets.[61]

There do not appear to be any Perepedil prayer rugs dating back earlier than the second half of the nineteenth century. The oldest Perepedil rugs are secular, featuring light-coloured grounds and a much greater variety of colours than is found in prayer examples.[62]

Of the 35 Perepedil prayer rugs in our sample (1.4 percent of the total), 30 have light grounds and five (all late examples) have dark grounds. The 'Kufic' border predominates, but other border designs are also used (see plates 47–50). (See Appendix E for database summary.)

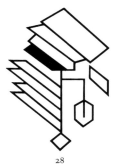

28

CHICHI There is much confusion over the origin of the appellation Chichi. It is shown as a village on some rug maps, but not others.[63] It has been suggested that the name 'Chichi' derived from the Chechens,[64] although this is not entirely convincing since Chechnya is northwest of Daghestan and is not known for its rug production (see caption to plate 51). What we do know is that Chichi rugs were made in the Kuba area and have great similarities in structure and colouring to Perepedil and Konaghend rugs. All three are tightly woven with the backs having a rippled appearance, a feature that is most pronounced in Chichi rugs.[65] A greenish hue is common to all three, as is the use of characteristic slate blue. Other colours tend to be sombre: madder red, cobalt blue, azure blue and moss green. Cotton wefts are relatively common.

There are 66 Chichi prayer rugs in the database, 3.2 percent of the total. The most common type employs an all-over design of geometric floral motifs that Kerimov called 'khirdagyd',[66] on a blue ground. Of the rugs in our sample, 37 are of that type, with 26 of them featuring the characteristic Chichi border of alternating diagonal bars and rosettes (see plate 51, fig. 30). Other types include a geometric design with latchhooked motifs,[67] boteh with latchhooked motifs,[68] a trellis design with 'arrowhead' polygons[69] and a gold-ground 'khirdagyd'.[70] 'Head and shoulders' keyhole designs[71] and multiple-niche examples[72] are also found. (For database summary see Appendix E.) The typical Chichi arch is illustrated in figure 31.

29

KARAGASHLI The small village of Karagashli is located on the coast of the Caspian Sea, south of Derbent, in the Kuba weaving area. Karagashli rugs are distinctive and highly prized. Prayer rugs are

XXIII Fire worshippers in the Baku temple in 1865. (Published in *From Constantinople to the Home of Omar Khayyam* by A. V. Williams-Jackson.)
XXIV Portal and tower of the eastern wall of the Fire Temple at Baku. (Published in *From Constantinople to the Home of Omar Khayyam* by A. V. Williams-Jackson.)
XXV Water vendor near the Palace of the Khans in Baku. (Published in *From Constantinople to the Home of Omar Khayyam* by A. V. Williams Jackson.)

30

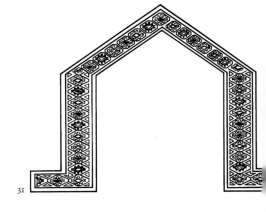

31

extremely rare and of quite different design to that found elsewhere; none features a conventional mihrab or gabled arch. The few Karagashli examples that can be considered prayer rugs employ a system of multiple squared-off and bracketed forms, arranged vertically, not unlike the stepped-mihrab prayer rugs of Karapinar in central Anatolia.[73]

Two major design motifs are typical of Karagashli weavings: a vertical arrangement of slanting lozenges, often mingled with palmette forms,[74] and a medallion on a blue field with fiery pendants.[75] (Both types share the characteristic minor border of box flowers on a dark ground and guard borders of 's' forms on an ivory ground.) Neither type, however, is known in a prayer format. Probably due to their high knot count, cotton wefts are often used.[76] Only five Karagashli prayer rugs are included in our sample, reflecting their rarity. The oldest known example is illustrated as plate 52.

ZEIKHUR Zeikhur (Seichur, Seychour) prayer rugs are very rare, with only ten examples known to me. Although no two are alike, four of the ten feature a 'Zeikhur rose' or 'cabbage' design[77] and three feature lattice fields.[78] The other three designs are vertical stripes, diagonal crosses and the 'Alpan-Kuba' pattern (see plate 54).[79] Zeikhur rugs are from the Kuba district and can be distinguished, apart from their designs,[80] by their highly consistent palette with a high incidence of salmon, 'Zeikhur' pink, yellow, green and light blue colours. Selvedges are usually blue and the ends bundled macrame style. Most are wool wefted, with brown weft quite common.[81]

DAGHESTAN 'Daghestan' means 'Land of Mountains'. The area lies north of Kuba along the western shore of the Caspian Sea. Its population is an ethnic mix of 32 groups, including Avars, Lesghians, Chechens and Tats.[82] Daghestan was a Persian province until Peter the Great of Russia took Derbent, the capital of Daghestan, in 1722.[83] From then, until the final 'pacification' of Daghestan in 1859, Russia fought the mountain tribes, whose most prominent leaders were the Imams Kazi Mullah and Shamyl, 'The Lion of Daghestan'. According to *Encyclopaedia Judaica* the name 'Daghestan' is thought to be derived from 'mountains of Jews', or *Chufut oz Dzubud Dag* in the Tat language. In a Russian chronicle of 1346, the entire eastern Caucasus was called 'Zhidy' ('land of the Jews').[84] Many 'Mountain Jews' (Tats) became dye makers and could be recognized by the permanent indigo dye which stained their lower arms and hands.

Many rug books and dealers have applied the name 'Daghestan' indiscriminately to most rugs from eastern Caucasus, often incorrectly. Eiland suggests that this is because Daghestan is the proper name for most of the northeast region bordering the Caspian Sea, where many different rug types, including Kuba, were woven. Thus, decades ago, the various types from this region (including Kubas and Chichis) were incorrectly labelled Daghestan, which became an almost generic name.[85] This situation was corrected to a great degree with the publication of Schürmann's *Caucasian Rugs* in 1964.

Prayer rugs labelled 'Daghestan' number 332 pieces in our sample and account for 16.4 percent of the total.[86] The lattice design is the most common. Superficially, lattice Daghestans are very similar to lattice Shirvans from further south. How does one distinguish between the two? Apparently no one is quite sure. Bennett declares that 'distinguishing between Shirvan, Kuba and Daghestan, especially prayer rugs … is a task so subjective as to be almost meaningless,'[87] and Stone writes that the structural characteristics of prayer rugs with lattice design from Daghestan, Kuba and Shirvan are 'virtually identical for all three, with a slightly higher incidence of cotton weft for Shirvans'.[88] (While I agree with both authors' conclusions, I disagree with the inclusion of Kuba rugs, which I feel have sufficient distinct characteristics to enable them to be distinguished from Shirvan or Daghestan products.) Jo Kris, the carpet expert at Skinner's auction gallery in Boston, suggests that a Daghestan may have a more depressed warp, slightly longer pile and a stiffer handle than a Shirvan. Walter Denny, in *Sotheby's Guide to Oriental Carpets*, describes Daghestan carpets as 'among the finest in weave, and supposedly identifiable by a two-level warp giving them a slightly stiffer "handle".'[89] Mary Jo Otsea, the carpet expert at Sotheby's New York, is of the opin-

32

32 So-called 'dragon' border, most common on Daghestan and Shirvan prayer rugs but used throughout the Caucasus.
33 'Eagle's beak' border design, also called bird's beak.
34 The 'Lesghi' star.

ion that Shirvan prayer rugs are somewhat finer than Daghestans, which she feels are coarser to the touch.

The majority of 'Daghestan' prayer rugs in the database are of the light-ground lattice type, but there are a small number of dark-ground lattice examples.[90] Other field designs are stylized tulips (see plates 60 and 61), palmettes (see plate 59), boteh,[91] stripes (see plate 58), latchhooked diamonds[92] and star-like forms (see plate 63). Three additional and unusual field designs, 'syrga', 'anchor' and 'palm', can only be tentatively attributed due to the lack of comparative data.[93] A variety of borders are used, including dragon (fig. 32), latchhooks and triangles (fig. 19), crab (fig. 20), 'eagle's beak' (fig. 33), boteh and asterisk. (For database summary see Appendix E.)

LESGHI   The term 'Lesghi' is a stylistic one and refers to rugs woven in Daghestan bearing the characteristic 'Lesghi star'. The large Lesghian community resides in southern Daghestan and north Azerbaijan. The Lesghi star (fig. 34) is a distinctive and complex design quite similar to the Turkoman gul, although its origins are uncertain. The tendency is to call every rug bearing that symbol a 'Lesghi', but in fact the motif has been used throughout the Caucasus. Designs travel, and the Lesghi star appears on rugs from Daghestan, Kuba and Shirvan, even on Kazaks and Genjes, as well as on sumakh flatweaves. Some experts have suggested eliminating the 'Lesghi' name as a place of origin.[94] These proposals show no signs of being accepted, however.

Although the 'star' is the signature feature of the so-called Lesghi rugs, Schürmann attributed a wonderful example with two blue and two green stars to Kuba,[95] but assigned two prayer rugs without out the star as Lesghi.[96] Schürmann sees colour as an important distinguishing feature, writing that 'Lesghi rugs can be recognized at a distance by their splendid yellow and emerald or bottle green.'[97]

Of the 19 'Lesghi'-type prayer rugs in the database, 14 have the typical stars and the other five have lattice fields. No one border design should be considered characteristic; the sample rugs show nine different border designs, with the most popular being the 'leaf-and-calyx'.

SHIRVAN   The Shirvan district lies south of Daghestan. The two areas are separated by the Greater Caucasus mountain range which diagonally traverses the entire Caucasus from the Caspian to the Black Sea. Shirvan is a mountainous region which was part of the Persian empire until 1805, when it was conquered by Russia. It is possible that the name stems from the Sassanian King Anushirvan the Just (AD 531–579) who was responsible for much of the fortification at Derbent.[98] The capital is Shemakha, a name that until early in the twentieth century was used generically to describe a type of rug. (Early rug nomenclature tended to name rugs after the major or capital city of the region, or after their place of exportation.) G.G. Lewis, in 1911, listed these synonyms for Shemakha: 'Soumak, Sumak, Kashmir, Cashmere… made by the nomadic tribes of Shirvan.'[99] The place-name Shirvan has been similarly attached to rugs made outside the region. Rugs have been identified as Kuba-Shirvan, Moghan-Shirvan, Lesgi-Shirvan, Akstafa-Shirvan, and so forth.

Shirvan rugs are among the most finely woven in the Caucasus. They did not always enjoy such high regard, however. Early this century the name Shirvan was used in an almost derogatory sense to describe weaves inferior in quality to Daghestan. Here are some examples:

Close, neighbourly relationship, no doubt, is the cause of the similarity between Shirvan and Daghestan rugs, but Shirvan rugs do not come up to the standard of the old antique Daghestans. They are coarser in quality, thinner in texture, and not quite so rich in colour; besides, the weavers of Shirvan seem to be ambitious and progressive to a dangerous degree … the texture, and in many cases the colourings, have the plain stamp of 'haste' marked upon them. (Garabed Pushman, 1902)[100]

[Shirvan] rugs, made in the district south of Daghestan, are somewhat coarser in weave than the Daghestans, and the colourings are less mellow … The old Shirvans were of excellent workmanship, but the modern rugs are hardly up to the ancient standard. (Levon Babayan, 1925)[101]

XXVI Derbent, an ancient city dating to the time of Alexander the Great. (Published in *From Constantinople to the Home of Omar Khayyam* by A. V. Williams-Jackson.)
XXVII The Lesghinka, the fast and furious traditional dance of the Lesghians. (Courtesy Ron O'Callaghan / *Oriental Rug Review.*)
XXVIII Anushirvan the Just, also known as Khusru or Chosroes, reputed to be the builder of the strongest bulwarks of Derbent. (Published in *From Constantinople to the Home of Omar Khayyam* by A.V. Williams-Jackson.)

XXVIII

34

Caucasian Prayer Rugs

35

Unusually fine for Shirvan. This rug is in the century class. The three borders are not often seen, but are characteristic of the older rugs of the Daghestan district. (Anonymous collector, 1920)[102]

There are 357 prayer rugs attributed to Shirvan in the database, the largest single group at 17.5 percent of the total. A wide variety of designs was employed by Shirvan weavers, with the most common design being the floral lattice on an ivory field (see plate 82). Other field designs include stylized tulips (see plate 80), boteh,[103] floral patterns,[104] latchhooks (see plate 77), keyhole or 'head and shoulders' (see plates 68 and 69), stripes (see plates 72 and 73) and serpents or animals.[105] Other, less frequently encountered designs include Ashik,[106] mosque designs,[107] dark-ground lattice,[108] 'Persian' designs (see plate 71), saffs[109] and designs with a central medallion (see plate 70). Border designs include dragon (fig. 32), 'Kufic' (see plate 78), floral motifs (fig. 35), latchhook (fig. 36), 'eagle's beak' (fig. 33) and geometric 'c' motifs (fig. 37). (For database summary see Appendix E.) Shirvan rugs are wool warped. Wool and cotton wefts are used in equal frequency.

BIJOV The classic Bijov (Bidjov) design consists of a highly intricate pattern of rising palmettes and other floral forms. The design takes its name from the village of Bijov in the Shirvan area, southwest of Shemanka. Strangely, while recent maps show the location of the village, older maps show no such place.[110] The oldest rugs with this design come from farther north, from the Zeikhur weaving area in the Kuba district.[111] Traditional colours are coral, pink, red, green, yellow and blue.

There are 12 prayer rugs in the database with the characteristic Bijov design. All are relatively late (after 1875) and from the Shirvan district. The 'bird' border appears on eight of the pieces. There are no known Bijov prayer rugs from the Zeikhur area with the typical colours.

AKSTAFA While there is a village called Akstafa in the Kazak weaving area,[112] rugs bearing that name are woven in eastern Caucasus in the Shirvan district. Exactly how they got the Akstafa name is unclear. To clarify matters, they are often designated as Shirvan/Akstafa. Typical secular Akstafas have a field design of four eight-pointed medallions interspaced with peacocks.[113] Although there are no known prayer rug versions of that design, a few rugs come close. An Akstafa prayer rug with four quatrefoil medallions alternating with peacocks, and with the typical kotchak border design of horned rectangles, is illustrated as plate 52 in Denny and Walker, *The Markarian Album*.[114]

The typical Akstafa prayer rug is long and narrow (average size about 1 × 2 metres / 3′ × 6′) and has a dark, usually blue, lattice field and a squared prayer arch (fig. 38). Of the 60 pieces in the database,[115] 46 conform to this model.[116] Borders vary, but the dominant design is a motif composed of linked, hooked 'bird's beak' elements (fig. 39). That motif, also known as 'kotchak' or ram's horn, is rarely seen in other rugs and could almost be considered an identifying feature of Akstafa pieces. Other Akstafa prayer rugs feature stripes (plate 87), linked medallions (plate 88) and boteh (plates 85 and 86).

MARASALI Marasali is a village south of Shemakha, in the Shirvan district. Rugs with the characteristic Marasali 'flaming boteh' design, were woven throughout the Caucasus, variously assigned to Shirvan, Daghestan and Kuba.[117] Liatif Kerimov illustrated a rug with the Marasali design from the village of Sor Sor, located near the Kura river.[118] Some maps show the village of Marasali, while others include Mereze (Maraza) only,[119] and still others show both places. Sotheby's, London, used to catalogue all Marasalis as Merezes.

The origin of the Marasali 'flaming boteh' is uncertain. It is possible that the Zoroastrian fire worship of Baku was an early inspiration for the design.[120] In addition to the boteh, another distinguishing feature is the use of a distinctive 'Marasali' red, a luminous, flame-like hue somewhere between salmon, orange and madder.

Even a cursory glance at the plates in this book will expose my bias towards Marasali rugs. In my opinion the best Marasalis are the most beautiful and majestic of all Caucasian prayer rugs. I am convinced that a small group of Marasali prayer rugs, probably dating to the late eighteenth or the early

36

35 One of the many variants of the floral motif border design.
36 Latchhook border design.
37 Geometric 'c' motif border design.
38 Typical 'Akstafa' prayer arch.
39 'Kotchak' (ram's horn) border motif, more rarely interpreted as composed of hooked bird's beak elements.
40 'Gold' Marasali flower motifs.
41 'Gold' Marasali cartouche border design.

37

38

XXIX

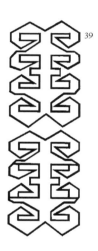

39

nineteenth centuries (represented by plates 89, 90 and 91) were different from other Marasalis, in that they were commissioned pieces, woven by master weavers from cartoons.

Besides the previously mentioned elite group, Marasali prayer rugs that closely adhered to the traditional design and colours continued to be made throughout the nineteenth century. Some wonderful examples were created during the mid- to late nineteenth century. Many Marasali-design rugs have been attributed to other areas, but for comparative purposes I have included all such rugs in the Marasali section of the database. There are 232 'Marasali' prayer rugs in the files (11.3 percent of the total). These may be divided into groups by field colour, as each colour has its own typical design.

Black Marasalis The so-called 'Black' Marasalis in fact have fields of very dark indigo. The oldest black Marasalis are the small number that have curved prayer arches (see plates 89, 90, and 91). The boteh in early pieces are randomly placed, face in alternate directions and are filled with a great variety of designs including honeycombs, stripes and zigzags. They also feature a wealth of colours in superb juxtapositions.[121] In later pieces the boteh usually all face in one direction and are considerably less imaginative in their use of colour and design.

Gold (or yellow gold) Marasalis This group may be divided into two-sub groups: floral lattice fields and boteh fields.[122] The lattice type features diagonally striped and vertically bisected geometric flowers arranged in 'v'-shaped rows (fig. 40). A characteristic border for this type contains latchhooks enclosed by hexagonal cartouches (fig. 41). There are 52 'gold-field' rugs in the database, of which 31 are latticed and 21 have boteh fields.

Ivory Marasalis Although the 'ivory-field' group can also be divided into the lattice and boteh subgroups, ivory-field rugs are designed very differently from their 'gold' cousins. The border shown in figure 41 is never employed; rather the dragon border predominates, with the 'Marasali' bird border design (fig. 39) being used in the prayer arch. There are a total of 34 'ivory-field' rugs in the database, of which 28 are of lattice design and four with boteh.[123]

Red- and green-field Marasalis These are extremely rare. There are four 'red fields' in the database,[124] and only one green-field Marasali known to me (sold at Sotheby's, London on 17 October 1984, lot 621). All are of different designs. A few 'unique' Marasalis do not conform to the typical designs outlined above.[125] These have been classified by field colour.

XXIX *Veiled Circassian Lady* by the French artist Jean-Léon Gerome (1824–1904), showing an Akstafa prayer rug very similar to the one illustrated in plate 55. (Published in *Christie's International Magazine*, Jan./Feb. 1997, p. 58. Reproduced courtesy Christie's International, NY.)

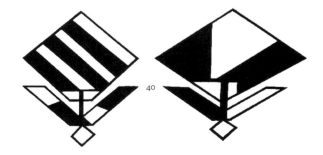

40

41

3

THE PLATES I

I

BORCHALO

early 19th century

0.96 × 1.09m (3′2″ × 3′7″)

This pretty little Kazak from the Borchalo region has some unusual features. Although it also has many typical Borchalo characteristics, such as the brown and white trefoil reciprocal main border and the blue re-entrant mihrab on a red surround, it is a distinct and very charming piece. Double-hooked lines project laterally from the mihrab into the field, forming a variant of the usual trefoil reciprocal design. Similar hooks project diagonally from the upper corners of the mihrab, a design variant apparently unique to this rug.[1] Another unusual feature is the two red polygonal medallions in the mihrab, which are centred among quatrefoil flowerheads. These medallions enclose cruciferous forms similar to those pictured in Gantzhorn's *The Christian Oriental Carpet* (which the author calls 'light symbol crosses'[2]). A similar diagram is also published in Kerimov's *Azerbaijanski Kovjer*, where he assigns the symbol to Karais(?).[3] These designs are also evocative of a certain type of Anatolian zile technique called 'vertical float', which produces a corded effect (called 'fitilli').[4] The rug was shown in the *Passages* exhibition at California State University, Hayward during the 1990 International Conference on Oriental Carpets (ICOC) in San Francisco.

2

BORCHALO

dated AH 1287 (1871)

1.50 × 1.78m (4′11″ × 5′9″)

With its vertically arranged hexagons filled with latchhooked diamonds, this rug deviates from the usual field design of Borchalo prayer rugs (double diamonds in an iterative pattern). It belongs to a small sub-group of prayer and secular Borchalo rugs that almost invariably feature a frame of multi-coloured slanted stripes surrounding the prayer niche or field. Most examples in this group have dates inscribed in a cartouche in the upper border, and feature geometric flowerheads in the niche. This example, however, has the rare variant of three latchhooked diamonds. The rug has a date cartouche (AH 1287) to the left of the arch, and an inscription in the upper border.

3

BORCHALO

1st half 19th century

0.96 × 1.22m (3′2″ × 4′0″)

Although this rug is in a very worn condition, it is included here because it is one of the oldest of its type that are known to have survived. Its owner, Wells C. Klein, has been studying the design of Caucasian prayer rugs for a number of years and has identified specific indices of age. A number of these appear here: the high prayer arch; the octagons containing 'c' motifs; the polychrome diamond-filled poles in the centres of the two diamonds, and the precision of the drawing. The soft, mellow colours showing the patina of age are consistent with an early date. The dark blue wool is used sparingly – in the prayer arch, in some of the outlining and in some minor details; the other colours are madder red, green, yellow, brown and ivory. The rug has wool warps and wool wefts of medium grey brown. Out of nearly 100 double-diamond Borchalo prayer rugs in the database, no exact analogy with this combination of features could be found.

41

4

BORCHALO

c.1865

1.04 × 1.17m (3′5″ × 3′10″)

Prayer rugs from the mountainous regions of southwestern Caucasia (especially from the Borchalo and Fachralo districts) are profoundly influenced by older Anatolian examples in which the mihrab, often with a re-entrant motif, takes up most of the field. This is in contrast to eastern Caucasian pieces where the prayer arch is generally free-floating. While rugs from the eastern Caucasus take their cue from the floral designs of Persia, the layout of rugs from southwestern Caucasus (such as those shown here) is architectural in its inspiration.

▷

5

BORCHALO

c.1875

1.02 × 1.14m (3′4″ × 3′9″)

The two examples presented here are paired for good reason. Colour-wise they are reverse images of each other, and they also represent two examples of a very rare design variant of Borchalo rugs: the single central diamond. This motif appears only on about three percent of the known prayer rugs from the district. At first glance, the rug with the blue niche appears to be a good deal older that the red niche example – it is better drawn, with every element confidently and precisely draughted. There are also some signs of age in the other rug, however. Although it is not drawn with the sureness of the former, the intricate reciprocal trefoil border with heavily corroded browns, and the octagons containing 'c' motifs flanking the prayer arch, suggest a date of around 1875.

6

BORCHALO

late 19th century

1.07 × 1.50m (3′6″ × 4′11″)

This prayer rug is typical of the Borchalo region. It features the characteristic Borchalo colouring, border and field design. The design comprises two hexagons arranged vertically, with a design of decorated rectangles inside. Nicolas Fokker published this piece in *Caucasian Rugs of Yesterday*,[1] calling the design inside the hexagons 'a rudimentary Tree of Life'.[2] While this may well be so, the design is similar to and most likely evolves from the crosses used in medieval Armenian churches and monasteries. (Examples are the crosses-within-crosses on the walls of the Church of Spitakawar, and the cross formed by a window with another cross above it at the Monastery of Sagmosavank.[3]) Many Armenian symbols and designs are incorporated into Caucasian weaving, and it is possible that many of these rugs were woven by Armenians. The motifs might also have a spiritual significance. Reviewing a similar rug for *Hali*,[4] Wilfred Stanzer referred to the motifs within the hexagons as 'tamga' signs, and to the two radiating diamonds as 'suggestive of windows to the universe'.[5]

The rug shown here is made from lustrous, silky wool and feels very soft to the touch. This is typical of Borchalo rugs since the wool comes from high-grazing mountain sheep and is thus very high in lanolin content, making it soft and pliable.

7

BORCHALO

2nd half 19th century

1.14 × 1.30m (3′9″ × 4′3″)

The condition of this rug is intriguing. Although it has holes and is tattered around the sides, the pile itself is lustrous and velvety, without signs of erosive wear. It is possible that the rug sustained rodent or water damage as one of a layer of unattended pieces piled in a mosque or warehouse. This is fairly common among rugs acquired (like this example) in Turkey. This particular Borchalo design of all-over hexagons and octagons is rare and much sought after.[1]

A number of analogous examples exist, but none has the unusual border displayed here. The parallel pieces feature variations on the trefoil border considered standard for this type, while this example features a narrow chequerboard main border that I have not seen on any Caucasian rug. (The main border is flanked by a more typical 'running dog' motif.) It is also the only one in the group with a re-entrant motif, here containing confronting dragons. The quality of red, green and blue dyes is superb, and there is also an unusual light avocado green in the octagons in the spandrels. While the inscribed date of AH 1315 translates to 1897, the rug appears to be considerably older.

8

FACHRALO

late 19th century

1.14 × 1.42m (3´9˝ × 4´8˝)

Although at first glance this red-ground Fachralo prayer rug appears to be a typical example, a closer examination reveals some unusual features. The 'c' gul motifs inside the diamonds in the spandrels are uncommon in Fachralos, although frequently seen in other rugs from the Kazak area. The confronting dragons inside the niche have been stylized to such a degree of abstraction as to be no longer recognizable. They flank the re-entrant arch, which contains almost identical stylized motifs; the motifs inside and outside the arch are near mirror-images of each other. The leaf-and-calyx border is the most popular border design for Fachralo prayer rugs, appearing on over one-half of such rugs in our database.[1] The alternating 'barber pole' treatment of the guard borders is also common throughout the Kazak weaving area.

9

FACHRALO

1st half 19th century

1.19 × 1.30m (3′11″ × 4′7″)

The main identifying feature of Fachralo carpets is the prominent central medallion; sometimes this is eight-pointed and at other times it lacks its lateral points, as in this example. The origin of this medallion may date back to Anatolian carpets of the sixteenth century or even earlier.[1] This rug is characteristic of the Kazak group, which is closely related to the traditional Turkish style. The geometric mihrab takes up most of the field and the bold, well-designed prayer niche is flanked by zoomorphic motifs. Typical waterbug palmettes surround the re-entrant niche. While the majority of the known Fachralo prayer rugs feature variants of the serrated leaf border, this example is distinguished by its use of a 'meander-and-cross' pattern. Such borders are uncommon, although a few related Fachralos do exist (see analogies).

IO

FACHRALO

2nd half 19th century

1.07 × 1.37m (3′6″ × 4′5″)

II

FACHRALO

2nd half 19th century

1.14 × 1.45m (3′9″ × 4′9″)

These two Fachralo Kazaks make an interesting comparison. While they share many characteristics, each displays some unique features. Both employ identical colour palettes of predominantly red, white and blue, combined with yellow and green – a combination favoured by Fachralo weavers. Both have blue mihrabs, lacking re-entrant arches, which enclose white, star-like medallions containing hooked cruciforms. The borders are virtually identical and comprise serrated leaves without the usual chalices or calyxes. The red surrounds are filled with waterbug palmettes of the type that Schürmann calls a 'chafer' design because of its resemblance to a beetle or a scarab.

There are also some marked differences between the two rugs, however. One mihrab has a peaked apex, while the other is squared off. The rug with the peaked apex is better drawn, with generous spacing. It is likely, therefore, that this rug is the older of the two; the other rug hints at the rather cluttered design that tends to afflict later pieces. Nevertheless, both represent highly collectable types, and demonstrate the fidelity to traditional elements and motifs that is found in village weavings.

12

FACHRALO

2nd half 19th century

1.20 × 1.31m (3′ 11″ × 4′ 4″)

This is a fine example of a typical Fachralo prayer rug. It embodies many of the signature features of the type including the star-like central medallion with hooked motifs, the 'chafer' or waterbug palmettes in the corners, and a re-entrant arch with confronting dragons flanked by animals and tree forms. This type of field design can be combined with a variety of borders that are indigenous to this weaving area. These include the serrated leaf, the meandering vine with crosses and the 'meander' palmette. The meandering floral border featured here is very similar to that in plate 17.[1]

13

FACHRALO

dated AH 1245 (1829)

1.07 × 1.17m (3´6˝ × 3´10˝)

This early, rare and rather important piece belongs to a small group of Kazak prayer rugs often assigned to Fachralo, although the palette and ornamentation are more consistent with Borchalo weavings. Rugs in this group feature large areas of undecorated colour and a particular shade of light, mottled green; dotted blue spandrels often feature above the prayer arch. The first publication of a similar example was in Kendrick and Tattersall's *Handwoven Carpets, Oriental and European*, of 1922 (plate 138). Like Kendrick and Tattersall's piece this rug has a 'pinwheel' or swastika within an ivory polygon, and bird-like ornaments which have been likened to imperial Russian eagles. The borders on the two rugs are identical. Our rug, however, is distinguished by its extraordinarily well-balanced design. It also differs in that it features a very broad madder mihrab, surmounted by a yellow prayer arch with a plain green polygon beneath it. Aesthetically, our example – with its pure, bright colours and wonderful use of space – should be considered to be a 'best of type' within this small, elite group.

14

FACHRALO

mid-19th century

1.17 × 1.52m (3′10″ × 5′0″)

White-ground Fachralo prayer rugs are extremely rare. This piece was created in the middle of the nineteenth century, perhaps even earlier, and with its clear, uncompromising lines is extremely impressive. Only two comparable pieces from this period are known.[1] The white re-entrant mihrab of undyed wool is dominated by a typical Fachralo medallion, composed of a smaller red stellar medallion inside the larger blue eight-pointed star. Small spikes project from the sides, and latch-hooks emerge from the top and bottom. Pairs of elaborate red rosettes appear above and below the medallion. The only other decoration in the mihrab is the polychrome cruciform motif underneath the prayer niche. The border is the characteristic 'leaf-and-calyx' pattern. The owner of the rug, Mike Tschebull, is of the opinion that the white wool in this and similar Fachralos has been bleached, which would explain why it has not yellowed – even a little – like most white wool.

White-ground Fachralo prayer rugs are attributed by some authorities to Lori-Pambak. Perhaps it is because of their white fields or a similarity of colours and their arrangements, or like border designs, or simply the geographical proximity of the two regions. In recent years a number of white-ground Kazak carpets with herald-like Lori-Pambak drawings have been found.

15

FACHRALO

c.1885

1.13 × 1.60m (3′9″ × 5′3″)

This is an intriguing and unusual example as it combines design elements from both the Fachralo and Borchalo areas (John Eskenazi assigned the rug to Fachralo in 1983.[1]) The colours and major border are typical of Fachralo (see plate 10), while the two large radiating diamond medallions are a signature motif of Borchalo rugs. The minor borders of small cruciform motifs on a sky-blue ground are used throughout the Kazak weaving area. In Fachralo pieces the subsidiary motifs surrounding the mihrab are usually 'chafer' or waterbug palmettes (as seen in plates 10 and 11); here, however, that role is filled by unusual hooked elements, a variant of the ram's horn motif. John Eskenazi likens these to the 'kotchak' horn motifs associated with Turkoman (Central Asian) weavings.[2] All of the design elements in this rug work together and complement each other, creating a cohesive whole that is quite unusual among such hybrids.

16

KAZAK

dated AH 1253 (1837)

0.96 × 1.24m (3′2″ × 4′1″)

Turkoman ancestry is evident in this highly unusual Kazak prayer rug, which was purchased by the owner's grandfather as an old rug in about 1900. (Turkish-speaking tribes, particularly Yomut and Chodor, often use octagons in a similar manner in their rugs.) While no analogous Kazak examples are known, similar octagons appear on a group of finely woven prayer rugs assigned to Moghan or Shirvan,[1] as well as on a Baku rug.[2] The sides of the prayer arch extend vertically into the field. This feature, while unusual, is known on a number of rugs of various types. The palette comprises the red, white and blue colours typical of southwestern examples, but green and yellow are also used sparingly and the red has a blueish tinge, tending to maroon.

Although classified as a Kazak, based on structural criteria, the rug has some Genje characteristics. The border, while identical to some Kazak examples, is typical of Genje pieces,[3] while the geometric 's' forms that dot the field, and the economical use of yellow, green and brown, are also Genje characteristics. The date is difficult to read but can be deciphered as AH 1253, translating to 1837, which, considering the rug's provenance and appearance, is credible.

I7

KAZAK

2nd half 19th century

1.26 × 1.58m (4′2″ × 5′2″)

An example of a rather rare type of Kazak prayer rug, this piece contains motifs indigenous to a variety of Kazak weaving villages and has not been attributed with certainty to a specific area. The first publication of a similar piece was by Lefevre in 1974;[1] further examples were published in 1978 by Spuhler, König and Volkmann and by Herrmann the following year.[2] While Lefevre's rug and this one have identical floral meander borders, Spuhler's and Herrmann's feature borders of star designs. (In Spuhler's case, the stars alternate with 'ram's horns'.[3]) All of the rugs feature large, free-floating mihrabs containing 'chequerboard' cruciforms with projecting 'kotchak' horn motifs. The mihrabs and borders of these rugs are virtually identical to those in a vertical Turkish saff attributed to Kagizman/Kars.[4] This surely establishes beyond doubt the strong connection between Caucasian rugs of this type and their Anatolian cousins.

18

KAZAK

mid-19th century

1.19 × 1.30m (3′11″ × 4′3″)

This is an extraordinary rug. Its stark, 'minimalist' look is extremely unusual and is one reason why the rug has fetched such a high price at auction.[1] Described by Detlef Maltzahn in the auction catalogue notes as 'one of the rarest remaining prayer carpets',[2] the rug's tremendous impact comes from its perfectly balanced design and pure, saturated colours. The green praying area, which stands on a bare red background, is strongly delineated and extremely simple in conception; Maltzahn likens it to a window which opens onto another world. The pronounced abrash[3] of this 'window' helps create an illusion of three-dimensional depth. Anatolian inspiration is evident in the rug's design, as is its architectural relationship to a small group of prayer rugs (featuring 'bug' medallions within the mihrab) attributed to Lori-Pambak.[4] Maltzahn has attributed the rug to the Fachralo area.

19

KAZAK

dated AH 1221 (1806)

0.74 × 1.30m (2′5″ × 4′3″)

This is the earliest known Kazak prayer carpet that can be precisely dated.[1] (The earliest dated secular Kazak is nine years older.[2]) The rug's unusually small size and its long, shiny pile – characteristic of the finest Kazaks – give it a jewel-like appearance. Although evenly worn, it still possesses the lustre that only the finest and softest wool can produce. The mottled field gives the impression of great depth, as does the abrashed light blue of the bottom compartment. Here, the appearance is one of an endless night sky. The wonderfully archaic white-ground border is evocative of Turkish and Central Asian antecedents.

Formerly in the collection of John Webb Hill of San Francisco, this piece is now owned by James Burns of Seattle. It was shown at the De Young Memorial Museum, San Francisco in the exhibition *Prayer Rugs from the Near East and Central Asia* (24 November 1984–28 April 1985) and published in *Hali* 26, p. 63. It was later shown in the *Passages* exhibition at California State University, Hayward, during the 1990 ICOC in San Francisco.

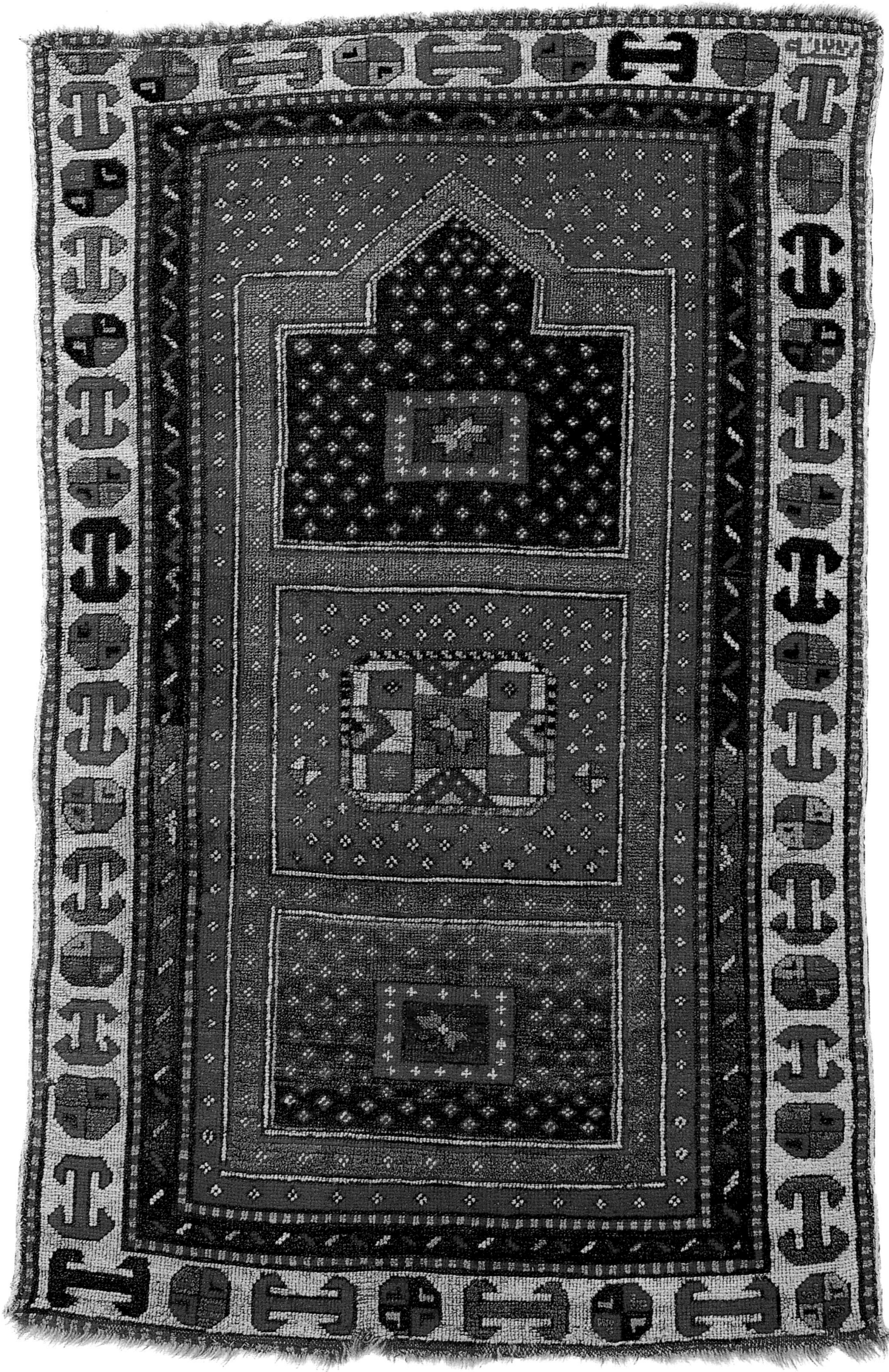

20

KAZAK

1st quarter 19th century

1.12 × 1.60m (3′8″ × 5′3″)

This prayer rug is wonderfully archaic in appearance. The green re-entrant mihrab is filled with bold polychrome rosettes. Prayer rugs with rosettes of this type have usually been assigned to the Borchalo district of the Kazak weaving area, but this example combines features indigenous to various districts. The mihrab, which is small in relation to the overall dimensions, floats on a madder field surmounting a row of five 'chafer' palmettes. These palmettes are a feature of many districts, including Fachralo. Surrounding the mihrab are heart-shaped, horned motifs which are in fact the detached top portions of the palmettes – a very unusual design treatment. While the top and bottom borders are virtually identical to those of the Kazak rug shown in plate 19, the side borders depict a more geometric, derivative rendering of the pattern.

21

KAZAK

c.1875

0.90 × 1.33m (2′11″ × 4′4″)

This rug belongs to a small group of mid- to late nineteenth-century south Caucasian pieces usually attributed to the Kazak weaving area. It shares a number of design characteristics with the rugs in plates 23 and 31. Describing a similar example sold in his gallery on 17 July 1981, Jean Lefevre suggested that some details of the ornamentation recall the decorative style of seventeenth- and eighteenth-century silk embroideries made in Shemaka, and that other aspects of the decorations (as well as the wool and handle) point to the southern regions of Talish or Moghan. The Lefevre rug was without doubt the model for a modern Turkish copy that was exhibited at the 1983 ICOC in London.[1] Another very similar example, dated 1865, was sold at Skinner's in 1991. That example, however, had the stylized cartouche border associated with early related pieces (such as that shown in plate 31).

There is a large group of related Kazak rugs that utilize central medallions very similar to that seen here. These rugs differ, however, in that they feature free-floating gabled prayer arches rather than the stylized mihrabs of this group and its ancestors. They also generally have an arrowhead border rather than the scrolled 's' border of these pieces. A hybrid example was published in Hawley, *Oriental Rugs, Antique and Modern*, plate 50.

22

KAZAK

c.1880

1.14 × 2.08m (3′9″ × 6′10″)

Designs travel. The borders, arch and floral field of this rug are influenced by east Caucasian designs, but it is without doubt a Kazak, with the red weft, full pile and hefty feel typical of that area. The red and white minor guard stripe is also an indication of southwest Caucasian origin. The field design is somewhat unusual in that it lacks a latticed grid, and the almost mushroom-like depiction of the flowers is uncommon as well. This could be a case of a weaver attempting to emulate a Shirvan pattern without a clear understanding of the design, or it could simply be an original design without specific antecedents. The rug has the clear colours typical of Kazak weavings, including white, red, two blues, two greens, yellow and light blue.

A very similar example, with an identical field and border system but with a notched prayer arch and hand prints in the spandrels, was sold to a leading German dealer at Skinner's in 1986.[1] Another, virtually identical, piece was offered at auction by Rippon in 1996. Other white-ground examples, similar in design but with naturalistically drawn flowers, have been assigned to the eastern Caucasus.[3]

23

KAZAK

dated AH 1278 (1861)

1.12 × 1.63m (3′8″ × 5′4″)

This rug is distinguished by its strong drawing and attention to detail, its use of saturated colours (including touches of aubergine in the border and field ornaments) and its two rather unusual green-ground medallions. The motif of vertically linked medallions is quite often found in other types of oriental carpet. In prayer rugs, however, it is quite rare – other than on Caucasian Kazaks, Karabaghs, Genjes and Akstafas.[1] A close analogy to this example, which shares its leaf-and-calyx border (characteristic of rugs from the Kazak district), can be seen in O'Bannon's *Oriental Rugs*.[2]

When this rug was sold at Rippon it was assigned to Fachralo by the auctioneers.[3] This designation was probably based on the shape of the medallions, as well as its typical border, although similar examples have not always been so attributed.[4]

24

The soft red ground of this attractive prayer carpet, the shape and decoration of its ivory prayer arch and the latchhooked polygonal ivory central medallion clearly follow the 'benchmark' example of this rare type, which is in the Rudnick Collection, as do both the subsidiary motifs scattered throughout the field and the polychrome triangles framing it. The Rudnick rug was published as plate 14 in *Through the Collector's Eye*, the catalogue of the first American Conference on Oriental Rugs, held in 1991. Commenting on the Rudnick rug in the catalogue, Mark Hopkins wrote that 'this prayer rug belongs to a rare group believed to have appeared in the early decades of the nineteenth century.' Indeed, the Rudnick rug bears a totally believable date of AH 1243 (1827) and appears to be the oldest in this small group, notwithstanding the earlier dates inscribed on other analogous examples. It differs from the present piece not only in its radically different border design of hooked cartouches, but also in the archaic style of its drawing. Our rug appears to be a generation or two later.

This rug may also be compared to the example in plate 31 below, 'the mother of this type', which belongs to a comparable but different sub-group. This sub-group is characterized by a rigid and square white central medallion and has other design and structural differences, such as silk wefting.

25

Whether or not this charming Tree of Life rug was intended for prayer is open to question: directional rugs often serve a dual purpose, employed both for prayer and as decorative pieces. A large green cypress tree dominates the madder field, and is flanked by a pair of fabulous birds and pairs of animals. Two related examples are more overtly for prayer use: one, belonging to Gérard Boëly of Aix-en-Provence, has a red mihrab surrounding the central cypress tree;[1] the other, with an even more clearly defined mihrab, is shown in plate 26 opposite. An example that may have been a Kazak copy of this rug was offered at Christie's, London on 16 April 1984, lot 39. As Boëly indicates in his discussion of the rug cited above (in *Hali* 54), these Tree of Life designs were probably inspired by eighteenth-century silk ikats (resist-dyed textiles) or velvets from Central Asia and Persia. *Hali* published a silk ikat velvet of identical size and virtually identical design to Boëly's rug, even down to the borders, and wrote that such pieces have been made 'as wide apart as Bukhara and Kashan'.[2]

The south Caucasian attribution of Karabagh seems correct for our example, while Boëly prefers Shirvan for his. The narrow border of this rug is very similar to the borders of Karabagh animal prayer rugs, while the colours and technical features are also consistent with that attribution. A comparison between this rug and Boëly's is discussed in the 'Auction Price Guide' section of *Hali* 61.[3]

26

While this very interesting prayer rug shares many features with the 'tree' Karabagh in plate 25, it appears to be more closely related to a contemporaneous prayer rug (dated 1879) from the collection of Gérard Boëly, published as a 'Connoisseur's Choice' in *Hali*.[1] While Boëly's has the more unusual palette, which includes a rare turquoise, the similarities in use of colour and overall design are striking. Both rugs feature a central tree divided into vertical stripes (eleven stripes in Boëly's piece, seven here) against a red ground beneath blue spandrels. Here, the blue of the spandrels is darker than the blues used elsewhere. Smaller trees flank the central one, and the 'grounds' of the trees are decorated with stepped lozenges. While in Boëly's rug the tree motif is repeated in the spandrels, here the prayer niche is flanked by fabulous birds. Other small animals dot the mihrabs of both rugs. Both employ unusual border designs: Boëly's uses a stylized 'Kufic' variant (a design presumed to have evolved from the Kufic script); while the rug shown here features segmented florettes in yellow, red, blue and teal.[2]

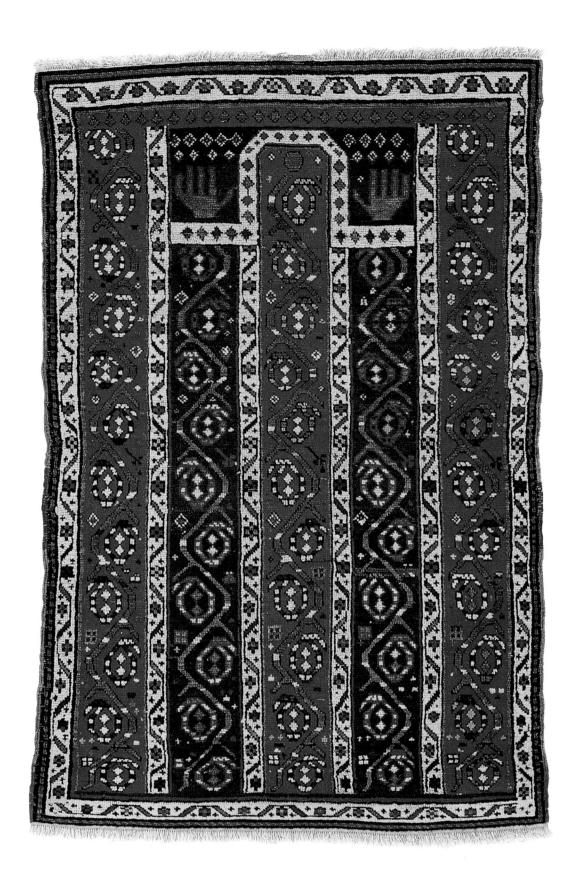

27

KARABAGH

2nd half 19th century

0.84 × 1.30m (2′9″ × 4′3″)

One distinguishing feature of Karabagh prayer rugs with striped fields seems to be that the area containing the prayer arch and the spandrels is of a different pattern than the field.[1] This example, however, belongs to a related sub-group which does not share this peculiarity. Both groups feature the design of broad vertical bands containing boteh with angular meandering vines. In some, the central and lateral bands are outlined by an ivory guard border so as to form a mihrab, following Anatolian tradition.[2] The owner of this rug, Raoul Tschebull, has pointed out that its red is quite unusual for the type; madder red (and aubergine) is used rather than the usual 'cochineal' colour. He suggests that this rug may be from a pre-cochineal period (cochineal was introduced around 1850); or perhaps cochineal was not available to the weaver for another reason.

While most of the rugs in this group are undated, a similar, unillustrated example, dated 1884, was sold at Sotheby's New York in 1984,[3] while another (see analogy 1) bears dates of 1814 or 1834, which seem too early by at least a generation.

28

KARABAGH

dated AH 1312 (1894)

0.84 × 1.17m (2′9″ × 3′10″)

This is one of those atypical rugs which occasionally emerge from Caucasia or Turkey. While no precise analogy to this rug has been identified, either in literature or by anyone with whom I have discussed it, Danny Anavian, a New York antique rugs dealer, has examined the piece and proposed that it is Kurdish work from the environs of Shusha in Karabagh. The offset depiction of the flowers in conjunction with the vertical stripes, the use of a particular shade of yellow, and the overtly Islamic character of the rug (with its stylized mosque), as well as some technical characteristics, have led him to this conclusion. Shusha was a major stop on a trade route between Persia and Caucasia that was used by Kurdish travellers, and the presence of large Kurdish communities in the area is indicated on a number of ethnographic maps.[1]

The configuration of vertical stripes is typical of south Caucasian Karabagh rugs, while the polychrome zigzag border is consistent with Kurdish work.[2] The inclusion of a mosque is quite rare, however, and the horizontally drawn lacy filigree is another unusual feature.[3] Whilst Caucausian prayer rugs with depictions of mosques are uncommon, there is a group of late Shirvan rugs that feature very realistic depictions of famous mosques.[4]

29

KARABAGH

late 19th century

0.89 × 1.58m (2′11″ × 5′2″)

Prayer rugs in this small group from south Caucasia have been variously assigned to Genje, Karabagh and its Persian neighbour, Karadagh. This group of rugs is characterized by a large medallion dominating the field, and an angular prayer niche; most examples also have hands in the spandrels. A related example, with an arched prayer niche and the central medallion on a latticed field, has been assigned to both Karadagh (where it was grouped with Persian examples) and the Caucasus.[1] A related example was assigned to Karabagh by Rippon[2] and to Saliani by Skinner.[3] Both these rugs have floral roundels in the field, whereas the example shown here has four square reserves, containing Memling guls, surrounding the central medallion. This rug was exhibited at the *Art of the Hordes* exhibition in San Francisco, July–September 1993.[4]

75

30

KARABAGH [?]

dated AH 1257 (1841)

1.09 × 1.50m (3′7″ × 4′11″)

Only three rugs of this type are known. One example (unpublished) was included in a 1984 exhibition at the De Young Memorial Museum, assigned to Karadagh;[1] the other was published in *Hali* in an advertisement for Konzett Teppichekunst.[2] Konzett assigned his rug to Shirvan, while the owner of this rug prefers a more general eastern Caucasian designation. Both attributions are less than certain, since the rugs combine design and structural elements from many rug-weaving districts. A Karabagh attribution seems the most likely, indices being the 'waterbug' palmettes, the gable under the arch and the central diamond, which is characteristic of Chelabi rugs from Karabagh. Nevertheless, both rugs have the multicolour selvedge typical of Kazak rugs, and the diamond design is quite different from the latchhook diamonds of Chelabi. In addition, the cotton weft of this rug is unusual – although not completely unknown – for a Karabagh.

This rug and Konzett's share a number of features with a small group of early, elite prayer rugs variously assigned to Karabagh, Turkey and southwest Caucasia.[3] Shared motifs include the hook decoration on the prayer arch and central medallion, and the cartouche above the bottom border. This group of rugs, pre-dating the rug shown here by about 30–40 years, is a very probable ancestor.

3I

KARABAGH

dated AH 1222 (1807)

1.0 × 1.40m (3′3″ × 4′7″)

This rug is one of a very small group of remarkably similar carpets bearing early dates and woven on all-silk foundations, all-cotton foundations, or combinations of both. Shared design features include the corner-bracketed central medallion, the unusual treatment of the prayer niche, and the distinctive cartouche border. Various provenances have been suggested for these pieces, ranging as far afield as Anatolia, the Talish group, Kazak and more recently Karabagh. However, it is most probable that this group of rugs, of which only six complete examples are known, is the work of a single workshop of Armenian weavers from Karabagh. Although the design is related to the seventeenth- and eighteenth-century embroideries of Azerbaijan, this design has no clear antecedents among Caucasian pile weaving. Another group of medallion prayer rugs subsequently evolved from these rugs (see plate 70) and the design continued to be woven well into the twentieth century.[1]

The first publication of this type of rug was in the Textile Museum, Washington, catalogue of 1974, *Prayer Rugs from Private Collections,* plate 26 (all-cotton foundation). Here an Anatolian influence, specifically the sixteenth-century 'Holbein' design group, was suggested.[2] The rug shown here was the second to be published (by Lefevre) where a connection to the Talish group was proposed.[3]

32

CHAN-KARABAGH

2nd half 19th century

0.85 × 1.44m (2′9″ × 4′9″)

This piece has many of the signature features of the group of rugs that Liatif Kerimov has termed 'Chan-Karabagh'.[1] Typical Chan-Karabagh features include a white-ground dragon border; a field of boteh or crab-like floral bouquets; and a single arrowhead motif under the prayer arch, with a box-like square ornament immediately beneath. An example virtually identical to ours was published in Bausback 1973, p. 72; another at Sotheby's, New York, 5 March 1982 (lot 82). An example with a border of linked 's' hexagons (typical of Shahsavan) was illustrated as plate 33 in Macey, *Oriental Prayer Rugs*, where it was described as a product of 'the warlike Kossak tribes which settled mainly in the Circassian area of the Caucasus'. Other typical borders for this type of rug include latchhooked diamonds on an ivory ground, linked arrowheads, 's' figures and stepped flowerheads.[2]

This example was offered at Lefevre in 1980, dated to the second half of the nineteenth century, with the colours described as 'brilliant shades of crimson, green, azure, yellow, violet-brown and white'.[3] It was subsequently offered at Rippon,[4] assigned to Talish, where it was acquired by its current owner.

33

GENJE

dated AH 1244 (1828)

0.96 × 1.52m (3′2″ × 5′0″)

A rather mysterious rug, with no known close analogies. Loosely woven, it has the look of south Caucasian pieces, possibly from the Karabagh district, although it is not a 'Karabagh' in the sense in which the trade uses the designation. The owner suggests a Genje attribution.

The prayer arch is formed simply by the intrusion of the spandrels into the latticed field. The sky-blue guard borders are typical of south Caucasian weaving, but the yellow-ground main border presents an enigma. The blue, green and red border elements represent some type of heraldic motif, possibly a double eagle or another kind of confronting bird form. They are vaguely reminiscent of the field ornaments of a white-ground Caucasian carpet in the Victoria and Albert Museum, London.[1] The rug is dated AH 1244 (1828), which is consistent with its look and feel.

34

GENJE

c.1800

0.76 × 1.60m (2´6˝ × 5´3˝)

A configuration of completely unadorned stripes, in solid colours, is extremely unusual among Caucasian prayer rugs.[1] Generally the stripes are decorated with crosses, dots or other miniature elements (eastern Caucasus) or small 's' forms (southern Caucasus). The rug shown here has been assigned to Genje on the basis of its colour scheme (the incidence of yellow and blue), the shape of its prayer arch, and its boxflower border design, which appears on Genje rugs as well as on other south Caucasian pieces. Identical borders can be seen on two rugs assigned to Genje by Ian Bennett[2] and on other Genje rugs.[3] (Lenkoran prayer rugs, from southeastern Caucasia, also feature this border.)

The most closely analogous example to this rug, in overall terms, is probably that illustrated in Schürmann, *Caucasian Rugs*, plate 74. Although assigned to Shirvan, with a sombrely striped field of blue and ivory diagonals, it has a very similar polychrome border. In his commentary, Schürmann points to the influence of the Genje district, although he still attributes it to 'the south of Shirvan region'. A very similar design and palette may also be seen in a Kuba bag face published by Herrmann.[4]

35

late 19th century

0.91 × 1.68m (3′0″ × 5′6″)

This is an interesting rug on a number of counts. Although the design is atypical for the region, its south Caucasian origin may easily be discerned. The distinctive polychrome rosettes are a feature of rugs throughout southwest Caucasus and are particularly prevalent in the weavings of Genje, Karabagh and, further east, Moghan. The mellow colour palette is consistent with Genje pieces and can be compared to a diagonally striped Genje published as plate 68 in Dodds et al, *Oriental Rugs from Atlantic Collections*.

While the rug's overall design is superficially similar to that of the Karabagh shown in plate 26, it has a number of singular components. The bottom panel (or 'elem') is unusual. The medachyl reciprocal inner border featured here and in the spandrels is rarely seen in south Caucasian prayer rugs, and the weaver's technical skill is evident from the way the design has been executed (particularly in the spandrels around the arch). The small sprinkle of white dots may have been intended to evoke a night sky, or a feeling of depth. The unusual and colourful zigzag border is coincidentally quite similar to that seen on the Karabagh in plate 28.

36

MOGHAN

2nd half 19th century

1.13 × 1.83m (3′8″ × 6′0″)

This carpet presents us with an intriguing conundrum. As pictured, it reads as a conventional prayer rug. The oblique white lines suggest a rudimentary prayer arch, while the little arrows pointing upwards to an apex recall similar, enlarged motifs in the fields of some Anatolian rugs. The field below the arch is filled with geometric renditions of floral forms, in the familiar pattern of prayer rugs. If examined the other way up, however, the 'arch' becomes an abstract flowering vase. The 'eagle's beak' border can be read in either direction. The owner, Jim Dixon, is convinced that the weaver's primary intention was to make a prayer carpet; he points out that all mihrabs are reflections of heaven and, as such, are sometimes rendered like a mirror. Many early Anatolian prayer rugs feature upside-down vases, lamps and ewers. (How this convention made its way from Anatolia to the Caucasus is a subject for interesting speculation.)

A possible 'dual purpose' for this rug cannot be discounted, however. Although the soft wool and dyes are of the highest quality, as is typical of Moghan work, the execution is experimental, not following convention or a cartoon. It is possibly a unique rug, or made for a client who wanted a dual-purpose piece. It is likely that more that one weaver was involved in making this rug.[1]

37

MOGHAN

1st half 19th century

1.14 × 1.87m (3′9″ × 6′2″)

This rug was one of the first to be attributed to Moghan.[1] Jean Lefevre identified this type in 1982 as a distinctive group of prayer rugs, with a strong geometric style, which he assigned to the mountainous Moghan region. The region borders present-day Iran and was the last of the Caucasian provinces to be ceded to Russia, in 1829. Three further examples of this type have subsequently been published.[2] All four examples feature a white-ground field with octagon pattern and kochanak or 'horn' crosses under the prayer arch. (In this rug kochanaks also appear in the spandrels.[3]) The border systems are identical, featuring triangles with arrowhead motifs. An early Shirvan runner with a main border of identical octagons was sold at Skinner's in 1991;[4] a Kazak example with very similar octagons is shown in plate 16 above.

THE EASTERN CAUCASIAN GROUP

THE PLATES II

38

BAKU-SHIRVAN

3rd quarter 19th century

1.25 × 1.76m (4´1˝ × 5´8˝)

The field of this rug is a rich golden yellow and the design is a highly stylized, geometric version of the Avshan pattern (an all-over floral repeat). This particular drawing of the prayer niche, with the vertical arms descending almost to the mid-point of the field, is rare in Caucasian weaving. The stylized version of the Avshan design, with the stepped polygons containing cruciferous flowers on a stylized arabesque trellis, is a feature of rugs from Baku. (Some Karagashli examples also exist.) There is a definite relationship between this rug and a group of rugs from eastern Caucasia that feature similar stepped polygons flanking a keyhole or 'head and shoulders' motif (variously assigned to Baku, Shirvan and Chichi). When this rug was sold at Rippon it was attributed to Shirvan and dated mid-nineteenth century.

39

BAKU

last quarter 19th century

1.21 × 1.40m (4′0″ × 4′7″)

Prayer rugs with the geometric keyhole ('head and shoulders') motif were produced throughout eastern Caucasia during the nineteenth century (see plates 68 and 69 for Shirvan and Daghestan examples). Although superficially similar, these rugs differ in structure, colouring and border systems according to their region of origin. The example shown here was assigned to Baku by John Eskenazi.[1] The border system is related to a slightly darker rug, with a tripartite mihrab, assigned to the Baku region by Peter Bausback in 1976.[2]

An unusual feature of this rug is its three borders of equal width. These comprise a central stripe of geometric motifs on a white ground, flanked by borders of stepped diamond shapes. The minor borders of this rug and that of Bausback's comprise strips of meandering ribbon on a sky-blue ground. The diamond borders and 'ribbon' minor borders are both typical of Chichi rugs. (The Bausback rug also features a very unusual central border of white dots with blue and red centres on a blue ground.) The slanted 'barber pole' is the more common border design among Baku prayer rugs with the 'head and shoulders' motif.

40

K U B A

2nd half 19th century

1.12 × 1.41m (3′8″ × 4′8″)

This rare prayer rug was purchased by its present owners in the 1980s from a small antique shop in New England – fostering renewed hope that great pieces may yet be found in unconventional venues (although the days of star Kazaks being discovered at flea markets by torchlight in the early morning hours have receded into myth). The chevron pattern is very unusual, and the vivid colours in the rug combine to create an effect of mobility and cheeriness. The 'v'-shaped 'base' of the field uses only three colours (red, dark blue and ivory); in concert with the polychrome field this creates an effect of depth and the illusion of a third dimension.

Although multicoloured striated patterns are common in Caucasian rugs, the most common arrangement is diagonals, followed by verticals – a configuration usually found on Karabaghs (see plate 34 for further comments on striped prayer rugs). Narrow stripes are generally used in east Caucasian rugs, with broader stripes being more typical of south Caucasia. A Genje prayer rug with an unusual zigzag arrangement of stripes is also known.[1] This example was published as plate 23 in the catalogue of the New Boston Rug Society's exhibition, *Through the Collector's Eye*, 1991–92.[2] Mark Hopkins, in the catalogue caption, identifies a Kazak with a similar configuration.[3]

41

K U B A

mid-19th century

1.07 × 1.35m (3′6″ × 4′5″)

This rug, with its naturalistic flowers in a latticed field, is a later version of the type shown in plate 42. The field is of similar colouring to that example, and both rugs also share the elaborate arabesque variant border (heavily corroded in this piece) and the medachyl (reciprocal trefoil) guard borders. Its double-niche format is apparently unique for a Kuba rug. The flowers are drawn with none of the idiosyncratic peculiarities one expects from rugs in this group, such as the tripartite tulip and flowers with leaves on one side of the stem;[1] instead they display certain Daghestan characteristics such as diamond-shaped flowerheads (see plate 55). The rug also has the marked depression of alternate warps, another Daghestan characteristic; indeed the rug's owner, Ross Winter, prefers a Daghestan attribution. The original knotted mesh ends are typical of the Kuba group, however, and the rug displays many other Kuba features. The direction of the flowers would seem to indicate that the taller of the two arches was intended as the top.

42

KUBA

early 19th century

1.02 × 1.32m (3'4" × 4'0")

Kuba prayer rugs of floral lattice design are considered to be among the earliest from this region. Some types within the Kuba group (notably Konaghend and Chichi) tend to have dark grounds, but the lattice rugs of Kuba itself are more or less evenly divided between dark and light. The two rugs shown here are virtual reverse images of each other, with one having a dark lattice field and a light border and the other a light-ground lattice with a blue-black border. Kuba lattice rugs are characterized by their naturalistic depiction of flowers; most feature an idiosyncratic three-part flower (possibly a tulip) and another flower with leaves only on one side.[1] A related group of Kubas, of very fine weave and often with silk or cotton wefts, has only the latter feature; this group is exemplified by an eighteenth-century secular carpet illustrated as plate 64 in Schürmann's *Caucasian Rugs*. Both groups share the characteristic border design, an early and complex version of the stylized 'Kufic' script.

The rug shown in plate 42 here is probably somewhat older than that in plate 43; the drawing is more spacious and the floral lattice rendered in a wonderfully naturalistic manner (a feature of the ▷

43

KUBA

early 19th century

1.06 × 1.36m (3′6″ × 4′5″)

earliest examples of this type). It is quite closely related to the Schürmann example cited above and to an example illustrated as plate 25 in *Orient Stars* and sold at Sotheby's, New York in 1992.[2] *Hali* described the latter as 'a very beautiful rug with excellent colours and well-drawn flowers, very finely knotted on wool warps and cotton wefts'.[3] Although Schürmann and Sotheby's attribute their examples to Shirvan, current scholarship would suggest Kuba as the proper origin for these pieces.

The rug in plate 42 is virtually identical to an example published in Burns, *The Caucasus: Traditions in Weaving* (plate 28). From an Italian private collection, it was previously published in John Eskenazi's *L'arte del tappeto orientale* (plate 141). Like other ivory-lattice pieces in this group it features minor borders composed of a repeat pattern of small diamonds of alternating colours, creating an illusion of oblique stripes. Dark-lattice Kubas, on the other hand, generally feature very finely drawn medachyl guard borders, as in plate 42 shown here.

44

KUBA

late 18th/early 19th century

0.75 × 1.45m (2′5″ × 4′9″)

The blue field of this Avshan-pattern Kuba prayer rug is designed on a triple vertical axis. It contains most of the elements typical of the late eighteenth-century floral carpets from the southern Caucasus attributed by Charles Grant Ellis to the Shusha area of Karabagh.[1]

This is the only known prayer carpet to employ the earlier naturalistic rendering of the Avshan pattern; the three known analogous examples are drawn in a much more angular, geometric style with larger, right-angled leaves and stepped cruciform flowerheads.[2] The pattern in the prayer arch is typical of Kuba rugs. The main border is also characteristic of prayer rugs from this area, employing a spacious, well-drawn version of the 'Kufic' border on a rich red ground. The flowering vine minor border is uncommon in east Caucasian rugs and is more frequently seen in south Caucasian pieces.[3] It is also used as the main border in an early Avshan carpet published by Yetkin.[4]

45

KONAGHEND

mid-19th century or earlier

0.91 × 1.50m (3′0″ × 4′11″)

The characteristic Konaghend field design is a repeat pattern of conjoined hexagons. These typical designs vary greatly in complexity, however, usually as a result of the rug's age – the more recent designs are generally more static, and less interesting. Ian Bennett graphically illustrates this regression through eight examples in *Oriental Rugs: Vol. 1, Caucasian*.[1] Only one of his examples is a prayer rug, but the field composition is identical in both prayer and secular examples.

Konaghend prayer rugs from before 1850 are extremely rare. The rugs shown in plates 45 and 46, both in the collection of Jim Dixon, are contemporaneous. It is unusual for one collection to possess two such similar examples of a rare type. Both share so many features – the blue tracery outlined in ▷

46

KONAGHEND

mid-19th century or earlier

1.04 × 1.80m (3′5″ × 5′11″)

white, the abstract 'animal' shapes, the light blue inner ground borders, the shape of the niches, and so on – that the likelihood of them having been woven by one extended family is quite strong.

Pre-1850 Konaghend prayer rugs nearly always have red fields, as in the examples shown, whereas later rugs tend to have indigo fields. In addition, early pieces feature 'Kufic' borders and five of the seven known examples feature a stepped cruciform medallion beneath the prayer arch. The pattern of small repeated crosses within the prayer arch occurs in all but one of the known examples; after 1850 this usually changes to a pattern of linked diamonds similar to that found in Kuba and Chichi rugs.

47

PEREPEDIL

dated AH 1281 (1864)

1.22 × 1.42m (4′ 0″ × 4′ 8″)

Two divergent schools of thought exist on the development of the Perepedil design. The established theory is that it is derived from traditional dragon and animal forms, whereas a newer idea (put forward by Christine Klose[1]) proposes that it is linked to the floral patterns of seventeenth- and eighteenth-century embroideries. A design anomaly present in this rug (also in plate 37) would tend to support Klose's opinion. The 'ram's horn' motif in the lower left is 's'-shaped rather than 'ε'-shaped; such a deviation would be unthinkable if the motif were truly meant to symbolize animal horns. It would, however, be acceptable and logical if the weaver's intent were to depict what Klose calls 'calycinal blossoms'.[2] These different theories, however, only serve to confirm the syllogistic nature of rug studies, and neither enjoys full acceptance.

The older Perepedils have light grounds of white, ivory and (much more rarely) yellow.[3] Although reliably dated to 1864, our rug has the spaciousness and boldness of these earlier examples.[4] Another anomaly is that it lacks the 'animal' or 'lily blossom' figures usually found in Perepedils. The border, comprising light-coloured serrated 'winecups' separated by hooked figures on a dark blue ground, is a variant on the 'leaf-and-winecup' pattern.[5]

48

PEREPEDIL *or* SHIRVAN

*c.*1870

1.19 × 2.57m (3′11″ × 8′5″)

This rug was exhibited at the *Oriental Rugs from Pacific Collections* show during the sixth ICOC conference in San Francisco (17–20 November 1990). It was published as plate 180 in the accompanying catalogue, where Murray Eiland wrote: 'The graceful rendition of geometric forms that are often cramped together in these rugs gives this example an unusual appeal. It provides an excellent example of how successful a rug can be, even with a small amount of synthetic mauve, which does not in the least upset the composition or colour scheme... The Perepedil design is often associated with rugs of the Kuba district, but this example, with no depression of alternate warps, seems typically Shirvan in weave.'

Be that as it may, the rug's design features are consistent with Perepedil rugs down to the smallest details. Two light blue squares containing animals near the bottom end of the rug are unusual for this type. Perepedil prayer rugs of such length are rare, with some examples being of the double-niche variety (see plates 49 and 50). There is a single-niche unpublished example in the collection of Ross Winter of Canada, and a somewhat smaller example (measuring 1.10 × 1.80m / 3′7″ × 5′9″) was sold at Rippon in 1987, dated to the mid-nineteenth century.[1]

49

PEREPEDIL

early 19th century

1.07 × 2.31m (3′6″ × 7′7″)

Illustrated in this plate and in plate 50 opposite are both of the known double-niche Perepedils.[1] The example illustrated here has different decoration in the spandrels at either end and also features the characteristic Perepedil 'ram's horn' design. Despite its damaged condition, the rug was described by *Hali* as 'one of the most beautiful and archaic examples [of the ram's horn design] we have seen'.[2] An unusual design feature is the 's'-form rendering of the upper pair of 'ram's horns', an anomaly also seen in plate 47 above.

50

PEREPEDIL

c.1870

0.98 × 2.22m (3′2″ × 7′4″)

Perepedils were rather harshly treated by Nicolas Fokker in his book *Caucasian Rugs of Yesterday*, where he wrote, 'If you've seen one of these, you've seen the lot. All appear to have been made on a single model.'[1] While this damning description may be appropriate for some late nineteenth- and early twentieth-century examples, it certainly does not describe the earlier pieces. The format of this rug, for instance, is quite eccentric, with prayer niches at either end. It has been suggested that this and similar examples were woven for export to the West, rather than for prayer.[2] I would question this theory on two counts, however: only one other double-niche Perepedil is known to me (plate 49), and Western demand did not materialize until very late in the nineteenth century.

The earliest pieces, some of which date from the early nineteenth century, generally have a white ground as in this example. James Burns, in *The Caucasus: Traditions in Weaving*, illustrates a wonderfully archaic ivory-ground rug – possibly a benchmark piece for this type – that he dates to the first third of the nineteenth century.[3] Christine Klose has proposed that the Perepedil design has its roots in seventeenth- and eighteenth-century Azerbaijan silk embroideries, and places the type shown here as the fourth and final phase of the design's development.[4]

5I

CHICHI

dated AH 1298 (1881)

1.22 × 1.52m (4′0″ × 5′0″)

This example represents the most popular type of Chichi prayer rug, executed in an abstract floral design that Liatif Kerimov has termed Khirdagyd. The field of this rug achieves an illusion of depth by the pronounced use of abrash and by the uncluttered positioning of the floral and star motifs.[1] The gently arched golden yellow mihrab appears to float on a cerulean blue field, enhancing the impression of depth. Khirdagyd Chichi prayer rugs most often feature one of two border designs: the pattern of slanted bars and rosettes of this rug, or the stylized 'Kufic' border.[2] The guard borders of hexagons containing stepped flowerheads, and the narrow minor border in an undulating ribbon pattern on a light blue ground, are typical features of Chichi rugs.

Although 'Chichi' is a corruption of 'chechen', rugs bearing this name have no connection to today's Chechnya. They were woven in the Kuba district on the coast of the Caspian Sea; Chechnya is an inland area north of Daghestan and south of the Terek river. In 1882 the Chechnya area was known as the Terek province.[3]

52

KARAGASHLI

early 19th century

1.12 × 1.73m (3´8˝ × 5´8˝)

This rare Karagashli is one of the very few of this type that can be designated as a prayer rug with any degree of confidence.[1] The Victoria and Albert Museum in London started acquiring their collection of Caucasian rugs in 1878, and this rug was purchased soon after (in 1880), along with six other Caucasians. The prices paid ranged from £5 to £9 10s.[2] Robert Pinner and Michael Frances describe this rug as follows: 'This beautiful prayer rug, unusual in having two niches, and woven with long pile in rich colours, is reminiscent of Kazak rugs; however, the construction, particularly the five blue double cords of the selvedge, as well as the border arrangement, is characteristic of pieces attributed to Karagashli, although the pattern is unusual for this area.'[3]

As stated earlier, the multiple arch motif is extremely rare in Caucasian prayer rugs and is more often found in Anatolian weavings.[4] The rug is in wonderful condition for its age, as the technical analysis by Jackie Stanger, of the Victoria and Albert Museum, confirms (see notes to this plate).

53

ZEIKHUR

2nd half 19th century

1.14 × 1.43m (3´9˝ × 4´8˝)

Zeikhur is a village in the Kuba district. Prayer rugs asigned to Zeikhur are extremely rare; only ten examples are known to me, of which no two are alike. The latticed field of this rug is similar in colouring and design to certain Kuba rugs, such as that shown in plate 42.[1] The prayer arch is also similar in shape and ornamentation to Kuba arches (see plates 41, 42 and 43). Unlike the Kuba pieces, however, the entire field of this example is enclosed by a minor border of the same width, colour and design as the arch. The Zeikhur origin of this piece can be inferred from the floral design and colouring of the main border, which uses the characteristic Zeikhur tones of coral and pink.[2]

54

ZEIKHUR

dated AH 1312 (1895)

0.71 × 1.19m (2′4″ × 3′11″)

Zeikhur area prayer rugs are extremely uncommon and this, to the best of my knowledge, is the only prayer example with the 'Alpan-Kuba' pattern. This design evolved from the eighteenth-century silk embroideries of Azerbaijan and Karabagh.[1] In his auction catalogue notes (Rippon, 28 March 1992) Detlef Maltzahn remarks on the rug's small format, its designation as a prayer carpet and the presence of an inscription and date in the border, which may indicate that the rug was a commissioned piece, probably intended as a gift.[2]

The bottom border differs from the others. Although at first glance it may appear that the original concept was simply abandoned in favour of the more standard 'running dog' motif, a closer examination shows that the weaver had a definite purpose: hexagons from the bottom border are repeated as decorations in the spandrels flanking the 'Zeikhur rose' prayer arch. The rug's palette is quite similar to that of a late nineteenth-century Alpan-Kuba example illustrated as plate 33 in Keshishian, *The Treasure of the Caucasus*.

Eastern group   105

55

DAGHESTAN

1st quarter 19th century

0.97 × 1.38m (3′2″ × 4′6″)

This rug was listed as a Kabistan in the inventory of the collection of C. Meyer-Müller, *Der Orient-Teppich*, in 1917.[1] It still has two of Meyer-Müller's identifying brass discs attached to its corners. A number of factors indicate an early date for this rug. The serrated latticed field is generously spaced and the drawing of the flowers exhibits great imagination and variety. The dragon border is more complex than later versions of this design. Perhaps the most important sign of age, however, is the intense saturated tone of the madder red. With a blueish tinge, it is almost a deep magenta – a depth of colour associated with early pieces. The design features shield-like ornamentation beneath the prayer arch, and 'H' forms in the spandrels (related to the abstract animal forms found in early Anatolian animal rugs). These motifs are found on a few analogous Daghestans, but all appear to be later examples.

56

DAGHESTAN

1st quarter 19th century

1.04 × 1.32m (3′5″ × 4′4″)

This early Daghestan prayer rug and that pictured in plate 55 are very similar and probably contemporaneous. They do differ in several aspects, however. The Meyer-Müller rug in plate 55 has an unusually intense, highly saturated dark red tending to crimson. Although the rug illustrated above has wonderful wool and glowing colours, its red is lighter and more conventional than that of plate 55. The field is filled with serrated latticed lozenges, beautifully rendered in a naturalistic manner. Despite their number (69 in total), the rug does not feel overcrowded. The Meyer-Müller rug features fewer lozenges (40), drawn in a somewhat more geometric, abstract style. The main borders are identical, each employing versions of the dragon 's' found in many border guards, and a blue and black medachyl inner guard. The other guard borders differ, however. Together, the rugs offer an interesting comparison between two very good, early examples.

57

DAGHESTAN

3rd quarter 19th century

1.12 × 1.32m (3′3″ × 4′4″)

Striped designs were employed on prayer rugs throughout the Caucasus region, with the possible exception of the Kazak weaving area. Various configurations are used, including vertical stripes, diagonal stripes and chevron bands. Other examples of striped rugs can be seen in plates 27, 28, 34, 40, 72, 73 and 87. This rug is of a somewhat unusual design, with its riot of colours (a total of 15 are used) and the alternating pattern of boteh and quartered diamonds within the bands. The field is filled with 25 polychrome vertical bands, while in the spandrels narrower bands, on a diagonal bias, are employed.

A slightly smaller but otherwise virtually identical rug is illustrated as plate 110 in Bennett, *Oriental Rugs, Vol 1: Caucasian*.[1] The two pieces are so similar that they may well have been woven as a pair; they are almost certainly the work of the same weaver. Although Bennett's piece was placed in the Karabagh section of his book, he wrote that 'I cannot help feeling that a more northeasterly attribution is likely'. (Bennett's book was essentially an English commentary to an earlier German book by Doris Eder, and Bennett was committed to the prior attributions.) The main borders of both rugs, as well as the blue-black medachyl inner border, are typical of Daghestan, as are the technical features of this example.

58

DAGHESTAN

late 19th century

0.81 × 1.80m (2′8″ × 5′11″)

Vertical bands are uncommon on prayer rugs from northeast Caucasia, although they do appear with some frequency on rugs from the south, particularly Karabagh (see plate 27). The weaver's economical use of colour does not lessen this rug's considerable appeal. The red vertical panels match the main border and contain bird-like, diagonally striped Marasali boteh; the ivory panels contain larger polychrome boteh of a different type in a variety of designs, while the two black panels feature a meandering vine with floral motifs and serrated leaf forms.

The rug has much in common with the wonderful, full-pile example published by Eberhart Herrmann in *Von Uschak bis Yarkand* (plate 44). Both share the design of vertical panels with ascending vines, boteh, blossoms and horizontal leaf forms, framed by a Marasali-type boteh border. While Herrmann's rug has a somewhat greater range of colour, the similarities are nonetheless compelling. This carpet was one of 16 pieces from the collection of Harold Zulalian, Sr, which were dispersed at Sotheby's, New York, on 3 December 1988 (along with 11 pieces from the collection of Dr and Mrs Hans Zimmer).

59

DAGHESTAN

3rd quarter 19th century

0.94 × 1.37m (3′1″ × 4′6″)

The colouring and drawing of the field of this very pretty palmette Daghestan are quite similar to those of a rug sold at Christie's in 1990, which deservedly quadrupled its auction estimate.[1] The employment of palmettes in Caucasian rugs is an old, unbroken tradition dating back to the classical Dragon and Blossom carpets of the seventeenth century. By the nineteenth century, this motif had developed into the geometric, abstract version seen here.

Most palmette Daghestans bear reasonably credible dates from the second half of the nineteenth century. The guard borders are always of alternating oblique stripes. The main borders most frequently feature the floral 'crab' design and less often a design of hexagonal lozenges containing hooked motifs.[2] The present 'leaf-and-calyx' border is uncommon for prayer rugs of this group. One other such example, virtually identical to ours (although less colourful) was published in Nagel (auction catalogue), 7 June 1980, lot 264, colour plate 96. Both pieces feature a Persian-style inner guard border, of floral design with a blue ground, that frames the field and matches the pattern of the gabled prayer arch. This is a rather unusual feature; in most of the parallel pieces the prayer arch is free-floating and of a pattern not connected with the guard borders.

60

DAGHESTAN

c.1800 or earlier

0.71 × 1.35m (2′4″ × 4′5″)

This is a very old Daghestan, possibly pre-1800. The intense burnt orange of the main border is unusual in east Caucasian weaving, but James Burns, the owner of the rug, states that it is a feature of very early Daghestans. The array of wonderful colours includes a deeply saturated aubergine. The wool is glossy and very fluffy, giving the rug an ethereal, almost weightless feel. In terms of design motifs it falls within a small group of Daghestan prayer rugs that feature a powerfully articulated, exaggerated lattice field. None of the other rugs in this group approaches the spaciousness of this example, however. The field contains stylized tulips, unlike analogous pieces which feature latch-hooked elements or rosettes. The other examples in this group also feature the arrowhead or 'ram's horns' main border employed here.

61

DAGHESTAN

1st quarter 19th century

0.86 × 1.07m (2′10″ × 3′6″)

This is an early, well-crafted Daghestan with wonderful drawing and a range of mellow colours. Rugs with palmettes such as these were woven in the Caucasus throughout the nineteenth century, but the older examples have an instantly recognizable look. This rug is distinguished by its small size and almost square proportions. The arch is quite large and wide in relation to the field, occupying almost all of the the top half of the rug.[1] The indigo-ground border has dragon 's' forms piled in three shades of red plus aubergine, yellow, blue-green, brown and ivory. The overall symmetry of the rug is remarkable and points to the work of a master weaver. While a number of analogous examples are known, this is one of the earliest and best of its type.[2] A somewhat later rug of comparable quality, with a yellow field and multiple borders (from the Glencairn Museum collection in Bryn Athyn, PA) was published on the cover of *Oriental Rug Review* 9/5 (June/July 1989).

62

DAGHESTAN

late 19th century

1.04 × 1.22m (3′5″ × 4′0″)

This rug and three others form a very small, distinct sub-group among the numerous examples of northeastern Caucasian ivory-ground prayer rugs. The four rugs share so many characteristics that they must be closely connected, possibly as the products of one workshop. The general layout of this rug, with its wide, crisply drawn prayer arch, is common to all; they also share an identical main border of dragon 's' forms framed by two minor borders containing 'Solomon' (eight-pointed) stars enclosed by octagons. Although the flora varies, all four feature unusual fringed diamonds in the field, seen here in the third row down from the apex of the arch. Two of the rugs (this example included) have an added border of stylized 's' forms on a golden ground.

The example published by Herrmann (*Kaukasische Teppichkunst*, plate 12) has been attributed to Kuba, while the others are assigned to Shirvan or Daghestan. The ends of Herrmann's and the present piece consist of fine white kilims finished in macramé-like multi-knotted warp fringe, a feature of both Kuba and Daghestan rugs.

63

DAGHESTAN

2nd half 19th century

1.14 × 1.44m (3′9″ × 4′9″)

The design of this rug is simple but charming, with a rustic and homespun feel to it. It is indeed surprising that such a design is not encountered more often. According to its Lefevre catalogue entry, the rug has 'a dense pile, in wool of excellent quality. It is in very good condition with original selvedges and braided ends. It is free of repair, except for a few sections of selvedges which have been rebound.'

After the West 'discovered' Caucasian rugs around 1875, a thriving cottage industry developed to supply the export market. Most of these rugs followed predictable patterns and adhered to safe, popular designs. This rug, however, does not follow any of these established styles and it is likely that it would have been made for personal use or for local trade. Most rugs of this type would wear out without ever leaving home, and it has been estimated that the average lifespan of such a rug was around 30 years.[1]

64

DAGHESTAN

mid-19th century

0.55 × 1.20m (1′8″ × 3′4″)

The tradition of silk weaving in the Caucasus is an old one. Early travel chronicles refer to the sericulture of the region,[1] and some splendid examples of seventeenth- and eighteenth-century silk embroidery survive from Azerbaijan, Karabagh and Daghestan. Early Caucasian prayer rugs piled in silk are extremely rare, however.

This example is most likely from Daghestan, by virtue of its design and the fact that we know that silk was readily available in the area. (Some Kaitag emboideries – a type of silk embroidery now identified as coming from Daghestan – date from the seventeenth century and thus offer conclusive proof of a long tradition of silk weaving in the area.) The rug is small, with a light yellow field. The ascending lattice traces the shape of the free-floating prayer arch, a rare feature among lattice design rugs. The rug has been woven 'upside down', with the palmettes pointing towards the bottom and the pile slanting towards the top. The practical reason for this technical feature, more typical of Turkish weavings, is to enable the faithful's palms and knees to be placed with (rather than against) the pile during the act of prayer. This charming rug was almost certainly a very special piece commissioned for a specific occasion.

65

SOUTH CAUCASIAN

KILIM

early 19th century

0.88 × 1.62m (2′1″×5′4″)

Antique prayer flatweaves from the Caucasus are extremely rare. A prayer sumakh from the Arthur D. Jenkins Collection was the first such example to be published, in 1969,[1] and as far as I know only 12 such pieces have been published to date (four vernehs, two sumakhs and six kilims). This example was the first (and to my mind best) of the kilims to appear at auction (at Lefevre in 1977).[2] As the accompanying catalogue points out, the absence of Caucasian prayer kilims is intriguing, given the relative abundance of other types of kilims from the area. This kilim is made from wool using the slit-tapestry technique on a mixed brown and ivory woollen warp. Some of the small ornaments in the spandrels and in the borders are embroidered. The boldly latticed ivory field evokes the lattice prayer rugs from Shirvan.

The kilim performed well at auction and, as so often happens, this brought other such pieces out of the chests and closets of collectors. One of these was sold at Edelmann in 1981.[3] Both rugs are very similar in concept, size, colouring and design, down to the smallest details.[4] (Eberhart Herrmann immediately recognized their scarcity and acquired both pieces.) A third kilim appeared at auction a year later.[5] While all three examples are obviously inspired by pile rug designs, their main borders employ traditional kilim motifs.

66

DAGHESTAN

1st half 19th century

0.89 × 1.51m (2′1″ × 5′0″)

This example belongs to a small group of Daghestan prayer rugs made in a long, narrow format – sometimes over two metres (6½ feet) in length. These long rugs almost invariably feature the stylized dragon border of this piece.[1] This rug is analogous to an example from the Meyer-Müller Collection sold at Christie's, New York in 1991,[2] but in my opinion is older and more beautiful. While most rugs of this type were probably made in the third and fourth quarters of the nineteenth century, a pre-1850 date for this piece is likely. The loss of the rug's outer guard stripe does not diminish its visual appeal. Its outstanding features include a range of wonderful, luminous colours; a great variety of flowers in the latticed field; generous spacing in the overall design, and outstanding draughtsmanship. The narrow dark blue prayer arch echoes the design of the guard stripes and adds a pleasing symmetry.

67

DAGHESTAN

2nd half 19th century

0.97 × 1.47m (3′2″ × 4′10″)

The so-called Lesghi star is a complex, unique and easily recognized motif based on the eight-pointed star. It appears throughout the Caucasus on pile rugs and, equally frequently, on the flatwoven sumakh bags of eastern Caucasia. This rug is a rare example of the motif's successful integration into a prayer rug design. It features one green and two large ivory stars on an indigo field, with a smaller and somewhat distorted green star wedged under the prayer niche. 'Memling' motifs adorn the spandrels, and the ivory-ground border features the 'kotchaks' (horns) usually identified with Akstafa rugs. The sections piled in brown are deeply corroded.

How the Lesghi star became identified as the signature symbol of the fierce Lesghi people[1] is not known. The star may at some time have been a totemic symbol, but this is a subject for speculation. East Caucasian pile weavings with the Lesghi star motifs were most probably woven in Daghestan,[2] Shirvan or even Kuba.[3] Ulrich Schürmann identified three prayer rugs as Lesghi, but they are of an entirely different design and bear no resemblance to this 'star' type.[4]

68

SHIRVAN

2nd half 19th century

1.23 × 1.35m (4′0″ × 4′5″)

Rugs with a mihrab in the shape of a keyhole or a stylized 'head and shoulders' figure were woven throughout east Caucasia, with published examples from Baku, Kuba, Shirvan, Daghestan and Chichi. Unlike most Caucasian prayer rugs those in the 'keyhole' and 'head and shoulders' group do not have a separate gabled or squared prayer arch; instead, the mihrab floats on the field. This design principle is more closely related to the style of prayer rugs from Anatolia. The 'head' or prayer arch in these rugs is virtually identical in shape to the re-entrant arches of Anatolian 'Bellini-type' rugs of the fifteenth to eighteenth century.[1] (These rugs are so called because of the paintings of Gentile Bellini, c.1429–1507, who depicted rugs with keyhole or re-entrant motifs.) The more immediate influences are the later keyhole rugs from Bergama and Konya.[2] A wide variety of borders is employed in this group of rugs, varying primarily by origin. Border patterns include a polychromatic slanted 'barber pole' (Baku), slanted bars-and-rosettes (Chichi), geometric guls with 'c' motifs (Kuba) and 'crab' borders (usually Shirvan or Daghestan) as in the pieces shown here.

The common thread connecting all the rugs in this group is the use of polygonal medallions inside the mihrab (rugs with this medallion design have been designated Ordutch-Konaghend by Liatif ▷

69

DAGHESTAN

2nd half 19th century

1.23 × 1.45m (4′1″ × 4′9″)

Kerimov[3]). An article published in *Oriental Rug Review* proposes that these medallions resemble Kerbala stones (grey prayer stones, usually octagonal in shape), an observation consistent with the predominately Shia persuasion of the population.[4] Other common characteristics of this group are hand prints flanking the prayer arch, and stepped flower heads within the field. Both elements feature in the examples shown here. The mihrab itself is divided into two or three compartments beneath the 'head', each containing a typical medallion.

A very intriguing rug from this family was formerly in the Jerome and Mary Jane Straka Collection. It has adjacent double mihrabs, each containing four compartments, and a border of stepped square forms.[5] This 'side-by-side' arrangement is extremely unusual, possibly unique, and the only such example in the 'keyhole' group. The rug in plate 69 was published in Eiland, *Oriental Rugs*, and exhibited at Mills College, Oakland, California in 1990.[6]

There is much ambiguity surrounding Shirvan and Daghestan attributions. Although plates 68 and 69 differ only marginally from one another, one has been attributed to Shirvan and the other to Daghestan by their owners.

70

SHIRVAN

dated AH 1233 (1820)

1.23 × 1.42m (4′1″ × 4′8″)

The design of this prayer rug is related to a small group of rugs with very early dates, an example of which is illustrated as plate 31. (This group was previously attributed to Kazak but is now generally seen as the product of Armenian weavers in Karabagh.[1]) Most rugs from this group have silk and/or cotton in their foundation, which indicates that these were weavings of the highest quality made for presentation or other special occasions. This derivative example is from Shirvan. Its ivory wool warp and red woollen weft correspond exactly to a very similar rug sold at Lefevre in 1979;[2] this rug was also assigned to Shirvan and dated to the first half of the nineteenth century. Another very similar example was acquired by the Austrian collector Peter Trimbacher for Schloss Plankenstein;[3] yet another was published by Skinner's in 1989.[4] All four rugs share the same leaf-and-calyx border and a hexagonal cartouche with stylized confronting dragons.

Trimbacher points out that rugs with this design continued to be made into the twentieth century, variously assigned to Kazak, Fachralo or Genje.[5] (The design had probably become a popular one for export.) These later examples are coarser in weave and material, less refined in their drawing, and usually feature borders of arrowheads (ram's horns) or scrolled or dragon 's' forms.[6]

71

SHIRVAN

2nd half 19th century

1.24 × 1.80m (4′11″ × 5′7″)

'What a riot of imagination lies in this small prayer rug,' wrote Ulrich Schürmann of a rug very similar to this one.[1] In fact, both rugs belong to an exclusive family of four rugs with strictly conforming designs, strongly influenced by north Persian weaving.[2] The field is dominated by a central cypress tree and filled with fantastic animals – including elephants, peacocks, lions and roosters – and human figures. The rugs in this small group also share a predominantly blue palette and are of similar dimensions. The peacocks are quite similar in design to those in some Caucasian animal carpets.[3] The theme of a mound and cypress tree motif flanked by peacocks also occurs in certain types of nineteenth-century Persian prayer rugs, such as Mosul, Malayer and Feraghan.[4] The lion with the sword (in the top border) is a symbol of imperial Persia.

This example was first published in Herrmann, *Seltene Orientteppiche II*, plate 38. In his text, Herrmann points out the peculiarity of the absence of a main border at the top and bottom, which occurs in all four examples.

72

SHIRVAN

2nd half 19th century

0.96 × 1.32m (3′2″ × 4′4″)

Caucasian weavers were able to take the simplest elements, such as adjacent stripes, and turn them into a variety of interesting and intricate designs. Striped rugs were woven mostly in Shirvan, Daghestan, Kuba, Genje and Karabagh. Sometimes only a small number of colours were employed, as in the red, white and blue diagonals of this piece; at other times an extensive palette would be used (see for example plate 40, with its riot of colours in a chevron design). Vertical stripes were rarely used in Shirvan weavings, being more typical of Karabagh and Daghestan.[1]

This rug is quite similar to one illustrated in Schürmann, *Caucasian Rugs* (plate 74), although with a totally different border. In his commentary on that rug, Schürmann points to the influence of the Genje districts and notes the care that has been taken to run the diagonal stripes in the opposite direction on the right side above the prayer gable – an arrangement also seen in this piece. An example virtually identical to the present rug, assigned to Kuba, was published as plate 38 in Herrmann, *Seltene Orientteppiche* VI. Both examples feature arrangements of tiny elements within the diagonal stripes which create an illusion of horizontal stripes intersecting the diagonals. Another similar example was published in Gombos, *Old Prayer Rugs*, plate 6.

73

SHIRVAN

last quarter 19th century

0.89 × 1.31m (2′11″ × 4′6″)

The design of this Shirvan prayer rug, with its wide diagonal stripes, is heavily influenced by similar rugs from the Genje district. The Genje rugs, however, have cooler colours (tending to blues, greens and whites) and usually feature 'hand prints' in the spandrels.[1] While the arrangement of the small hooked squares inside the stripes is typical of both Genje and Shirvan, this is not the only decoration to be used. Boteh and stars are employed in Genje pieces,[2] while small crosses or dots are used in Shirvan rugs.[3] Our rug is a very good example, albeit of a type that is not particularly rare.

74

SHIRVAN

2nd half 19th century

1.0 × 1.41m (3′3″ × 4′7″)

The field design of this unusual white-ground Shirvan prayer rug is obviously inspired by an earlier group of Kuba rugs. Its pattern of stylized trees in vertical rows almost exactly matches that of a Kuba rug published in Volkmann, *Old Eastern Carpets II* (plate 64), which the author suggests may have developed from Persian textile designs. Examples in this Kuba group almost invariably feature golden yellow fields with highly stylized arabesque borders piled in blue and black or ivory and black. Although no prayer examples with that exact classic Kuba design are known, a small number of related prayer pieces with variant designs exist. The most widely published of these (catalogued as Kuba and Baku) has a yellow ground with a single narrow border and an understated prayer arch shaped like an inverted 'U'.[1]

75

SHIRVAN

2nd half 19th century

1.14 × 1.22m (3′9″ × 4′0″)

This unusual Shirvan has some interesting and distinctive features. Its squarish dimensions are uncommon, but the focus here is on the spandrels which contain 'jewellery' motifs and three additional prayer arches. Depictions of jewellery pieces, specifically the triangular pendants (*daghdan*) or amulet cases (*turmar*) evocative of Turkoman craft,[1] are rarely used as ornamentation in Caucasian weavings, although an instance of similar use in the spandrels of a Marasali prayer rug is known.[2]

Multiple prayer arches in Caucasian rugs are very rare. Karagashli pieces feature a vertical arrangement not unlike the stepped progression found in the Karapinar prayer rugs of central Anatolia, but a horizontal multiple distribution is extremely unusual. (A horizontal arrangement does appear in saffs, but they are rare in their own right.) An apparently unique example, with three vertical panels each containing two adjoining prayer arches, was published in *Oriental Rug Review*,[3] while the Strakas once owned a prayer rug with two adjacent 'head and shoulder' mihrabs.[4] To date, no similar depiction of a combination of prayer arches and pendant in the spandrels of a Caucasian prayer rug is known to me.

76

S H I R V A N

c.1875

0.96 × 1.90m (3′2″ × 6′3″)

The field design of this rug, with its pattern of highly stylized shield-like medallions, is common in Caucasian kilims, where it has many variants. It is rarely employed in pile carpets, however, and this example is the only known instance of its use in a prayer rug. Ignazio Vok identifies the design as 'pashali',[1] and Yanni Petsopoulos speculates that it may have its origin in an earlier group of 'Shield' carpets[2] (such as the examples illustrated in Schürmann, *Caucasian Rugs,* plates 6, 62 and 94). The border is also evocative of kilim designs, but the floral decoration flanking the central medallions is typical of eastern Caucasian pile weaving. The pattern also includes Akstafa birds and two realistically depicted samovars.

77

SHIRVAN

c.1865

1.14 × 1.63m (3′9″ × 5′4″)

The ivory field of this example is beautifully framed by an unusual deep yellow and red border of highly stylized dragon 's' forms. (There is a theory that, since the letter 's' in the Armenian alphabet stands for 'D', many 's' borders were intended as homage to 'dios' or God.) This piece shows how effective the simplest designs – here an all-over repeat of latchhooked diamonds – can be, when thoughtfully executed. The spacing of the quartered diamonds with their masterful juxtaposition of colours, and the contrast between field and border colours, all contribute to this rug's special appeal. The edges of the field are scattered with small 's' forms, combs, ewers and crosses. Various inscribed Islamic dates flank the deep blue prayer arch; these read 1252, 1302, 1320 and 1220 (translating to AD 1836, 1884, 1902 and 1805). Since none of these dates can be considered reliable, they are best discounted.

78

SHIRVAN

c.1875

1.12 × 1.55m (3′8″ × 5′1″)

This piece belongs to a small group of Shirvan rugs with similar design, colouring and detail. All feature 'Kufic'-type borders, usually on blue grounds; a polychrome inner border of boxed swastikas; unusual flowers in the lattice field; and inscribed dates, usually to the right of the prayer arch. This example is dated AH 1252, which translates to 1837 – probably 40 years earlier than when the rug was actually made. (Most of the analogous examples bear dates between 1875 and 1900, and there is no reason to suppose that this rug is any older.) Although essentially a typical Shirvan prayer rug, the dark 'Kufic' border and the swastikas of this piece give it a very different overall appearance. The 'Kufic' border is more a feature of rugs from the Kuba area (such as Perepedil, Konaghend and Chichi) and is very rarely seen on Shirvan rugs other than those in this group. A very similar example, though with a more crowded design, was sold at Bonham's, London in 1993.[1]

79

SHIRVAN

late 19th century

1.02 × 1.65m (3′4″ × 5′5″)

Thousands of Shirvan and Daghestan prayer rugs were made in the last decades of the nineteenth century. Most of them adhered fairly strictly to the most popular formula of flower-filled lattice field with dragon border. There were, of course, exceptions – such as this example, which appears to have started out as a conventional floral lattice piece but then changed to a rudimentary pattern of multi-coloured 'x' forms. The simplicity of the design suggests that this rug might have been made for personal use rather than for export, as rugs made for overseas markets generally employed the more popular patterns. Although the design appears rather crowded, the green prayer arch and the border of animal-filled 'birds' give it a certain character and charm.

80

SHIRVAN

early 19th century

1.17 × 1.32m (3′10″ × 4′4″)

This piece gives us an insight into the beauty of early Caucasian prayer rugs, which are so rarely found today. Although extensively damaged, the rug still hints at its former glory. The drawing is very bold and spacious; the stylized tulips are beautifully executed and the border is drawn with the refinement and selection of dyes seen only in older pieces. The projecting hooked horizontal lines that decorate the field are uncommon. A Genje prayer rug published in Franses, *An Introduction to the World of Rugs* (plate 17) has similar lines radiating from the prayer arch. The main border of interlocking birds is sometimes referred to as the 'eagle's beak' design; later versions of this design are much more angular and geometric. The field has lost much colour due to extreme wear, but the upper part and the main border still retain much of their original, deeply saturated hues.

81

SHIRVAN

c.1860

0.81 × 1.68m (2′8″ × 5′6″)

A distinctive feature of this rug is its field pattern of 'rising' palmettes. This design occurs primarily in Shirvans, Daghestans and, more rarely, Kubas. Two basic versions exist. In one version, arguably the earlier, the palmettes resemble floral shields; Ian Bennett has proposed that this pattern may be connected to the stylized lotus palmettes of eighteenth-century Caucasian 'Shield' carpets, which may be from Shirvan. In the other (possibly later) version, as seen here, the pattern is highly stylized (Bennett has likened these palmettes to huge insects).[1] Not everyone agrees with Bennett's evolutionary theory; an example owned by Eberhart Herrmann and featuring the 'stylized' version is dated c.1800 and assigned to Kuba (see analogies).

The rug shown here is missing its outer guard border. The red and blue barber-pole stripe framing the rug is unusual, and cochineal dye is used extensively. All of the brown is camel hair, which points to a southern Shirvan origin. An example with a similar field was depicted in an 1877 painting by Henri Fantin-Latour, now in the Musée des Beaux-Arts in Lyon (see p. 18).[2]

82

S H I R V A N

1st quarter 19th century

0.96 × 1.35m (3´2˝ × 4´5˝)

By all criteria, this is a 'classic' Shirvan prayer rug. In spite of its condition it has all the qualities of the best pieces: precise draughtsmanship; high-quality, finely spun wool; saturated colours, and an over-all dignity of design and execution. The polychrome 'eagle's beak' border contrasts beautifully with the ivory field, which contains a great variety of naturalistic flowers. The prayer arch, which is very fine and carefully rendered, picks up the 'crosses and sevens' pattern of the guard borders but is on a green ground. This subtle use of green draws additional attention to the prayer arch.

Naturalistic flowers and fine, precise prayer arches without serrated edges are widely believed to be a characteristic of older Shirvans. This example lends support to that theory. Two gold-ground examples with similar prayer arches are also known to exist;[1] these probably date to a generation later and are perhaps an attempt to emulate the earlier ivory-ground pieces.

83

SHIRVAN

dated AH 1310 (1892)

1.19 × 1.27m (3′11″ × 4′2″)

This rug features a rare simplified version of the classic Konaghend design, an intricate mosaic of interwoven elements based on conjoined hexagons (see plates 45 and 46). The Konaghend pattern is arguably the most intricate and complex of all Caucasian field designs. It is almost certainly rooted in the 'Lotto' designs of sixteenth-century Ushak rugs from Anatolia (an intricate lattice tracery pattern featuring conjoined hexagons; so called because of its depiction in paintings by the sixteenth-century artist Lorenzo Lotto). Various bird and animal forms may be identified in Konaghend patterns; whether these were intentional *trompe l'oeil* or accidental imagery on the part of the weaver is as yet an unresolved issue.

It is surprising that this rug was produced in the Shirvan area. No similar Shirvan rug is known. It is dated AH 1310 (1892), a date fully consistent with the rug's appearance and feel. It has some unusual features, such as the almost-square format and the field design of confronting chicken or rooster forms. It seems unlikely that such an unconventional rug would have been made for export; it could possibly have been made by a weaver who had moved to Shirvan from neighbouring Konaghend and was thus familiar with the designs from that area.

84

SHIRVAN

2nd half 19th century

1.07 × 1.25m (3′6″ × 4′1″)

Not every boteh rug from the north Caucasus can be automatically assigned to Marasali. Although this rug was catalogued as Shirvan in the Sotheby's auction catalogue of 1991,[1] *Hali* elected to review it as a Marasali, commenting on its 'good design, generous drawing, but not very inspirational colour'.[2] This colouring is the very reason why the rug should be assigned to Shirvan. Colour, as much as design, is a constant of Marasali rugs, particularly the salmon or 'Marasali red' which gives these rugs their characteristic fiery glow. This example, however, has the cooler and more restrained palette of a Shirvan. The 'free floating' boteh on an ivory field are unusual, as most ivory Marasalis have latticed fields, the former pattern being a feature of 'black' Marasalis. (A black Marasali with a border identical to that shown here was offered at Sotheby's in 1981.[3])

85

SHIRVAN AKSTAFA

2nd half 19th century

0.94 × 1.85m (3′1″ × 6′1″)

The town of Akstafa is situated in the Kazak weaving area, near the rail line that runs parallel to the Kur River between Tiflis and the town of Genje (Elizavetpol) in the eastern Caucasus. It has little or nothing to do with a group of rugs named Akstafa, which were woven in south Shirvan (although Ulrich Schürmann mentions the town in connection with a Kazak rug, published as plate 26 in *Caucasian Rugs*).

The rug shown here combines features from so many east Caucasian weaving areas that precise attribution is difficult. While it has various Marasali characteristics – flaming boteh, a 'bird' border and the typical Marasali palette – other features indicate a different origin. The 'boteh-inside-boteh' (or 'pregnant' boteh) is not a Marasali feature and is found in Akstafa and Daghestan boteh rugs.[1] The square prayer arch filled with 'x' motifs is another Akstafa feature, as is the comb and square beneath the arch. The guard borders, back and structure appear to be Shirvan, but the double-bundled blue cotton overcast selvedges are more typical of Kuba and Daghestan, although occasionally a feature of Akstafas as well (see plate 88). To my knowledge there are no close published analogies.[2]

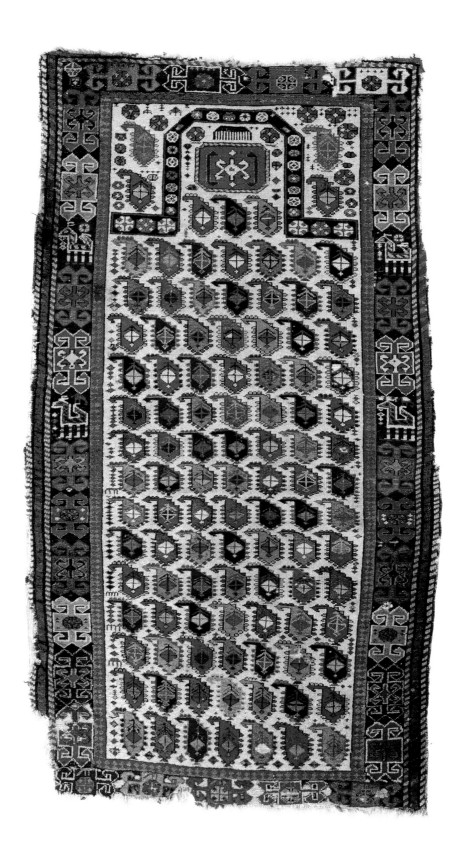

86

AKSTAFA

3rd quarter 19th century

0.91 × 1.68m (3′0″ × 5′6″)

This rug features a 'pear design' boteh. This type of boteh, characteristically surrounded by a bead-like border, has a full body and well-developed upper 'tail'. Rugs of this design were attributed by Walter Hawley to Kutais,[1] an appellation that has now fallen into disuse. Nowadays they are usually assigned to Akstafa, and sometimes to Daghestan. The boteh in rugs of this type contain smaller boteh, floral and plant forms, or animals. Herrmann illustrates a rug with all four types of boteh in alternating rows in *Seltene Orientteppiche IV*, plate 25. Commenting on this rug, Herrmann writes, 'while the pattern is basically simple, interest is provided by the diagonal colour progression and the changing motifs within the boteh.' In the rug shown here the boteh are arranged in a random fashion, without a systematic rationale based on colour – somewhat similar in style to Marasali rugs. Unlike Marasalis, however, the boteh on this type of rug always face in the same direction.

The borders of rugs in this group typically feature 'latchhook and dice' designs or latchhooked lozenges.[2] This example, however, has a kochanak and animal border, which is quite rare. The field of this rug, with the large red octagon beneath the prayer arch, is also unusual. In a typical configuration the boteh field would continue beneath the arch, which is sometimes augmented by a comb.

87

AKSTAFA

1st half 19th century

1.01 × 1.61m (3′4″ × 5′3″)

This rug is unusual for its striped field. No other such Akstafa example is known to me. A number of characteristic Akstafa features are also included, however: the hooked border, the dotted arch, the 'hand prints' in the spandrels, the comb beneath the arch and the light blue selvedge. This rug is a good illustration of the talent of Caucasian weavers to freely borrow major design elements from other districts, whilst still producing pieces with a strong indigenous character and integrity.

Writing about a similar example, which he assigned to Karabagh, Eberhart Herrmann explained that the five fingers in the hand prints symbolize five important religious personages of Shi'ite Islam: Mohammed, Ali, Fatima, Hassan and Hossein.[1] His example, dated AH 1293 (1876), has a very similar vertically striped field but is decorated with boteh instead of the geometric motifs of our example, and also differs in the shape of the arch.[2]

88

AKSTAFA

3rd quarter 19th century

0.84 × 1.40m (2′9″ × 4′7″)

Akstafa prayer rugs, with a few exceptions (such as plate 87), feature three basic field designs: all-over boteh; lattice designs, frequently on a blue field (these rugs tend to be long and narrow and to have double-hook or kochanak borders); and three or four linked medallions beneath a square prayer arch. This rug is of the third type. The characteristic Akstafa 'peacock' motif, although fairly common in secular long rugs, is rare in prayer pieces, appearing only in two of the listed analogies (nos 5 and 7). The example shown here is small and jewel-like, with wonderful colours. The border, an abstraction of the 'crab' floral motif, appears on only one other known Akstafa prayer rug.[1] It does, however, feature on other types of prayer rugs from the Shirvan region.[2]

89

MARASALI

early 19th century

1.06 × 1.38m (3′6″ × 4′6″)

The 'curved arch' black Marasali is the rarest and earliest of the Marasali type. Berdj Achdjian, the owner of this piece and co-author of *Tapis et textiles Arméniens*, has a theory about them. Fewer than ten such pieces are known, and Achdjian proposes that we multiply them by a factor of five to arrive at the probable number that were produced. We could then assume that about 50 such pieces were made. Even 100 pieces could very probably be the work of one extended family of master weavers over a generation. The similarity of dyes, structure, detailing and design, and even the way the poly-chrome boteh are placed in sequence, puts such a theory very much within the limits of probability.

The Marasali boteh is arguably the earliest representation of that motif in Caucasian rugs. 'Boteh' means 'cluster of leaves' in Farsi (sometimes translated as 'cluster of flowers') and there are many and greatly divergent theories concerning its evolution. What is certain is that it is descended from seventeenth- and eighteenth-century Kashmir (and later Kerman) 'paisley' shawls.[1] The 'glow' sur-rounding some versions of the boteh (notably Marasali) has been interpreted as suggestive of a reli-gious experience.[2] In the nineteenth century the use of this motif had been widespread throughout Persia, the Caucasus, on Baluch rugs and in Central Asia, particularly on Ersari rugs.[3]

90

MARASALI

early 19th century

1.06 × 1.40m (3′5″ × 4′7″)

This is the second of the 'curved arch' black Marasalis published here. Although obviously from the same family as the carpets pictured in plates 89 and 91, this rug has a very unusual shade of abrashed celadon green in one of the boteh. The prayer arch is narrower and more compressed than in parallel pieces. As the owner, Jim Dixon, has pointed out that this rug was probably made in a workshop as a commission for an affluent client.[1] The materials are of the highest quality, with brilliant colours, finely spun warps and strong, shiny pile. The weaver was obviously extremely skilled; indeed, as Dixon says, there are very few Caucasian carpets of this calibre left in the world.

91

MARASALI

early 19th century

0.89 × 1.14m (2´11˝ × 3´9˝)

This is possibly the most famous and most published Caucasian prayer rug of all time. *Oriental Rug Review* described it as 'the finest Marasali in the world, with fabulous colours',[1] while Murray Eiland says of the rug, 'this must be the most finely woven of the Marasali type, and the lustrous wool gives it an unusual glow'.[2] Louise Mackie in the Textile Museum, Washington, catalogue, *Prayer Rugs*,[3] declares that 'the superb juxtaposition of colours, detailed drawing and the lustrous quality of the wool must qualify the rug as one of the finest of its type… The beauty of the rug is greatly enriched and enlived by the random use of colours and designs on each buta.'

This piece was acquired by Jerome and Mary Jane Straka in Krakow, Poland in 1937.[4] Of more than two hundred rugs in their collection, it was always their favourite. This rug, more than any other, inspired our own passion for rug collecting. Although the Strakas donated a large part of their collection to the Textile Museum in Washington DC, this rug stayed with the family until Jerome Straka's death in April 1986. When it came on the market at Sotheby's, New York, later that year, Linda and I were delighted to be able to acquire it. We were later honoured to receive a letter from Mary Jane Straka in which she talked about her affection for the rug and the history of its acquisition.[5]

92

MARASALI

3rd quarter 19th century

1.12 × 1.52m (3′8″ × 5′0″)

Early black Marasalis with curved prayer arches (see plates 89, 90 and 91), although very special, are by no means the only Marasalis of merit. Some later examples – such as the rug shown here – have been wonderfully crafted, with large, bold, alternately facing boteh in a panoply of designs. In this example the boteh are so large that only five horizontal rows are needed to fill the field. (In most later examples, which are more crowded and with less variation in boteh designs, the boteh face the same direction.[1])

Marasali designs tend to be fairly standardized, usually featuring more or less geometric botehs on a blue field. Within this formula, however, some surprising variations can be found. In this example 11 colours are used and the 46 boteh display six different designs, including crosshatch, honeycomb, diagonal stripes, a central axis, diamonds and double diamonds. A total of 37 design variants can be seen. The typical Marasali 'bird' border is flanked by characteristic blue-ground guard borders, then framed by a supplementary guard border of angular floral design, on a yellow ground.

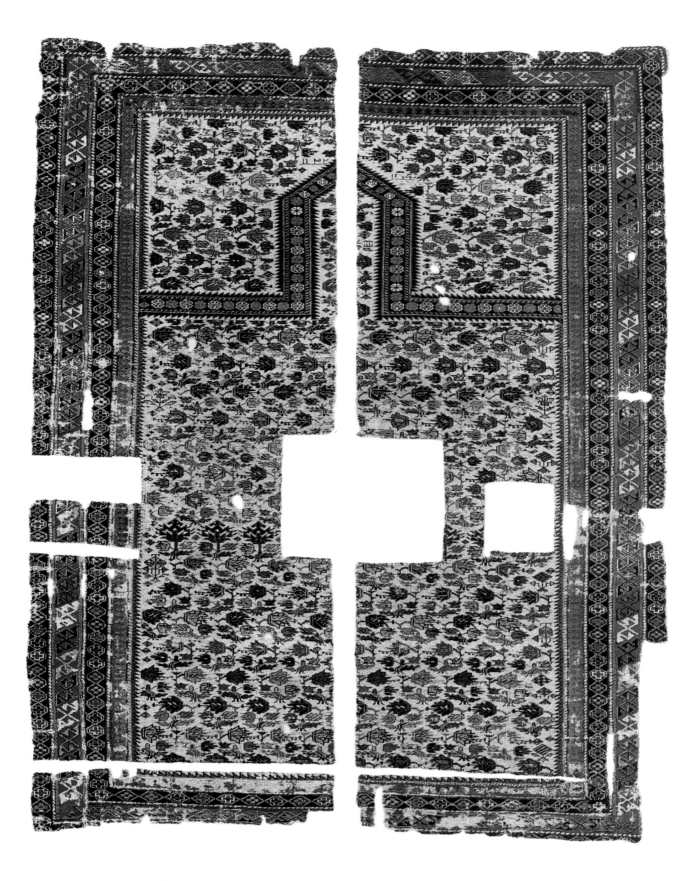

93

MARASALI

1st quarter 19th century

0.86 × 1.12m (2´10˝ × 3´8˝)

With its naturalistic flower design, and lack of a geometric lattice framework, it is quite probable that this piece represents a very early style of Caucasian prayer rug. Very few rugs of this design now exist. The rug is extremely finely woven, with 525 knots per square inch, and uses silk wefting. It is published as plate 8 in *The Caucasus: Traditions in Weaving* by James Burns, the owner of the rug, where he calls it 'the most finely knotted Caucasian weaving I have examined'. Indeed, it is almost twice as fine as the 'Straka' Marasali (plate 91), which has 287 knots per square inch.

The tradition of silk wefting and extremely fine knotting endured throughout the nineteenth century. Caucasian weavers continued to produce very fine white-ground prayer rugs for special commissions. Maury Bynum of Chicago recently had two such examples, one dated 1854 with cotton weft and silk warp and one dated 1840 with silk weft, warp and highlights. Plate 7 in Burns, *Traditions in Weaving,* illustrates a silk-wefted Shirvan dated AH 1230 (1814) with 324 knots per square inch. Another very fine example, dated AH 1243 (1827) and with 260 knots per square inch, was sold at Lefevre in 1984.[1] These rugs were special presentation pieces, often intended as gifts or bridal dowry.[2] The rug shown here has an interesting recent history.[3]

94

MARASALI

early 19th century

1.02 × 1.30m (4′3″ × 3′4″)

This rug belongs to a small, elite family of very finely woven lattice pattern rugs, usually attributed to Marasali. Rugs in this group feature rows of flowers arranged in sequence to form a 'V' pattern. The depiction of some of those flowers is usually naturalistic, and red silk is often used in the pile. Yellow is used in greater proportions than in similar white-ground lattice pieces.

These pieces, along with certain black Marasalis, are among the most finely woven of all Caucasian prayer rugs.[1] They all date from the early nineteenth century. An example in the James Burns collection, formerly in the Yale University Art Gallery, is dated AH 1230 (1814) and has 324 knots per square inch, with woollen warp and wefts and selvedges of silk.[2] A very similar example, from the Andrew Dole collection, was sold at auction in 1976, misattributed to Senna.[3] An all-wool example, very similar in execution and colouring to the rug shown here and with 225 knots per square inch, was published by Herrmann and attributed to Kuba.[4]

95

M A R A S A L I

dated AH 1274 (1858)

0.92 × 1.20m (3′ 0″ × 3′ 11″)

Yellow Marasalis usually feature lattice fields with flowers or boteh or, less commonly, rows of boteh on an open field. This example has a most unusual design, however: a red trellis network enclosing hexagonal geometric figures which contain polychromatic depictions of plant forms. The arrangement of the white 'bird' motifs on the red ground of the arch and main border is also unusual, with the reverse colour scheme being the more general rule. The undulating drawing of the prayer arch is yet another odd feature. This rug is well known from its publication (in black and white) in the catalogue of the first post-war all-Caucasian exhibition, which was held in Germany at the Museum für Kunsthandwerk, Frankfurt in 1962.[1]

96

MARASALI

c.1800

1.24 × 1.45m (4′1″ × 4′9″)

The main focus of this striking rug is the three figures of elaborately attired warriors astride large horses, which are equally elegantly decorated. The rug also features a profusion of animals, deer and a few birds both above and below the prayer arch. This appears to be a unique design for a Marasali prayer rug, with no known analogies in rug literature except for a vaguely related example with a large horse and rider as a centrepiece.[1] It is quite possibly a commissioned piece, made for a family of hunters or warriors. Particular attention has been paid to details such as the riders' costumes and saddle covers. Special batches of dyes must have been made for the pale sky blue and golden yellow ochre of the horses, which are unusual colours for a Marasali.

Prayer rugs containing fabulous birds (see for example Volkmann, *Old Eastern Carpets*, plate 66) and lions have been attributed to Marasali.[2] Other prayer examples with birds are assigned to Akstafa. The Volkmann rug has a system of major and minor borders virtually identical to this piece. Volkmann suggests that the deer-like animals that also feature on his rug symbolize the Caucasian countryside. There are related secular Shirvan examples with naturalistic horses alternating with roosters.[3]

97

MARASALI

mid-19th century

1.17 × 1.52m (3′10″ × 5′0″)

Imagination and unpredictability are two aspects of Caucasian rugs that make collecting them such an exciting pursuit. Take this example. The octagon-filled field is a rare feature in Caucasian rugs (see plates 1 and 86) and virtually unknown in prayer pieces from the northeast. Indeed, this appears to be the only such carpet in existence. Aside from the unusual field, the border design is uncommon. It is an evolutionary variant of the Marasali 'bird' border, but the addition of four legs transforms the birds into exotic, llama-like animals. Similar borders coincidentally appear on rugs with other unconventional field designs. These include a rug advertised in *Oriental Rug Review* with animals, birds and humans amidst the boteh;[1] a rug with a row of six Mongol horsemen and their leader, auctioned at Skinner's;[2] and a rug pictured in Volkmann, *Old Eastern Carpets* with humans, deer-like animals, naturalistic small birds and three large 'Akstafa' fabulous birds.[3] Volkmann's comment about rugs of this type is worth repeating: 'These immensely fine and noble prayer rugs, whose patterns with likelihood were accommodated to Persian tastes, were probably already intended for Persian export in the early nineteenth century.'

4

APPENDICES

This essay is an attempt, in a very brief space, to look at carpets in general and prayer rugs in particular as reflections of some deeply felt Islamic conceptions about the universe. The plates in this book testify to the extraordinary prevalence of the design schemes discussed below.

The European fascination with oriental carpets – dating at least as far back as the twelfth century and the crusades – has produced remarkably little writing about the origins of the designs and their interpretation. Travellers, from Marco Polo on, mention carpet production in one place or another, with little further comment. Although writing on aesthetic subjects became more common in the eighteenth and nineteenth centuries, it did not extend to carpets. From the time of the first museum holdings and exhibitions in the 1880s, increasingly scholarly attempts at classification – by place and materials of manufacture, structure, design and period – have taken a relatively prescribed form. This classificatory interest, however, inspired virtually no field research; there were consequently no accounts of the meanings of designs and symbols within the cultural and religious context of those who made and used the carpets. Occasionally, rug books of dubious scholarship and motive have addressed the subject in a fragmented way.

In the last two decades a relative abundance of theories concerning motifs, designs and symbols has appeared in print. We have been variously assured that most rugs are really Armenian or Christian in origin; that they are manuals of sexual instruction for the apparently perplexed villager; that their designs derive primarily from Luristan, or from Georgian or Zoroastrian art; and that they represent the modern survival of Neolithic design, and of the Mother Goddess. More interestingly, but probably of little help to the student of carpets, we have been urged to explore carpets as 'faces of God' and 'projections of our ideal selves'.

This pot-pourri of inventions, interpretations, anachronisms, half-truths and occasional genuine insight continues to ignore one fundamental question: what meaning do the designs and design elements of carpets – whatever their historical origin – have for those who design, make and live with them in the Islamic community?

The Western mind has shown itself ill-prepared to interpret the art of Islam. For, except in so far as everyone has access to 'universal symbols' through some faculty akin to the Jungian 'unconscious', Westerners are truly outsiders to the spiritual expression – esoteric and exoteric – of traditional Islamic culture and so tend to superimpose romantic projections and preconceptions on what they think they are seeing.

WORSHIP AND THE MOSQUE The orthodox canon of Islam is based on the Koran, together with sayings attributed to Mohammed not included in the Koran (the Hadith), the Hebrew Torah, and the Gospels. Surprisingly, the writings of Rumi and the works of great theologians and Sufi mystics are held in almost equal veneration. Islamic life is suffused in all its parts by the message of the Prophet. 'Islam' means, literally, to 'surrender', or 'submit' one's life and will to Allah. Because Allah is 'one', with no intermediaries, there are, ostensibly, no priests. Worship, performed five times a day, is very much a communal function, although a Muslim can also worship alone. The worshipper prostrates himself, facing Mecca, and touches his head and hands to the ground, after carefully prescribed ritual cleansing. Heeding the injunction to cleanliness, he performs these prostrations on cloth, or when affordable, on a prayer rug. Caucasian prayer rugs in particular often have hands drawn in the spandrels where the worshipper's own hands support his prostrate form; the mihrab nearly always has a device within its niche to mark the place where the worshipper's head should touch the carpet.

Most frequently this device appears as a 'niche within a niche' (see plates 30, 32, 45, 47–50, 55, 56, 74, 76, 80). Its position at the top of the niche is significant, as it represents the topmost, or next to topmost, element in a series of figures composing an ascending seven-tiered (occasionally nine-tiered) Tree of Life. In its upward-pointing form it may also represent a tray or reliquary containing earth consecrated by Mohammed or a saint, used as an object in Islamic rite. As a niche it provides orientation (towards Mecca and salvation) and thus represents the niche in the mosque. As a niche within a

APPENDIX A

DESIGN AND SYMBOLISM

Some observations with special reference to Caucasian prayer rugs

Jim Dixon

niche it is a holy of holies, emphasizing the ascending movement of Resurrection, and the means whereby it becomes possible.

The mosque floor itself – and by extension, the prayer rug – has an especially holy significance. As Nasr points out in *Islamic Art and Spirituality*:

> ...*the first mosque was the House of the Blessed Prophet, it was the forehead of the most perfect of God's creatures, of the Perfect man himself, about whom God has said 'were it not for thee I would not have created the heavens' that touched in prayer the floor of the humble room within which he prayed, thereby sanctifying the floor of the mosque and returning this floor to its inviolable purity as the original earth at the dawn of Creation...its primordial condition as the mirror and reflection of Heaven. This sanctification bestowed a new meaning upon the ground and the carpet covering it. The carpet...reflects Heaven and enables the Traditional Muslim who spends most of his time at home on the carpet to experience the ground upon which he sits as purified and participating in the sacred character of the ground of the mosque upon which he prays.*[1]

Thus, he who prays prostrate with his head on this representation of the earth consecrated by Allah, hopes also to be consecrated and restored to the 'primordial' condition, when earth was spiritually still like Heaven.

PLANES OF SPIRITUALITY From the eighth century on – beginning in the sophisticated court life of Baghdad – the classical heritage of Rome, and more particularly that of Greece, was translated, absorbed and reconciled with Islamic teaching. Plato and Aristotle were immensely important influences but so, too, were the doctrines of Pythagoras and the Hermetic corpus. The earlier traditions of Mesopotamia, Egypt and other Eastern civilizations had also found their way into Near Eastern and Greek thought. Despite innumerable doctrinal differences and variations, a world view emerged, generally consistent among Islamic writings of the tenth to the fifteenth centuries, combining earlier cosmological views with current elaborations and providing a general basis for a cosmogony that would be acceptable to Islam, with its insistence on absolute monotheism.

The Koran refers to the 'seven Heavens'. The eighth Heaven is the transition between the sensory and the suprasensory world. It can only be perceived spiritually: it is the 'lotus tree of the extremity'. It is in the eighth climate where all becomes possible; this is the abode of the fixed stars, the portal of the home-coming to Eden, the resurrection of the body of man in awakened, enlightened form. From this spiritual prominence, further ascent is possible to the immaterial and suprasensory ninth plane of the seraphim and the tenth plane of the throne of God. These heavens form concentric spheres with, for most Islamic writers, earth at the centre. In the tenth and eleventh centuries a highly allegorical form of literature developed that described spiritual ascents. In such writings (typified by the works of Suhrawardi, Semnani and Avicenna) the seeker encounters the seven Heavens of the seven Heavenly bodies. These planets have correspondences on earth and in man, for example the seven climates, minerals, gems, psychological states, kinds of animals, colours and musical tones.

The most important visual representation of these planes, or layers of reality, is the Tree of Life. This ancient form, as it appears on prayer rugs and on mosaics in the niches of mosques, usually has seven, though occasionally nine, tiers. Frequently a Tree of Life will have seven tiers of branches with an eight-pointed star, an eight-petalled lotus or an octagon floating above it. Alternatively it may have six tiers of branches surmounted by a seven-tiered palmette. The progression from seven to eight (sometimes from nine to ten) symbolizes the completion of the octave, the transition from the merely physical to the state of spiritual awakening. Many mosques have portals shaped as niches in which the walls recede in seven steps, forming a series of borders leading inwards to the door. The muqarnas (stalactites) which make the transition from the wall to the dome in mosques are seven-tiered, and examples exist in which the planets corresponding to each tier are named. Mosques themselves commonly have seven tiers, and their tile decorations are frequently elaborated in seven (or nine) ascending bands.

THE HEAVENLY ASCENT We have seen how the tree is a representation, or map, of the various planes of existence. The Koran suggests that the universe can be conceived as a tree whose roots are in the lower earth and whose trunk extends through the Ka'ba at Mecca to branch in the heavens. This tree is said to branch as the 'lotus-tree of the extremity' in the eighth Heaven. Representations of this cosmological idea are found from earliest times in Egypt, Mesopotamia (fig. 1), India and Greece. Sumerian representations of the caduceus, a staff around which two serpents twine, go back to 3000 BC. These serpents cross five times; at the sixth position is a winged solar disc and at the seventh position their heads face towards each other. Here they frame the top of the staff which terminates in one of several motifs, among them a lotus bud and a seven-lobed palmette. Above the staff, in the eighth position, there is often either an eight-petalled lotus or an eight-pointed star.

In India, this staff is articulated as two intertwined serpents around the channel of the Sushumna, a subtle energy channel coincident with the human spine; the serpents represent respectively the solar and lunar energies. This macrocosmic symbol echoes the microscosm of the 'subtle body', the human spine, and the plexuses of the human body. These plexuses or chakras are positioned at the crossing of the serpentine energies around the spine. As in the Heavens of Islamic thought, the seven chakras (or vortices or wheels) each have a corresponding planet, a musical tone, colour or geometric shape. When the chakras are 'open' the yogi experiences the first stages of enlightenment. Further nirvanas open with the further ascent of the yogi to the two extracorporeal chakras above his head. The seventh, or crown chakra is frequently represented by an eight-petalled lotus, or an eight-pointed star.

A similar scheme of subtle sensory organs and 'energy centres' can be seen in the Jewish tree of Kabbalah (fig. 2), which appears from at least the thirteenth century. This tree consists of ten spheres; their arrangement forms three vertical rows and seven stages from the lowest to the topmost sphere. Each stage, whether it comprises a single sphere in the central vertical axis or a pair – one on each side of the central axis – again represents one of the seven planets, days of the week, parts of the body, heavens, angels, letters, musical notes or colours.

In the Islamic world, a closely corresponding system of suprasensory organs (latifa) existed. Through these, the seeker might explore the more real but less visible world. Writing in the fourteenth century, Semnani describes the seven subtle sensory organs, their colours and the emanation of the Prophet to which they correspond. Although early Sufic texts have left little record of such matters, there is strong evidence for this tradition in eighteenth- and nineteenth-century verbal descriptions, for example in the works and translations of Henry Corbin.[2]

The earliest Islamic visual depiction of these 'subtle psychic organs' may be a palm tree – significant in the Sufi tradition – in a mosaic (fig. 5) from the Dome of the Rock in Jerusalem. Surely the eight circles depicted as an ascending column relate to an inner and an outer cosmology of Islam. An examination of early rugs from this cosmological perspective can be intriguing, as long as the issue is not confused by counting minor ornaments.

THE DESIGN OF PRAYER RUGS Prayer rugs contain some of the best evidence of this cosmology. Turkish prayer rugs often feature seven-branched trees surmounted by an eight-pointed star. Most of the rugs in this book show seven tiers of devices, or compartments. Some can be counted directly up the centre to the top of the niche; on plate 46, for example, the central of three columns is composed of seven hexagons, with the eighth position – in the niche – appropriately filled by a stepped octagon. Plate 50 has eight tiers of devices. The other Perepedil prayer rugs in the book (plates 47–49) seem to have either eight or nine. Plate 53 has seven ascending compartments. Plate 78 has eight compartments up the centre, as does plate 82.

The compartments in the rug on plate 75 are counted by another method, starting either in the column to the immediate left or in that to the right of the central column and zig-zagging to the centre and back. There are a total of eight compartments, ending in a talismanic eyed rhombus in the ninth position. Seven devices can be counted up the centre of plate 70, with two curved branches above the seventh device. About a dozen of the plates in this book show these same curved branches at the top

I ASSYRIAN RELIEF, NINTH CENTURY BC. This detail from a stone relief shows the Tree of Life with guardians. The tree has a central column with chevrons (ascending Waters of Life) surrounded by a seven-lobed palmette. Seven-petalled lotuses emerge from the smaller columns on either side of the central column. The crossings of branches between the columns – like the serpents twining on either side of the caduceus – form six layers, the six ascending lotuses on either side completed by the seventh and topmost lotus at the crown of the tree. This three-columned arrangement is common in innumerable classical carpets which incorporate three vertical rows each consisting of seven or eight guls. The Persian Garden carpet with three water channels also follows this format.

1

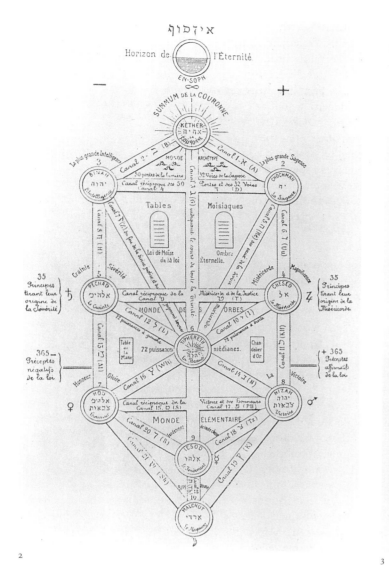

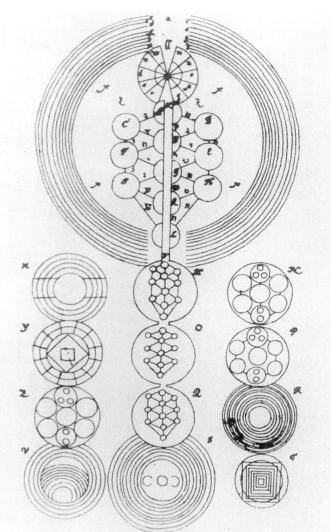

of the niche, sometimes rising into the spandrel. In plate 53 there are seven ascending stepped octagons (containing tree forms) on either side of the three-tiered niche. Plate 85 has a row of six boteh, a comb (a symbol of purity) in the seventh position and a rectangle, again possibly depicting the Ka'ba, in the eighth position with an eight-petalled lotus rising from it. Plates 55 and 56 have six clear compartments up the centre with the tray of sacramental earth in the seventh position and branches of the implied Tree of Life emerging from the top. Most of the remaining rugs have seven or eight boteh up the centre, including that in the niche, although a few have nine.

The layers of the Islamic cosmology have thus far been examined in profile or perspectival view. Many classical Islamic medallions can also be seen as a representation of this system, from an overhead view. The seven (or nine) Heavens exist in space as concentric spheres; the Tree of Life or axial pole connects them to the pole star. Looked at from above, the spheres become a series of concentric circles, or octagons, almost always with an eight-branched tree, eight-pointed star or eight-petalled lotus in the centre. A medallion almost always has six or seven concentric layers, counting from the

2 DIAGRAM OF THE KABBALISTIC TREE. This nineteenth-century diagram is a clearer presentation of a form whose earliest representations appear in twelfth- and thirteenth-century Spain. The Kabbalah – also composed of three columns and seven planes – purports to demonstrate the ancient Hermetic proposition, 'What is above is below, and what is below is above.' The Koran incorporates this dictum without explanation. Man is a microcosm of the whole, and his internal spiritual and psychological structure is like that of the universe, and vice-versa. Some Islamic diagrams of the *latifah* follow the same pattern as the Kabbalistic Tree.

3 THE KABBALAH BY ISAAC LURIA. Luria's seventeenth-century figure of the Kabbalah shows the Tree of Life at the top, in perspectival view, surrounded by the overhead view of ten concentric rings. The seventh and eighth rings are the widest.

centre, the field representing either the seventh, or when green, the eighth heaven. In classical medallions there are seven layers, with the field making eight; or nine, with the field making ten. (The single rows of outlining brown knots are not counted as part of the expanding concentric layers of colour.)

There is room within the tradition for considerable numerological variation. Plate 14 shows a typical eight-pointed Islamic star, the radiating branches of a tree expanding outwards from the star in the centre. Seven layers expand from the centre to float on an eighth layer, the white prayer niche. The eight-pointed tree-stars in plates 10 and 11 both have six layers that rest on the field, which represents the seventh layer. The water border of plate 10 at first looks like several borders, but proves to be a zig-zag floating on a white border (the eighth layer) separating the field of the niche from the ninth layer, the field of the rug.

Plates 3, 4, 5, 16, 19, 22 and 23 all have seven major and minor borders leading to the field. This format is typical of the majority of the plates in this book; interestingly, in the rugs with eight borders the fields are white. The obviously later rugs in this group typically have eleven or twelve borders, and often many tiers of design in the field.

For those who are inclined to doubt these observations about the relation between Islamic cosmology and the medallion, these further brief examples may prove useful.

Jocelyn Godwin remarks that in the dance of the whirling dervishes of Konya (introduced in the mid-thirteenth century by Rumi), the tall hats of the dervishes 'are said to be tilted at the same angle as the earth's axis, and their dance to symbolize the movements of the [seven] planetary spheres as

4 CIRCUMAMBULATION OF THE KA'BA. The rings of circumambulation of the Ka'ba (the four-sided building typifying 'earth' in its ancient signification) have a distinct marker in the eighth position. The ninth plane is that of the Garden of Paradise and the 'fixed stars', only be perceivable by the subtle senses of the psychically awakened.

5 MOSAIC, DOME OF THE ROCK, JERUSALEM. The palm tree in this sixth-century mosaic represents a mystical symbol much loved by mystical Islam and other Near Eastern religions. Here we see medallions within the trunk of the tree – eight in number – probably representing the subtle organs and their increasingly subtle characteristics. In most representations of palms there are seven or nine leaves.

they circle in perfect order and love for their Lord.'[3] Similarly, the pilgrimage to Mecca involves "The sevenfold circumambulation of the Ka'ba … and a sevenfold running between Safa and Marwa … But the central rite is the "staying" on the hill Arafat, a distance of eight miles from Mecca, on the ninth day of the month … on the way back the "stoning of Satan" is performed by casting pebbles three times at a certain place.'[4]

The repetition of sevens was pervasive in the ancient world. The ziggurats of Babylon, for example, were seven-tiered, each tier being of a different colour and representing a different heaven. The fifth-century Roman writer Macrobius makes a list of sevens that exceeds 30 pages in English; these entries were largely common to the entire ancient world.

THE QUEST FOR PARADISE It is the peculiarly intense Islamic urge for Resurrection and the return to the purity and perfection of the archetypal world that makes the yearning for paradise in Islamic art so deeply felt and that accounts for its essentially abstract quality. The flowers in the lattice field in the Marasali prayer rugs in this book are difficult to identify not because the weaver lacked skill in depiction, but because he wished us to reflect on the perfect flowers of the ethereal, archetypal world. These flowers are seen as overwhelmingly abundant, like the stars in the desert sky. The weaver would have us think of 'irisness' rather than of any particular iris.

The archetypal flower of the entire ancient world seems to have been the lotus. Hardly a classical Islamic rug fails to include an eight-petalled lotus, or an eight-pointed star. Seven is the number of the perfected human life; seven is the portal, the gate. Eight is the door to the relationship to the All: conventionally, to Resurrection, esoterically, to enlightenment in the literal sense of being filled with light. That state is symbolized by the eightness of the lotus, the octagon, the eight-pointed star or the eight-branched tree. Its transformative spiritual radiance is represented by the aureole that surrounds the saints, the prophets and all the forms of nature reawakened to their Edenic state. This aureole is symbolized by the palmette that surrounds the lotus when it is seen in profile. Not surprisingly the lotus, usually surrounded by a palmette, is the flower depicted most commonly in the prayer rugs in this book. Pre-Islamic palmettes have the same seven- or eight-tiered structure common to so many of the basic design elements in Islamic art.

The above remarks are a condensation of a careful analysis of an enormous amount of related visual material in an effort to see Islamic carpets in their cultural context. It is remarkable how widespread and consistent the design configurations seem to be from the fourteenth century, or earlier, to the mid-nineteenth century. It is difficult to determine the degree to which they represent repeated conventions, to which they represent the pervasive and ongoing traditions of Sufi workshops. But the evidence is not extraneous to the carpets. Their detailed visual analysis has hardly begun.

In so far as these carpets are maps of the cosmology of Islam, macrocosmic and microcosmic, they are all appreciations of paradise as it exists within us and around us at present; and they are anticipations, for an entire culture, of what might be. They are reference points in an ascending order of perception, intuition, and more complete participation. In the oft-quoted words of Rumi:

I died as mineral and became a plant
I died as plant and turned to animal
I died as animal and became man
What fear I, then, as I cannot diminish by dying?
Once when I die as a human I'll become an angel;
And I shall give up angelhood.
For Not-Being, 'Adam', calls with an organ like voice
'Verily we are his and to Him we return!'

(*Sura* 2 / 151)

NOTES

1 Seyyed Hossein Nasr, *Islamic Art and Spirituality* (State University of New York Press, Albany, New York 1987), p. 38.
2 Henry Corbin, *Spiritual Body and Celestial Earth* (Bollingen Series, Princeton University Press, Princeton, New Jersey 1977).
3 Jocelyn Godwin, *Harmonies of Heaven and Earth* (Arkana Press, New York and London 1986), p. 88.
4 Anne Marie Schimmel, *Islam* (State University of New York Press, Albany, New York 1992), p. 37.
5 Quoted by Anne Marie Schimmel from Nicholson's translation of the *Mathnawi* (Shambhala Publishing, Boston MA and London 1992), p. 156.

INDO-EUROPEANS	Slavs		3,183,870
	Other Europeans		163,036
	Iranians	Persians	13,929
		Talish	34,994
		Tats	95,050
		Ossetes or Ossetians	171,716
		Kurds	99,836
	Armenians		1,116,461
	Gypsies		3,041
ALTAIC	Turkic	Azeri Turks	1,509,785
		Osmanli Turks	139,419
		Nogai Turks	64,048
		Turkomans	24,522
		Karachais	27,222
		Kumyks	83,408
		Karapapaks	29,902
		Kalmucks (= Kalmyks)	14,409
		Other	1,620
	Finns		7,422
CAUCASIANS	Georgians		1,352,455
	Circassians		216,950
	Chechens and Ingushes		274,318
	Daghestanis	Avaro-Andians	212,692
		Darghins	130,209
		Kurins (= Lesghians)	159,213
		Other	98,300
SEMITIC			46,739

APPENDIX B

POPULATION OF THE CAUCASUS BY LANGUAGE GROUPS

Results of the Russian census of 1897; reproduced with permission, from Peter Stone, *Rugs of the Caucasus: Structure and Design* (Greenleaf Co., Chicago, 1984); adapted by Professor George Hewitt.

The following excerpts, taken in sequence from De Hell's chapter on 'The prohibitive system [of trade] and its pernicious results', amplify the deteriorating trade situation in south Russia and the Caucasus during the first half of the nineteenth century.

From the destruction of the Genoese colonies in the Crimea, in 1476, down to the treaty of Kainardji, a period of 300 years, the Black Sea remained closed against the nations of the West, and was the privileged domain of Turkey. Its whole coast belonged to the sultans of Constantinople, and the khans of the Crimea. The Turks, and the Greeks of the Archipelago, subjects of the Ottoman porte, had the sole right of navigating those waters, and all the commerce of Europe with that portion of the East with exclusively in the hands of the latter people. The conquests of Peter the Great, and subsequently those of the celebrated Catherine II, changed this state of things. The Russians advanced towards the south, and soon made themselves masters of the Sea of Azof, the Crimea, and all the northern coasts of the Black Sea.
...

About the year 1817 an increased duty was laid on all foreign goods in the Black Sea; but at the same period Odessa was definitively declared to be a free port, without restriction. Things continued thus until 1822; and it was during this interval that all those great foreign houses were established in Odessa, some of which exist to this day. The commerce of Southern Russia had then reached its apogee.
...

Dazzled by this commercial prosperity, till then unexampled in Russia, and, doubtless believing it unalterably established the government then chose to return to its prohibitive system, and, whether through ignorance or incapacity, the ministry deliberately ruined with their own hands the commercial wealth of Southern Russia. In 1822, at the moment when it was least expected, an ukase suppressed the freedom of the port of Odessa, and made it obligatory on the merchants to pay the duties on all goods then in the warehouses. This excited intense alarm, and as it was totally impossible to pay immediately such enormous duties as those imposed by the general tariff of the empire, the merchants remonstrated earnestly and threatened, all of them, to commit bankruptcy.
...

The Transcaucasian provinces enjoyed very extensive commercial freedom at this period by virtue of an ukase promulgated, October 20, 1821... Redoutkalé, on the shores of Mingrelia, was then the port to which all the goods were conveyed by sea. But all these promising elements of prosperity were to be annihilated by the narrow views of the minister of finance. The commercial franchise of the Caucasian provinces, after having lasted for ten years, was suddenly suppressed on the first of January, 1832. The most rigorous prohibitive system was put in force: Tiflis, the capital of Georgia, more than 220 miles from the Black Sea, was made the centre of the customs administration, and all goods had to pass through that town to be examined there and pay duty.
...

By these arbitrary and exclusive measures, the government thought to encourage native manufactures; and by prohibiting the goods of Germany, France and England, it hoped to force the productions of Russia on the trans-Caucasian provinces. The transit trade was, of course, proscribed at the same period. By a first ukase, the merchants were forced to deposit at the frontier in Radzivolof, double the value of their goods, and the money was only to be returned to them at Odessa, upon verification of their bales. It is obviously not to be thought of that merchants, however wealthy, should carry with them, in addition to the capital to be expended on their purchases, double the value of their goods in transitu. This new measure, therefore, was sufficient of itself alone to put an entire stop to the transit trade.
...

APPENDIX C

TRAVELS IN THE STEPPES OF THE CASPIAN SEA,

THE CRIMEA, AND THE CAUCASUS (EXCERPTS)

Xavier Hommaire de Hell (London, 1847)

The table below compares the number of Anatolian and Caucasian prayer rugs published by two leading rug dealers – Eberhart Herrmann and Peter Bausback – from 1978 to 1994. The figures illustrate the relative scarcity of early (pre-1800) Caucasian prayer rugs. Only piled examples were considered, and many double-niche designs, such as 'Transylvanians' and Karachophs, were excluded. There are no known Karachophs of small (prayer) size, or examples with a single directional niche. The prayer arch as used in the double-niche Karachoph is in my opinion purely a decorative device.

HERRMANN catalogue number/date	Anatolian prayer rugs		Caucasian prayer rugs	
	16–18th C	19th C	17–18th C	19th C
SOT I	2	2	—	1
SOT II	1	3	—	3
SOT III	2	8	—	5
SOT IV	2	4	—	6
SOT V	3	3	—	6
SOT VI	1	1	—	6
SOT VII	1	2	—	2
SOT VIII	2	3	—	9
SOT IX	3	1	—	2
SOT X	—	—	—	3
ATT 1	4	—	—	2
ATT 2	2	1	—	2
ATT 3	2	—	—	2
ATT 4	2	—	—	2
Kaukasische Teppichkunst	—	—	—	10
SUBTOTAL	27	28	0	61

BAUSBACK				
1978	7	6	—	10
1979	1	2	—	3
1980	—	5	—	6
1981	1	3	—	2
1982	—	1	—	4
1983	1	2	—	6
1987–88	1	1	—	4
SUBTOTAL	11	20	0	35

EARLY ANATOLIAN AND CAUCASIAN PRAYER RUGS

A comparison of exhibition catalogues

This database was originally conceived almost twenty years ago as a means of tracking auction performances of the types of rugs that were of personal interest. Over the years it developed into a much more extensive index of these rugs as published in all available sources, including books, auction catalogues and magazines. They are grouped by type, region of origin and design characteristics.

BORCHALO	149 rugs	number	%
Border design	Reciprocal trefoil or 'running dog' borders (figs 3, 4)	117	78
	Leaf-and-calyx (fig. 9)	21	14
	Other	11	8
Field design	Double diamonds in field (fig. 2)	96	64
	Single diamond in field (fig. 2)	5	3
	Multiple all-over hexagons (fig. 1)	13	9
	Other	35	24

FACHRALO	252 rugs	number	%
Border design	Serrated leaf (with and without calyx) (fig. 9)	151	52.6
	Zigzag (fig. 10)	50	17.4
	Leaf and branch (fig. 11)	29	10.1
	Asterisk rosette	12	4.2
	Other	45	15.4

KARABAGH	142 rugs	number	%
Field designs	'Crab' or floral field (fig. 20)	29	20.4
	Broad vertical bands with 's' motifs	13	9.15
	Animals or horses in field (figs 14, 15)	10	7.05
	Various narrow 'stripe' designs	10	7.05
	Boteh (including Chan-Karabagh)	9	6.3
	Chondzoresk (cloud band)	9	6.3
	Chelaberd (waterbug palmettes) (fig. 18)	10	7.05
	Chelaberd (sunburst or 'eagle' type)	1	0.7
	Stars	5	3.5
	Goradis	2	1.4
	Medallion (Fachralo type)	4	2.8
	Narrow vertical stripe with rhomboid medallions	5	3.55
	Linked medallion	3	2.15
	Herati	4	2.8
	'Ikat' design	3	2.15
	Kasim-Ushag	1	0.7
	Other	20	14.08

APPENDIX E

THE KAFFEL DATABASE

GENJE	73 rugs		number	%
Field design	Diagonal stripes		20	27
	Boteh		13	18.5
	Floral		12	16.5
	Lattice		10	14
	Linked 'head and shoulders' medallions		7	9.5
	Memling guls		2	2.5
	All-over stars		7	9.5
	Other		7	9.5

BAKU	26 rugs		number	%
Field design	'Head and shoulders' with octagons (fig. 24)		11*	42.3
	Avshan design with stepped polygons (fig. 26)		3	11.6
	Memling guls		3	11.6
	'Cemetery design'		8	30.8
	All-over stepped polygons		1	3.7

* 8 of these have 'barber pole' borders (fig. 25).

KUBA	42 rugs		number	%
Field design	Lattice		15*	35.7
	Stylized flowering plants		6	14.3
	Floral palmettes		10	23.8
	Kilim design		1	2.4
	Boteh		2	4.8
	Star flower		2	4.8
	Other		6	14.3

* 12 of these have arabesque borders (fig. 27).

PEREPEDIL	35 rugs		number	%
Ground colour	Light		30	85
	Dark		5*	15
Border designs	'Kufic'		17	48.5
	Latchhook-and-calyx		6	17.2
	Leaf-and-calyx (fig. 9)		4†	11.4
	'Crab' (fig. 20)		2	5.7
	Other		6	17.2

*all late examples. † 2 of these have yellow grounds.

CHICHI	66 rugs		number	%
Field design	Blue-ground 'Khirdagyd'		37	56.1
		with bar and rosette borders (fig. 30)	26	70
		with Kufic borders	7	19
		with leaf-and-calyx borders	2	5.5
		with other borders	2	5.5
	'Head and shoulders' keyhole (fig. 24)		11	16.7
	Geometric latchhooked motifs		7	10.6
	Gold-ground 'Khirdagyd'		4	6.1
	Boteh with latchhooked motifs		2	3
	Trellis with 'arrowhead' polygons		2	3
	Multiple niche		1	1.5
	Other		2	3

DAGHESTAN	332 rugs	number	%
Field design	Light-ground lattice (usually ivory, rarely golden yellow)	208	62.6
	Tulip design	47	14.2
	Palmette	17	5.2
	Dark-ground lattice	15	4.5
	Boteh	13	3.9
	Striped	11	3.3
	Latchhook diamonds	11	3.3
	Star field	7	2.1
	'Syrga'	1	0.3
	'Anchor'	1	0.3
	'Palm'	1	0.3

DAGHESTAN *The following table indicates the two most common border designs for each of the seven most common Daghestani field designs:*

field	border	number	%
Light-ground lattice (208 rugs)	Dragon (fig. 32)	184	88.5
	Bird or 'eagle's beak' (fig. 33)	8	3.8
Tulip (47 rugs)	Dragon (fig. 32)	26	55.3
	Latchhook (fig. 19)	9	19.1
Palmette (17 rugs)	Crab (fig. 20)	5	29.5
	'Ashik'	4	23.5
Dark-ground lattice (15 rugs)	Rosette	3	20
	Dragon (fig. 32)	2	13.3
Boteh (13 rugs)	Dragon (fig. 32)	4	30.7
	Latchhook	4	30.7
Striped (11 rugs)	Boteh	5	45.5
	Dragon (fig. 32)	5	45.5
Latchhook diamonds (11 rugs)	Asterisk	5	45.5
	Dragon (fig. 32)	4	36.3

SHIRVAN	357 rugs	number	%
Field design	Light-ground lattice*	142	39.8
	Tulip	36	10.1
	Boteh	33	9.2
	Floral	27	7.6
	Latchhooks	23	6.4
	'Head and shoulders' keyhole (fig. 24)	21	5.8
	Striped	16	4.5
	Animals, serpents, etc.	15	4.2
	Ashik	9	2.5
	Mosque	7	1.9
	Dark-ground lattice	6	1.7
	'Persian' design	4	1.1
	Saff	4	1.1
	Central medallion	4	1.1
	Other	10	3

* usually ivory, occasionally golden yellow.

The following table indicates the two most common border designs for each of the seven most common Shirvan field designs:

field	border	number	%
Light-ground lattice	Dragon (fig. 32)	105	74
(142 rugs)	'Kufic'	12	8.5
Tulip (36 rugs)	Dragon (fig. 32)	22	61
	Bird or 'eagle's beak' (fig. 33)	9	25
Boteh* (33 rugs)	Latchhook (fig. 36)	18	54.5
	Dragon (fig. 32)	5	15
Floral† (27 rugs)	Floral (fig. 35)	8	29.6
	Dragon (fig. 32)	5	18.5
Latchhooks (23 rugs)	Dragon (fig. 32)	11	47.8
	Bird	4	17.4
'Head and shoulders'	Crab (fig. 20)	8	38
keyhole (21 rugs)	Geometric 'c' motifs (fig. 37)	7	33.3
Stripes (16 rugs)	Dragon (fig. 32)	5	31.2
	Stepped polygons	4	25

* *Some of the boteh rugs have been assigned to Shirvan-Akstafa or Akstafa.*

† *There is no one border design that can be said to be typical of floral prayer rugs from Shirvan.*
Twelve different border designs appeared on 27 rugs, with variants of floral borders used eight times.

The table below indicates the two most common border designs for each of the three major groups:

group	border	number	%
'Black Marasali'		141	60.7
	Marasali 'bird' or boteh	113	80
	Dragon (fig. 32)	9	6.4
'Gold Marasali'		52	22.5
	Marasali 'bird' or boteh	28	53.8
	Cartouche (fig. 41)	21	40.3
'Ivory Marasali'		34	14.6
	Dragon (fig. 32)	20	58.8
	Marasali 'bird' or boteh	13	38.2

Full bibliographic references may be found in the Bibliography, page 187.

PREFACE

1 Julius Lessing, *Altorientalische Teppichmuster nach Bildern und Originalen des XV und XVI Jahrhunderts*, Berlin 1877 (English edition London 1879).
2 Denny and Walker, *The Markarian Album*, Appendix 2: Oriental Rug books 1877 to 1926.
3 *Hali* 91, p. 87, reporting on sixteenth- and seventeenth-century Persian 'Salting' carpets classified as nineteenth-century Turkish production.
4 The world's oldest known rug, the 2,500-year-old Pazyryk carpet, which was discovered in a frozen tomb in the Altai Mountains of Siberia in 1949, may well have been woven in the Caucasus. (See Schürmann, *The Pazyryk, Its Use and Origin*, pp. 28–33; Kerimov, *Rugs & Carpets from the Caucasus: The Russian Collections*, p. 16).

BACKGROUND

1 See Maclean, *To Caucasus, the End of all the Earth*, p. 11.
2 Benet, *Abkhasians, The Long Living People of the Caucasus*, p. 6.
3 Herodotus, *The Histories*, trans. David Greene (University of Chicago Press, Chicago, 1937). pp. 125–26.
4 Stone, *Rugs of the Caucasus: Structure and Design*, p. 46: '... the long-tailed sheep native to Mingrelia are called Colchian sheep. The tail of the Colchian sheep reaches the ground ... The Mingrelians preserved the curl character of the young fleece while the lamb grew by washing the lambs every day and pressing the fleece close to the skin.'
5 See Benet, *Abkhasians, the Long Living People of the Caucasus*.
6 Maclean, *To Caucasus*, p. 12: 'The Abkhazians, according to some the handsomest race of all, claim descent from Prometheus himself.'
7 See Schürmann, *The Pazyryk, Its Use and Origin*.
8 For more about Queen Tamar see Maclean, *To Caucasus*, pp. 20–21.
9 Stone, *Rugs of the Caucasus*, p. 50.
10 See Maclean, *To Caucasus*, pp. 55–90.
11 For further discussion, see Stone, *Rugs of the Caucasus*, pp. 55–58.
12 Pliny is quoted in Mounsey, *A Journey Through the Caucasus and the Interior of Persia*, pp. 20–21: 'It would appear that, in very ancient days, the products of the East found their way through the Caucasus. Pliny thus describes their route: "Arrived in Bactra [Balk] the merchandise descends the Icarus as far as the Oxus and thence is carried down to the Caspian. It then crosses that sea to the mouth of the Cyrus [Kyra], where it ascends the river, and on going ashore is transported by land for five days to the banks of the Phasis [Rion] where it embarks once more and is conveyed down to the Euxene."'
13 Hanway, *An Historical Account of the British Trade Over the Caspian Sea with a Journal of Travels*, 4 vols.
14 Keppel's writings, from 1824, are cited in Lefevre, *Caucasian Carpets*.
15 De Hell, *Travels in the Steppes of the Caspian Sea, The Crimea, The Caucasus, etc.* Writing of the 1932 closure of the Transcaucasian provinces, he states that 'while the people of Persia and Turkey in Asia were forsaking their old commercial routes for new markets, Russia has gone on making her prohibitive system [of trade] more and more stringent.' (For further excerpts from this work see Appendix C.)
16 Ellis, *Early Caucasian Rugs*, p. 9.
17 Lefevre, *Caucasian Carpets*, p. 19.

18 Bennett, *Oriental Rugs: Vol. 1, Caucasian*. Bennett writes that 'the majority of scholars take the view that the carpets with geometric designs which appear in Flemish and Italian paintings from the fifteenth century, are almost certainly Anatolian and not Caucasian', but goes on to state that 'the carpets which appear in fifteenth-century Flemish paintings with lozenge designs and hooked octagons ... resemble both Anatolian, and more strongly, Caucasian carpets of later dates.' (p. 9).
19 Kerimov, *Rugs and Carpets from the Caucasus: The Russian Collections*. Kerimov writes about carpets being made in Azerbaijan in ancient times, citing ancient documents such as the writings of Greek historian Xenophon (fifth century BC) and the Arab historian El Mukalasi (tenth century BC), among others. He goes on to say that 'by the thirteenth and fourteenth centuries ... carpets that were produced in Azerbaijan ... attracted the notice of ... Venetian merchants and travellers ... From the fifteenth century on we discover Azerbaijan carpets ... in paintings by Carlo Crivelli, Jan Van Eyck and Hans Holbein.' (A Russian carpet scholar from Baku, Kerimov codified the nomenclature of Caucasian rugs in his 1961 book *Azerbaijansky Kovjer*. This evolved into the 1964 definitive nomenclature by Ulrich Schürmann.)
20 Yetkin, *Early Caucasian Carpets in Turkey*, vol. 2, p. 3.
21 Schlosser, *The Book of Rugs, Oriental and European*. 'Some types of fifteenth-century rugs, such as the example with the dragons and phoenixes formerly in the Berlin Museum [the Dragon and Phoenix rug], or the fragment with a stylized tree and two small birds in Stockholm [the Marby rug], though generally described as Anatolian, may well have come from the Caucasus.' (p. 52).
22 An example is a rare and early rug acquired in 1995 by Heinrich Kirchheim for his Orient Stars Collection, published in *Hali* 82, p. 111, attributed to Anatolia sixteenth/seventeenth century, but now judged to be Caucasian.
23 Quoted in Lefevre, *Caucasian Carpets*, p. 42.
24 Hanway, *Historical Account*, vol. 1, p. 378; vol. 2, p. 48.
25 Published in *Hali* 75, p. 59.
26 See George Leland Hunter, 'The Truth About Doctored Rugs', *Country Life in America*, July 1906.
27 Kerimov et al., *Rugs and Carpets from the Caucasus: The Russian Collection*, p. 11.

NOTES TO

THE TEXT

28 Berdj Achdjian, letter to the author: 'When I was travelling in the Soviet Union, in 1980 and more recently 1992–93, [I saw] in north Armenia many cartoons, in very small villages of course, in the hands of women of 75 or 85 years old. Those cartoons were as old as those women. They were cartoons or designs for borders or for parts of the inner fields of a rug. They were in such a poor condition that I wondered how these women could weave from such a destroyed cartoon … But what remained was enough to count the knots and weave. And sometimes the women of the village would make exchanges between them, giving them variety in their work.'

29 Stone, *Rugs of the Caucasus*, p. 41.

30 For further discussion of Kerbala stones see Gombos, *Aszkéták, Dervisek, Imaszönyegek* (Ascetics, Dervishes and Prayer Rugs), p. 104.

31 Ibid., p. 105.

32 Blair and Bloom (eds), *Images of Paradise in Islamic Art*, p. 37.

33 Michael Craycraft and Anne Halley, *Belouch Prayer Rugs* (exhib. cat., Point Reyes Station, California, 1983).

34 Association Libanaise des Amateurs du Tapis Ancien, *Antique and Ancient Prayer Rugs dating from the Sixteenth to the Nineteenth Century*. (In spite of the title, no sixteenth-century rugs are listed in the catalogue.)

35 Fiske, *Prayer Rugs from Private Collections*, introductory essay.

36 Manuelain and Eiland, *Weavers, Merchants and Kings: The Inscribed Rugs of Armenia*, p. 24.

37 Gombos, *Aszkéták, Dervisek, Imaszönyegek*, p. 100.

38 Gombos, ibid., pp. 99–106: 'Most probably the use of prayer rugs was introduced by Mohammedan ascetics and Sufi dervish monks, who defined the roles and purpose of prayer rugs … The sufi (*suf* means wool in Arabic) – that is to say, hooded – dervish … must sit on a prayer rug, turn his face in the direction of Mecca …'

39 Published in *Turkish Handwoven Carpets* (Ministry of State and Ministry of Culture and Tourism of Turkey), vol. 2, pl. 0166. (Illustrated below.)

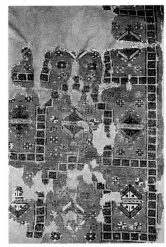

see note 39

40 Plate 7 in Ölçer et al., *Turkish Carpets from the 13th to the 18th Centuries*. (Illustrated below.)

see note 40

41 See *Hali* 58, p. 88.

42 Eiland, *Oriental Rugs: A New Comprehensive Guide*. p. 20.

43 Dimand, 'Prayer Rugs of Persia (Iran)', in Ettinghausen et al., *Prayer Rugs*, p. 84; .

44 See Mills, 'Carpets in Paintings', *Hali* 58, p. 88, fig. 3. Also published Ölçer, *Turkish Carpets*, pl. 128. (Illustrated below.)

see note 44

45 See *Turkish Handwoven Carpets* (Ministry of State and Ministry of Culture and Tourism of Turkey), vol. 3. (Illustrated below.) The Ka'ba (Arabic 'cube') is a small cube-shaped shrine in Mecca, believed to be the house of God built by Abraham (definition from Blair and Bloom, *Images of Paradise*, p. 112 and Ettinghausen et al., *Prayer Rugs*, p. 18)

see note 45

46 Denny, 'Saff and Sejjadeh: Origins and Meaning of the Prayer Rug', *Oriental Carpet & Textile Studies* 3/2, pp. 93–104.

47 Ibid. p. 92, pl. III, fig. 3; also p. 94.

48 Ibid. p. 100, fig. 20; also published as a seventeenth-century piece in Ölçer et al., *Turkish Carpets*, pl. 118.

49 Ibid. p. 101, fig. 22; also published as a seventeenth-century piece in Ölçer et al., *Turkish Carpets*, pl. 116.

50 Gantzhorn, *The Christian Oriental Carpet*, p. 477.

51 Ibid. p. 478 (see illustration 671, of an eighth-century floor mosaic from Beit Shean depicting a Torah curtain under an arch between two columns).

52 Ernst Kühnel, *Cairene Rugs and Others Technically Related, 15th Century–17th Century*, Textile Museum catalogue raisonné (National Publishing Company, Washington DC, 1957).

53 See *Hali* 69, p. 91.

54 Fokker, *Caucasian Rugs of Yesterday*, pp. 90–91, fig. 2.

55 Gantzhorn, *The Christian Oriental Carpet*, pp. 484, 485, illus. 680.

56 *Oriental Carpet & Textile Studies* 3/2, p. 94, illus. 2.

57 Gantzhorn, *The Christian Oriental Carpet*, p. 479, illus. 674.

58 Blair and Bloom, *Images of Paradise*, pp. 27–29, 87.

CAUCASIAN PRAYER RUGS

1 Volkman, *Old Eastern Carpets, Masterpieces in Private German Collections*, caption to pl. 66.

2 Cootner, *Prayer Rugs from the Near East and Central Asia* (McCoy Jones Collection pamphlet, M.H. De Young Memorial Museum, San Francisco, 1984).

3 Burns, *Caucasus: Traditions in Weaving*, p. 10.

4 Bennett, *Caucasian*, p. 9.

5 Schürmann, *Caucasian Rugs*, p. 97 (illustrated below). For more about this type, see *Hali* 2/1, p. 77, 'Rugs on the Market', fig. 11 (discussing a later rug from the same group).

see note 5

6 Bausback, *Alte und Antike Orientalische Knüpfkunst 1982*, pp. 46, 47.

see note 7

7 Erdmann, *Seven Hundred Years of Oriental Carpets*, p. 174. The rug is illustrated as pl. 95 in Breck-Morris, *James Ballard Collection of Oriental Rugs* (New York 1933). (Illustrated above.)

8 King, Pinner and Franses, 'Caucasian Rugs in the Victoria and Albert Museum', *Hali* 3/2, pp. 95–115.

9 SLO 21 Oct. 1992, lot 57.

10 Stanzer, review of 'Prayer Rugs and Meditation Stones' exhibition in *Hali* 6/1.

11 Manuelian and Eiland, *Weavers, Merchants and Kings*, p. 37, fig. 15.

12 Ettinghausen, *Ancient Carpets in the L.A. Mayer Memorial Institute*, pl. 11. The Munich rug is published in Gantzhorn, *The Christian Oriental Carpet*, p. 251.

13 Schürmann, *Caucasian Rugs*, p. 96.

14 See for example Herrmann, *Seltene Orientteppiche (SOT)* III, pl. 24.

15 See for example Herrmann, *SOT* VIII, pl. 25.

16 Phillips, London 13 Feb. 1990, lot 25; sold for £19,800 ($33,492). *Hali* 50, 'Auction Price Guide', p. 166.

17 Rippon 10 Nov. 1990, lot 166; sold for DM45,240 ($30,568). *Hali* 55, 'Auction Price Guide', p. 161.

18 Eiland, *Oriental Rugs: A New Comprehensive Guide*, p. 257.

19 Stone, *Rugs of the Caucasus*, p. 113.

20 Lefevre, *Caucasian Carpets*, p. 50.

21 Kerimov, *Azerbaijanski Kovjer* (Azerbaijani Carpets). The 13 names given to Kazak rugs were: Kazakh, Salakhy, Shikhly, Kemerli, Demirchiler, Gaimakaly, Gyoicheli, Dagkesemen, Oisuzlu, Borchaly, Karayazi, Kachagan, Karachop (names translated by Dr C. Mitchell in *Hali* 3/1, pp. 27–30). Of these names only Kazak, Shikly, Borchalo and Karachop (Karachov) are in general use. (Curiously, Kerimov lists Fachralo in the Genje group.)

22 Nagel Oct. 1976, lot 224 = Bennett, *Caucasian*, pl. 3; *Hali* 5/4 'Auction Price Guide', p. 539, fig. 28 = Bukowski, Zurich 15 June 1983, lot 234.; *Hali* 53, p. 186, ad. for George Gilmore, Costa Mesa, California.

23 Herrmann, *SOT* VIII, pl. 32; Nagel Nov. 1977, lot 149 = Bennett, *Caucasian* pl. 4.; SNY 22 Sept. 1993, lot 120 (an obviously late piece with a bright orange dye).

24 These include Hawley, *Oriental Rugs Antique and Modern*, pl. 50; Kerimov, *Azerbaijanski Kovjer*, pl. 27; Thompson, *Carpet Magic*, p. 125; Hasson, *Caucasian Rugs*, pl. 10.

25 Bailey and Hopkins, *Through the Collector's Eye*, pl. 14; *Oriental Rug Review*, Oct./Nov. 1989, p. 53 (Columbus Museum of Art); Lefevre 9 July 1976, lot 35; Skinner 23 April 1994, lot 6.

26 Other examples in this rare sub-group include: *Hali* 72, p. 125, 'Auction Price Guide' (Weschler Auction 16 October 1993, lot 24); Skinner 4 June 1989, lot 234; Nagel 12 November 1993, lot 94, exhibited at the 7th ICOC in Hamburg by Adil Besin, Vienna; SNY 18 May 1985, lot 35.

27 See Keshishian, *Treasure of the Caucasus*, pl. 18; *Hali* 2/4, p. 24.

28 Other examples include: Bernheimer 1987, lot 16; R. Benardout, exhib. cat. 1978, no. 8.

29 An unusual Kazak prayer rug sold at auction for $49,015 in 1990 (plate 18 below).
The 'top ten' can be listed as follows:
i) Star Kazak: The famous 'Abadjian' star, published Herrmann *ATT* 2, pl. 23, sold for $286,000, SNY 20 Jan. 1990, lot 88 (*Hali* 50, p. 167).
ii) Star: Weber, Zurich 20 Oct. 1990, lot 135, sold for $164,708 (*Hali* 55, p. 161).
iii) Star: Skinner 5 June 1988, lot 112, sold for $154,000 (*Hali* 40, p. 78).
iv) Karachov: Rippon 14 Feb. 1994, lot 147, sold for $129,735 (*Hali* 78, p. 128).
v) Star: SLO 9 Oct. 1991, lot 60, sold for $92,400 (*Hali* 60, p. 150).
vi) Lori-Pambak: Rippon 18 Nov. 1995, lot 114, sold for $91,145 (*Hali* 85, p. 135).
vii) Star: SLO 18 Oct. 1995, lot 48, sold for $88,705 (*Hali* 84, p. 135).
viii) Star: Rippon 16 Oct. 1991, lot 116, sold for $83,910 (*Hali* 61, p. 164).
ix) Star: SNY 15 April 1993, lot 135, sold for $68,500 (*Hali* 69, p.148).
x) Karachov: Rippon 14 Jan. 1992, lot 151, sold for $58,735 (*Hali* 67, p.130).

30 Stone, *Rugs of the Caucasus*, p. 94.

31 Schürmann, *Caucasian Rugs*, pl. 37, p. 130.

32 See King, *Prayer Rugs*, 8th pl. (pages not numbered), dated AH 1223 (1808).

33 Gerard Boëly, in *Hali* 54, pp. 104–5.

34 Kerimov, *Rugs and Carpets from the Caucasus*, p. 19. He lists the 'Gianja groups' as follows: (a) Gianja: Gianja, Gadim, Gianja, Samukh. (b) Kasum-Ismailor: Chaily, Shadly, Fakharly. (c) Kedabek: Kedabek, Chirakhly, Karagoyunly. Few of these names are in use in the West. 'Chaily' or 'Chajli' rugs are usually attributed either to Moghan or Shirvan, although the characteristic border is similar to that of Genje rugs. 'Fakharly' (Fachralo) is in the Kazak district. (See Bennett, *Caucasian*, pp. 173–74.)

35 Mumford, *Oriental Rugs*, p. 130.

36 Schürmann, *Caucasian Rugs*, p. 41.

37 Examples include: Fokker, *Caucasian Rugs of Yesterday*, p. 67; Schürmann, *Caucasian Rugs*, pl. 50; *Hali* 2/1, p. 62, ad. for Rahim Bolour; *Hali* 6/3, p. 48, ad. for Mark Keshishian.

38 Stone, *Rugs of the Caucasus*, p. 141.

39 See Bennett, *Caucasian*, pp. 168–73.

40 See Wright, *Rugs and Flatweaves of the Transcaucasus*, pl. 35, and Fiske, *Prayer Rugs from Private Collections*, pl. 23.

41 For examples of Talish prayer rugs see Hubel, *The Book of Carpets*, pl. 58; for examples of Lenkoran prayer rugs, see Edelmann, New York 14 March 1981, lot 361. A very similar rug, illustrated in 'Namazlyg or Mehraby-Prayer Rugs', *Oriental Carpet & Textile Studies* 3/2, is attributed by Kerimov to Bahmanli, Garabagh group (p. 151, fig. 7)

42 See Lefevre 15 July 1983, lot 31 for an example of a lattice-field Moghan prayer rug, and Bennett, *Caucasian*, pl. 202 for an example of a linked-diamond Moghan prayer rug (an almost identical example was sold at Sotheby's Arcade, New York, 28 March 1989, lot 32).

43 Stone, *Rugs of the Caucasus*, pl. 61.

44 Herbert Coxon, *Oriental Carpets*, pp. 46, 49.

45 Fokker, *Caucasian Rugs of Yesterday*, p. 68.

46 Hawley, *Oriental Rugs Antique and Modern*, Dover reprint, p. 210.

47 Wolfe and Wolfe, *How to Identify Oriental Rugs*, p. 24.

48 Schürmann, *Caucasian Rugs*, pp. 44, 45.

49 Wolfe and Wolfe, *How to Identify Oriental Rugs*, p. 23.

50 This particular octagon motif is reputed to be the representation of the Kerbala stone.

51 The 'cemetery design' refers to a group of rugs with a unique design resembling a geometric representation of a bier surmounted by a coffin. It has been suggested that these were burial rugs, while in some publications they have been designated as prayer rugs. For examples see Association libanais des amateurs du tapis ancien, *Antique and Ancient Prayer Rugs*, pl. 11; Bausback 1978, p. 247 (assigned to Shirvan); Christie's London, 8 July 1982, lot 36.

52 Ellis, *Early Caucasian Rugs*, p. 11.

53 John Wertime and Richard E. Wright, 'The Tabriz Hypothesis', *Hali Annual* II, Asian Art, pp. 30–35.

54 Hasson, *Caucasian Rugs*, p 11.

55 Pl. 74 depicts a Shirvan with a similar field. A yellow-field Kuba example is illustrated in Herrmann *SOT* V, pl. 25. Secular Kuba rugs also feature this design; see Herrmann *ATT* 4, pl. 46, and Bennett, *Caucasian*, pl. 328.

56 For examples of this motif see Bennett, *Caucasian*, pls 326, 327; Lefevre 15 April 1981, lot 44.

57 The tracery design probably evolved from a group of sixteenth-/seventeenth-century Anatolian rugs, called 'Lotto' because of their appearance in the paintings of Lorenzo Lotto, which employ a related field design of complex tracery pattern.

58 The remaining rug is of a type Liatif Kerimov called Ordutch-Konaghend (see Schürmann, *Caucasian Rugs*, p. 278). The major feature of these rugs is a particular octagon design, also found in many other types, including 'head and shoulders' prayer rugs (see fig. 24). A rare Ordutch-Konaghend prayer rug was published in a Rippon Boswell catalogue of 11 Nov. 1978, lot 208.

59 Examples include a Chichi prayer rug published as pl. 27 in Herrmann, *Kaukasische Teppiche* and a Shirvan prayer rug (pl. 83 below).

60 *Hali* 55, p. 111.

61 *Hali* 5, p. 113, fig. 7.

62 See Burns, *Caucasus: Traditions in Weaving*, p. 20; *Hali* 55, p. 115, fig. 9.

63 The maps of the Caucasus in Schürmann, *Caucasian Rugs*, and Bennett, *Caucasian*, show the village of Chichi slightly southeast of the town of Kuba. The maps in Kerimov, *Rugs and Carpets of the Caucasus* and *Azerbaijanski Kovjer* show no such place; nor does the map in Eiland, *Oriental Rugs, A New Comprehensive Guide*. Eiland suggests that Chichi may be a corruption of Divichi, a nearby village on his and Kerimov's maps. The map in Gans-Ruedin's *Caucasian Carpets*, however, shows both the villages of Divichi and Chichi. Eiland has travelled in the Caucasus and has no first-hand knowledge of such a village.

64 Stone, *Rugs of the Caucasus*, p. 134.

65 Neff and Maggs, *Dictionary of Oriental Rugs*, pl 11.

66 See Schürmann, *Caucasian Rugs*, pl. 110, pp. 288–89.

67 See Straka and Mackie, *The Oriental Rug Collection of Jerome and Mary Jane Straka*, pl. 109.

68 See Sotheby's New York, 1 Dec. 1984, lot 22, and *Hali* 59, p. 80, 'Letters'.

69 See *Hali* 5/3, p 10, ad. for Campana, Milan.

70 See Ettinghausen and Roberts, *Bulletin, Allen Memorial Art Museum*, p. 46.

71 See Lefevre 6 Feb. 1976, lot 1.

72 See *Oriental Rug Review*, Oct./Nov. 1989, p. 26, illus. 1.

73 See Werner Brüggeman and Harald Böhmer, *Rugs of the Peasants and Nomads of Anatolia* (Verlag Kunst & Antiquitäten GmbH, Munich 1983), pl. 46.

74 See Schürmann, *Caucasian Rugs*, pl. 108 for the first variant, and Bailey and Hopkins, *Through the Collector's Eye* (pl. 21), for the second.

75 See Herrmann, *SOT* III, pl. 48.

76 See Stone, *Rugs of the Caucasus*, p. 136.

77 DeCredico and Pickering, *Oriental Rugs from Members of the Oriental Rug Society of New England*, pl. 56; Sotheby's London 20 Oct. 1993, lot 34; Sotheby's New York 15 Dec. 1994, lot 6; Nagel 12 March 1981, lot 2861.

78 Pl. 53 below; Rippon 14 Nov. 1992, lot 84; Englehardt and Englehardt, *Orientteppiche der Sonderclasse* 1982, p. 87 = Edelmann 12 Dec. 1980, lot 236.

79 Vertical stripes: Denny and Walker, *Markarian Album*, pl. 73; diagonal crosses: Lefevre 15 April 1981, lot 45 = Edelmann 13 Dec. 1980, lot 92; 'Alpan Kuba': pl. 54 = Rippon 28 March 1992, lot 62.

80 For discussion of Zeikhur history, structural characteristics and designs see Tschebull, 'Zeichur', *Hali* 62, pp. 85–95.

81 Stone, *Rugs of the Caucasus*, pp. 134–36.

82 Stone (ibid., p. 69) writes that in 1897 the population of 587,000 included 158,000 Avars, 121,000 Darghins and 94,000 Kurins (Lesghians). Eiland (*Oriental Rugs, A New Comprehensive Guide*, p. 278) writes that Chechens (in the north) and Lesghi (to the south, and evidently used in the sense of Daghestanis) form the two largest population groups of northeastern Caucasus.

83 'Derbent' is really 'Darband' which in Persian means 'Closer of the door' or 'closed door'. Derbent was the 'Gate of Gates' or the key to Persia in ancient times (Jackson, *From Constantinople to the Home of Omar Khayyam*, pp. 60–61). The city produced rugs, but over the years the name 'Derbent' seems to have acquired somewhat pejorative connotations, and consequently few rugs are so attributed. As far as prayer rugs at auction are concerned, I recall one rug attributed to Derbent at a New York auction in 1981. It did not sell. (Edelmann 14 March 1981, lot 370.)

84 *Encyclopaedia Judaica*, vol. 12:478 (Macmillan, New York 1972) (Mountain Jews).

85 Eiland, *Oriental Rugs, A New Comprehensive Guide*, p. 272.

86 For the purposes of this book, I have gone along with the designations of Daghestan or Shirvan as they are listed in the sources used in the database.

87 Bennett, *Caucasian*, p. 308.

88 Stone, *Rugs of the Caucasus*, p. 155. Stone's criteria included mean knot density, mean rug area, mean knot ratio, mean shape ratio, types of warp and weft. As well as finding a higher incidence of cotton wefting in Shirvans (64 percent, with Kuba being 50 percent and Daghestan 57 percent) he also found a higher knot density (137 for Shirvan, 121 for Kuba and 125 for Daghestan).

89 Denny, *Sotheby's Guide to Oriental Carpets*, p. 83.

90 See Bennett, *Caucasian*, pl. 431, for a rare red-ground example.

91 Herrmann, *SOT* II, pl. 41.

92 Ettinghausen et al., *Prayer Rugs*, pl. XXXI.

93 'Syrga': Nagel 11 Nov. 1981, lot 294; 'anchor': Herrmann *SOT* VI, pl. 36; 'palm': Nagel 24 April 1979, lot 189 = *Hali* 1/4, p. 49, ad. for Nagel.

94 Eiland, for example, writes: 'What I propose is to simplify the matter, first by dropping the 'Lesghi' label, as I have no reason to believe that it has any relevance for carpets.' (*Oriental Rugs, A New Comprehensive Guide*, p. 272.)

95 Schürmann, *Caucasian Rugs*, pl. 101. The rug was sold at Rippon 16 Nov. 1996, lot 151 (attributed to 'Kuba-Lesghi') for DM 51.040 ($33,145). The hyphenated label could be viewed as an attempt to use 'Lesghi' as descriptive of design rather than of origin.

96 Schürmann, *Caucasian Rugs*. The first, pl. 129, featured a saturated yellow field filled with flowers and a border of bold hexagons on white ground. The second, pl. 130, had a design of latticed palmettes on brilliant yellow ground and an unusual blue prayer arch the width of the field. Also published in Erdmann, *Kaukasische Teppiche*, pl. 82 and Macey, *Oriental Prayer Rugs*, pl. 32. A virtually identical rug was published as pl. 81 in *Kaukasische Teppiche*. To date, they are the only two known examples of the type.

97 Schürmann, *Caucasian Rugs*, p. 328.

98 Jackson, *From Constantinople to the Home of Omar Khayyam*, p. 62.

99 Lewis, *The Practical Book of Oriental Rugs* (third printing 1922), p. 263.

100 Pushman, *Art Panels from the Handlooms of the Far Orient As Seen By A Native Rug Weaver*, p. 65.

101 Babayan, *The Romance of the Oriental Rug*, p. 44.

102 A collector describing his 'Rose' Zeichur, pictured as Shirvan opposite p. 266 in Lewis, *The Practical Book of Oriental Rugs*.

103 See DeCredico and Pickering, *Oriental Rug Society of New England*, pl. 39.

104 See Kyburz et al., *Alte Teppich aus dem Orient*, pp. 56–7.

105 See Herrmann, *SOT* IV, pl. 24.

106 See *Hali* 1/4, p. 26, ad. for D.W. Kinebanian.

107 See Sotheby's New York 13 Sept. 1989, lot 29.

108 See Rippon 20 May 1995, lot 199.

109 See Ettinghausen et al., *Prayer Rugs*, pl. XXX.

110 The village of Bijov is shown on the maps in Bennett, *Caucasian*, endpapers; Gans-Ruedin, *Caucasian Carpets*, p. 10; Schürmann, *Caucasian Rugs*, endpapers. It is absent, however, from Herrmann, *Kaukasische Teppichkunst*, map following p. 77.

111 Tschebull, 'Zeikhur', *Hali* 62, pp. 91–5.

112 Ulrich Schürmann illustrated a lattice field rug with an arrowhead border and hands in the spandrels, which he described as a 'Kazak prayer rug … woven in the south near Akstafa (*Caucasian Rugs*, pl. 16). Walter B. Harris, writing in 1896 (in *From Batoum to Bagdhad*) describes the village and its location thus: 'On a bright hot afternoon of April I left Tiflis by train for Akstafa, a small station on the Tiflis-Baku line, which forms the terminus of the great road, via Erivan, to Jalfa and the Persian frontier … The town of Akstafa, such as it is, lies a couple of miles or so to the south of the railway. It is a picturesque spot, quite oriental in appearance, with its mud-houses and gardens of tall poplar trees, its forges by the roadside, and its little yellow mosque and minarets.'

113 See Eskenazi, *L'Arte del tappeto orientale*, pl. 113, and Bennett, *Caucasian*, pls 210–18.

114 Other prayer rugs with peacocks are illustrated in: Nagel 2 Oct. 1992, lot 4535; Spuhler, König and Volkmann, *Old Eastern Carpets*, pl. 62; *Oriental Rug Review* 10/6, p. 9 (a prayer rug with eight-pointed 'Akstafa' medallions, without peacocks). Writing about rugs, absolute statements are demonstrably perilous however. O'Bannon in his 1995 book *Oriental Rugs: The Collector's Guide to Selecting, Identifying and Enjoying New and Antique Oriental Rugs*, captions an Akstafa prayer rug thus: 'Akstafa prayer rugs do not have peacocks …'

115 Boteh design rugs were tabulated in the Shirvan section.

116 For examples see Benardout, *Woven Stars*, p. 29; Bennett, *Caucasian*, pl. 219.

117 See Herrmann, *SOT* VI, pl. 35, assigned to Kuba.

118 Kerimov, 'Namalygor Mehraby – Prayer Rugs', *Oriental Carpet & Textile Studies* 3/2, pp. 148–53, fig. 4, Sor Sor (Shirvan group), fig. 6, Maraza (Shirvan group).

119 Eiland's map shows the villages of Sor Sor and Maraza, Gans-Ruedin's map shows Marasali only, and the map in Bennett shows the village of Marasali as southwest of the larger town of Maraza.

120 An early northwest Persian carpet with ascending palmettes is described as having a 'Zorastrian flame palmette design' (*Hali Annual* 1, p. 104–105, ex-collection Meyer-Müller, now Ronnie Newman collection, New Jersey).

121 The rug in pl. 93, although not one of the earliest, nevertheless employs 11 colours and six different designs for its 46 boteh.

122 The Strakas also had a penchant for Marasali prayer rugs. Their collection included one of each of these two types: a yellow boteh rug (pl. 103 in Straka and Mackie, *Collection of Jerome and Mary Jane Straka*) and a yellow floral rug (ibid., pl. 104).

123 The 'Burns' ivory Marasali (pl. 93) is in a class by itself, having an unlatticed floral field.

124 See Bausback 1982, p. 57.

125 The 'unique' Marsalis are:
i) A vertically striped example with a red field published in Hasson, *Caucasian Rugs*, pl. 27, from the collection of Voitech Blau. A similar rug attributed to Daghestan was sold at Sotheby's New York 10 Jan. 1977, lot 101.
ii) A rug with hexagons on a blue-black field (pl. 97 below) from the Dixon Collection.
iii) Two Marasali rugs on indigo fields with boteh around large lozenge panels: Christie's London 28 March 1985, lot 279; *Hali* 53, p.186, ad. for George Gilmore.
iv) A Marasali rug with large horses (pl. 96 below).
v) A 'black Marasali' with a boteh field containing a large panel with zigzag stripes (Herrmann, *ATT* 3, pl. 24).

Full bibliographic references may be found in the Bibliography, page 187.

Technical analyses are provided where available.

The following abbreviations have been used for dealers' and auction catalogues:

ATT	Eberhart Herrmann, *Asiatische Teppiche und Textilekunst*
CLO	Christie's, London
CNY	Christie's, New York
Lefevre	Lefevre & Partners, London
Nagel	Dr Fritz Nagel Auktionshaus, Stuttgart
PB 84	PB 84 (Sotheby's), New York
Rippon	Rippon Boswell & Co., Wiesbaden (also Munich & Frankfurt)
Skinner	Skinner's, Bolton, MA and Boston
SLO	Sotheby's, London
SNY	Sotheby's, New York
SOT	Eberhart Herrmann, *Seltene Orientteppiche*

1   BORCHALO
early 19th century
0.96 × 1.09m (3′2″ × 3′7″)

NOTES
1 Modified versions of this treatment appear in a Kazak prayer rug published in Engelhardt, *Orientteppiche der Sonderklasse*, pl. 51, and a Turkish prayer rug assigned to Kars, published in *Turkish Handwoven Carpets*, vol. 3 (Ministry of State and Ministry of Culture and Tourism of Turkey), pl. 204.
2 Gantzhorn, *The Christian Oriental Carpet*, p. 35, figs H1 and H2.
3 Kerimov, *Azerbaijanski Kovjer*, pl. 48, fig. 7.
4 See Belkis Balpinar Acar, *Kilim, Cicim, Zile, Soumak* (Eren Yayinlari, Istanbul 1983), p. 63, detail 15.

PREVIOUS PUBLICATION
Oriental Rug Review 11/3, p. 53.

TECHNICAL ANALYSIS
Warp ivory wool; z2s; 12 threads per inch (48 per dm)
Weft rose and undyed wool; s-spun, unplied; between 4 and 6 shoots, the 1st and 4th with rose wool; 7 knots per inch (28 per dm)
Pile symmetrical knot; 42 knots per sq. inch (672 per sq.dm)
Ends missing
Sides not original

Dixon Collection
Photograph: Don Tuttle

2   BORCHALO
dated AH 1287 (1871)
1.50 × 1.78m (4′11″ × 5′9″)

PREVIOUS PUBLICATION
Rippon 17 Nov. 1987, lot 92.

ANALOGIES
Prayer Analogies
1 Bausback 1977, p. 36.
2 *Prayer Rugs from the Near East and Central Asia* (McCoy Jones Collection pamplet, M.H. De Young Memorial Museum, San Francisco, Nov. 1984).
3 CNY 6 Dec. 1988, lot 19.
4 Skinner 4 June 1989, lot 60 (lacking slanted striped frame).

Secular Analogies
5 Hermann, SOT VII, pl. 29 = CNY 7 April 1990, lot 33.
6 PB 84, 25 June 1980, lot 311.
7 Skinner 16 Dec. 1986, lot 99.
8 Herrmann, SOT VI, lot 21.
9 Georg Butterweck et al., *Antique Oriental Carpets from Austrian Collections*, pl. 45.
10 Lefevre 29 Nov. 1974, lot 39.
11 CLO 15 Oct. 1981, lot 36.
12 Schürmann, *Caucasian Rugs* , pl. 12.
13 Eiland, *Oriental Rugs from Pacific Collections*, pl. 183.
14 Rippon 14 Nov. 1992, lot 102 = Herrmann, *Kaukasische Teppichkunst*, pl. 59.
15 Sotheby's Geneva 13 Nov 1981, lot 55.

TECHNICAL ANALYSIS
Warp natural brown wool; z3s; 13 threads per inch (52 per dm)
Weft red wool; z2s; 3 or 4 shoots; 7 knots per inch (29 per dm)
Pile wool; symmetrical knot; 46 knots per sq. inch (754 per sq.dm)
Ends not original
Sides 2 cords, each of 2 threads, overcast with blue cotton
Colours red, yellow, green, mid-blue, blue, dark brown, brown, ivory (8)

Exner Collection
Photograph: Herbert J. Exner

3   BORCHALO
1st half 19th century
0.96 × 1.22m (3′2″ × 4′0″)

TECHNICAL ANALYSIS
Warp white wool; z2s; 14 threads per inch (56 per dm)
Weft brown wool; unplied; between 2 and 4 shoots; 6 knots per inch (24 per dm)
Pile wool; symmetrical knot; 42 knots per sq. inch (672 per sq.dm)
Colours red, yellow, green, blue, brown, white (6)

Klein Collection
Photograph: courtesy Wells C. Klein

4   BORCHALO
c.1865
1.04 × 1.17m (3′5″ × 3′10)

PREVIOUS PUBLICATION
1 *Oriental Rug Review* 11/3, p. 53.

ANALOGIES
Bacharach and Bierman, *The Warp and Weft of Islam*, pl. 26.

TECHNICAL ANALYSIS
Warp ivory wool; z2s; 12 threads per inch (48 per dm)
Weft red wool; z2s; 8 knots per inch (32 per dm)
Pile symmetrical knot; 48 knots per sq. inch (768 per sq.dm)
Sides 2 cords overcast with wool
Colours dark red, yellow, light green, mid-blue, light blue, dark brown, ivory (7)

Kaffel Collection
Photograph: Don Tuttle

5   BORCHALO
c.1875
1.02 × 1.14m (3′4″ × 3′9″)

TECHNICAL ANALYSIS
Warp ivory wool; z2s; 12 threads per inch (48 per dm)
Weft red wool; z2s; 7 knots per inch (28 per dm)
Pile symmetrical knot; 42 knots per sq. inch (672 per sq.dm)
Sides 2 cords overcast with red wool
Colours dark red, indigo, mid-blue, light blue, dark brown, ecru, ivory (7)

Kaffel Collection
Photograph: Don Tuttle

6   BORCHALO
late 19th century
1.07 × 1.50m (3′6″ × 4′11″)

NOTES
1 Fokker, *Caucasian Rugs of Yesterday*, p. 52.
2 Fokker also says that the Tree of Life is 'extremely rare' in Caucasian rugs. This is not quite so; it is the dominant element in a large group of Kazak rugs (commonly known as the 'Tree Kazaks') of which the archetype is pl. 47 in McMullan, *Islamic Carpets*.
3 For a discussion of Armenian motifs see Manuelian and Eiland, *Weavers, Merchants and Kings: The Inscribed Rugs of Armenia*, p. 37, fig. 15 and p. 40, fig.19.
4 *Hali* 6/1, p. 8, ad. for Reinisch Rare Rugs and related review.
5 Stanzer, 'Prayer Rugs and Meditation Stones', exhibition review, *Hali* 6/1, pp. 52–3.

PREVIOUS PUBLICATION
Fokker, *Caucasian Rugs of Yesterday*, p. 52.

TECHNICAL ANALYSIS
Warp ivory wool; z2s; 12 threads per inch (48 per dm)
Weft red wool; z2s; 6 knots per inch (24 per dm)
Pile wool; symmetrical knot; 36 knots per sq. inch (576 per sq.dm)
Ends missing
Sides 2 cords, each of 4 threads, overcast with red wool
Colours red, indigo, light blue-green, brown, ivory (5)

Kaffel Collection
Photograph: Don Tuttle

NOTES TO

THE PLATES

---

7   BORCHALO

2nd half 19th century
1.14 × 1.30m (3′9″ × 4′3″)

NOTES

1 A secular red-ground example, with four rows each of hexagons and octagons and minor borders virtually identical to the present rug, sold for a respectable DM 60,000 ($32,000) in 1989 (Rippon 6 May 1989, lot 118.)

ANALOGIES

Prayer rugs

1 Bausback 1971, p. 49.
2 *Hali* 48, p. 42, ad. for Rascid Rahaim.
3 SNY 5 Oct. 1973, lot 69.
4 Eiland, *Oriental Rugs 1981*, pl. 41 (a hybrid piece containing hexagons, octagons, diamonds and flowerheads).

Secular rugs

5 Schürmann, *Caucasian Rugs*, pl. 10, dated *c*.1800.
6 Eskenazi, *L'arte del tappeto orientale*, pl. 82.
7 Benardout, *Woven Stars: Rugs and Textiles from Southern Californian Collections*, pl. 1.

TECHNICAL ANALYSIS

Warp   ivory wool; z2s; 24 threads per inch (96 per dm)
Weft   ivory wool; z2s; 9 knots per inch (36 per dm)
Pile   symmetrical knot; 108 knots per sq. inch (1728 per sq.dm)
Ends   missing
Sides   incomplete, but evidence of 2 cords overcast with brown wool
Colours   red, green, avocado green, blue-green, indigo, aubergine, rose, brown, light brown, white, blue-black (11)

Kaffel Collection
Photograph: Don Tuttle

8   FACHRALO

late 19th century
1.14 × 1.42m (3′9″ × 4′8″)

NOTES

1 The serrated leaf border, with or without the calyx or 'winecup', appears in 151 of the 287 Fachralo prayer rugs tabulated (see p. 165).

TECHNICAL ANALYSIS

Warp   undyed wool; z2s; 12 threads per inch (50 per dm)
Weft   red wool; z2s; 2 or 3 shoots; 7 knots per inch (28 per dm)
Pile   wool; symmetrical knot; 42 knots per sq. inch (700 per sq.dm)
Sides   3 cords, each of 2 threads, overcast with a variety of coloured wool
Colours   red, light yellow, mid-blue, blue, light blue, dark brown, mid-brown, ivory (7)

Exner Collection
Photograph: Herbert J. Exner

9   FACHRALO

1st half 19th century
1.19 × 1.30m (3′11″ × 4′7″)

NOTES

1 See Ettinghausen, *Ancient Carpets*, pl. 11. This refers to an antecedent in the sixteenth-century Anatolian Bergama rug in the Bavarian National Museum (published in Gantzhorn, *The Christian Oriental Carpet*, pl. 251). An even earlier design precursor is suggested by Michael Franses in his commentary to a similar rug in Kirchheim et al., *Orient Stars: A Carpet Collection*, pl. 21, who identifies the archaic fifteenth-century double-niche Anatolian rug published in pl. 200 (ibid.) as a Fachralo ancestor.

PREVIOUS PUBLICATION

Lefevre 22 April 1983, lot 27.

ANALOGIES

Fachralos with the 'meander-and-cross' border

1 Kirchheim et al., *Orient Stars*, pl. 21.
2 SNY 5 Nov. 1983, lot 129 (from the Karl Milde collection).
3 Tschebull, *Kazak*, pl. 22 (from the Dr William Price collection).
4 Dodds, *Oriental Rugs: The Collection of Dr & Mrs Robert A. Fisher*, pl. 53.
5 Crossley, *Unravelling the Rug Puzzle*, pl. 25. This example is very similar to ours. The book comments that 'this rug was probably made by Muslim Azerbaijani Turks of the southern Caucasus, rather than the Armenians who are Christian'.

Private Collection
Photograph: Lefevre & Partners, London; courtesy The Hali Archive

10   FACHRALO

2nd half 19th century
1.07 × 1.37m (3′6″ × 4′5″)

ANALOGIES

1 Lefevre 14 April 1978, lot 10.
2 Skinner 5 Dec. 1988, lot 225.
3 Nagel 23 April 1977, lot 143.
4 *Hali* 58, p. 63 ad. for Kailash Gallery.
5 Kirchheim et al., *Orient Stars*, pl. 21 (with a re-entrant arch and different border).

TECHNICAL ANALYSIS

Warp   wool; z3s; 14 threads per inch (56 per dm)
Weft   rose wool; z3s; 2 shoots; 7 knots per inch (28 per dm)
Pile   symmetrical knot; 49 knots per sq. inch (784 per sq.dm)
Sides   3 cords, each of 2 threads, overcast with rose wool

Dixon Collection
Photograph: Don Tuttle

11   FACHRALO

2nd half 19th century
1.14 × 1.45m (3′9″ × 4′9″)

ANALOGIES

1 Bennett, *Oriental Rugs: Volume 1, Caucasian*, pl. 24.
2 Rippon 14 May 1994, lot 40.
3 *Oriental Rug Review* 10/4, p. 58 (with re-entrant arch).

4 Nagel 3 Nov. 1979, lot 147A (with re-entrant arch).

TECHNICAL ANALYSIS

Warp   wool; z2s; 16 threads per inch (64 per dm)
Weft   rose wool; z2s; mainly 4 shoots, but sometimes 6; 7 knots per inch (28 per dm)
Pile   symmetrical knot; 56 knots per sq. inch (896 per sq.dm)
Ends   lower: upper: ⅜″ (1 cm) plainweave with rose weft
Sides   2 cords, each of 2 threads, overcast with rose wool

Dixon Collection
Photograph: Don Tuttle

12   FACHRALO

2nd half 19th century
1.20 × 1.31m (3′11″ × 4′4″)

NOTES

1 This border appears in 29 of the 287 Fachralo prayer rugs in the database (see p. 165).

ANALOGIES

1 King, *Prayer Rugs*, pl. 10 = Skinner 4 June 1989, lot 157 = *Hali* 32, 'Gallery', p. IV, ad. for Peter Pap Oriental Rugs. This is the closest analogy to our rug.

Some other analogies are

2 Wright, *Rugs and Flatweaves of the Transcaucasus*, pl. 8.
3 *Hali* 54, p. 190, exhibition review for Bernard Voloder, Salzburg = Phillips, London 22 Nov. 1988, lot 41.
4 Herrmann, *SOT* X, pl. 29.
5 Lefevre 14 June 1985, lot 4.
6 Skinner 2 Dec. 1989, lot 78.
7 Skinner 2 Dec. 1989, lot 177.
8 Skinner 4 June 1989, lot 138 = Rippon 16 Nov. 1991, lot 105.
9 *Hali* 84, p. 117, ad. for Storica, Lugano.
10 *Hali* 4/2, p. 67, ad. for Michail, Florence.
11 *Hali* 5/3, p. 352, review of exhibition at the Indianapolis Museum of Art.

TECHNICAL ANALYSIS

Warp   ivory wool; z3s; 13 threads per inch (52 per dm)
Weft   red wool; z2s; 2 or 3 shoots; 7 knots per inch (28 per dm)
Pile   wool; symmetrical knot; 46 knots per sq. inch (728 per sq.dm)
Ends   not original
Sides   2 cords, one of 2 threads and one of 3, overcast with a variety of coloured wool
Colours   red, yellow, light green, blue, light brown, ivory (6)

Exner Collection
Photograph: Herbert J. Exner

13   FACHRALO

dated AH 1245 (1829)
1.07 × 1.17m (3′6″ × 3′10″)

PREVIOUS PUBLICATION

1 SLO 23 April 1980, lot 120.
2 Engelhardt, *Orientteppiche der Sonderklasse*, 1980, p. 41.

ANALOGIES

1 *Hali* 50, p. 84 (review of Karim Khan and Robert Müller exhibition) = CLO 19 Oct. 1993, lot 441. Closely related in design, but a generation later and with more elongated dimensions; described by *Hali* as a 'Kazak pinwheel variant prayer rug'.
2 Schürmann, *Oriental Carpets*, pl. 173. Border variant of oblique linear design, assigned to Borchalo. Dated to first half nineteenth century.
3 Bausback, *Antike Orientteppiche*, p. 176. Another border of oblique linear design, virtually identical to Schürmann above. Also assigned to Borchalo and dated to first half nineteenth century.

TECHNICAL ANALYSIS

Warp   wool
Weft   brown wool
Pile   symmetrical knot; 49 knots per sq. inch (780 per sq.dm)

Private Collection
Photograph: courtesy Sotheby's, London

14   FACHRALO

mid-19th century
1.17 × 1.52m (3′10″ × 5′0″)

NOTES

1 A variant was published in Bausback, *Antike Orientteppiche*, p. 185. This rug has a rectangular white field with a blue medallion and a finely drawn prayer arch on a red ground, decorated with stylized tulips and a white-ground border with crosses. Tschebull, in his article 'The Development of Four Kazak Designs' (*Hali* 1/3, pp. 257–61), illustrates a white-ground prayer rug very similar to this example (fig. 34) with a white mihrab with a re-entrant motif on a plain red ground. While this example has the confronting dragon motif in the re-entrant archway, the *Hali* example has a latchhooked diamond. The two rugs share many aspects with the traditional small rugs of Lori-Pambak, which Schürmann described as 'favouring few colours and large areas of plain colours' (*Caucasian Rugs*, p. 8). Herrmann published a secular Fachralo rug with an octafoil central medallion (*ATT* 4, pl. 41) which, were the medallion replaced with the typical 'turtle' image (symbolizing longevity), would be virtually identical in all respects to a well-known Lori-Pambak (Jacobson, *Oriental Rugs*, p. 446 = *Hali* 1/3, p. 260, fig. 32 = *Hali* 5/3, p. 352 = CNY 8 Feb. 1992, lot 47). In his text, Herrmann refers to the connection between the two types, and states that a piece comparable to an early Fachralo piece is not known. He identifies two later white-ground analogies: *Hali* 5/2, p. 200 = SLO 12 Oct. 1982, lot 89; and *Hali* 6/2, p. 192.

TECHNICAL ANALYSIS

Warp beige wool; z3s; 16 threads
per inch (64 per dm)

Weft red wool; z2s; 2 or 3 shoots;
8 knots per inch (32 per dm)

Pile symmetrical knot; 64 knots
per sq. inch (1024 per sq.dm)

Sides 2 cords, each of 2 threads,
overcast with red wool

Tschebull Collection
Photograph: Don Tuttle

15 FACHRALO

c.1885
1.13 × 1.60m (3′9″ × 5′3″)

NOTES

1 Eskenazi, *L'arte del tappeto orientale*,
pl. 76.
2 A Fachralo single-medallion rug
features similar motifs (Nagel 7 Oct.
1992, lot 2071); these motifs feature
in the field and spandrels of a
Fachralo prayer rug (Bausback 1975,
p. 97).

PREVIOUS PUBLICATION

Eskenazi, *L'arte del tappeto orientale*,
pl. 76.

Private Collection
Photograph: courtesy John Eskenazi

16 KAZAK

dated AH 1253 (1837)
0.96 × 1.24m (3′2″ × 4′1″)

NOTES

1 Assigned to Moghan: see pl. 37
below = Lefevre 1 Oct. 1982, lot 29
= *Hali Decorative: A Buyer's Guide
to the Best of Decorative Carpets*
(London 1988), p. 36. Assigned to
Shirvan: see Georg Butterweck et
al., *Austrian Collections*, pl. 66;
Skinner 1 June 1991, lot 172 =
Herrmann, *ATT* 4, pl. 49; SNY
9 March 1994, lot 3.
2 Hubel, *The Book of Carpets*, pl. 57
(octagons with Memling guls).
3 For a Kazak example see Hubel,
The Book of Carpets, pl. 36 = Rippon
16 Nov. 1991, lot 155. For Genje, see
Hawley, *Oriental Rugs Antique and
Modern*, pl. 50.

TECHNICAL ANALYSIS

Warp white and brown wool,
sometimes plied together; z3s

Weft red and shades of brown
wool, sometimes plied
together; z2s; 2 or 3 shoots

Ends missing

Sides 3 cords overcast with a variety
of coloured wool

Colours red, yellow, green, 2 blues,
aubergine, mauve, brown,
white (9)

Klein Collection
Photograph: Wells C. Klein

17 KAZAK

2nd half 19th century
1.26 × 1.58m (4′2″ × 5′2″)

NOTES

1 Lefevre 5 July 1974, lot 22.
2 Spuhler, König and Volkmann,
Old Eastern Carpets, vol. 1, pl. 52;
Herrmann, *SOT* IV, pl. 39.

3 This border is identical to one on
a similar rug published as pl. 2 in
Carpets from the Orient, Dalhousie
Art Gallery, Nova Scotia
(exhib. cat. 1977).
4 *Turkish Handwoven Carpets*
(Ministry of State and Ministry of
Culture and Tourism of Turkey),
vol. 5, pl. 0057.

PREVIOUS PUBLICATION

1 Nagel 28 Sept. 1985, lot 4399.
2 *Hali* 29, 'Auction Price Guide', p. 70.

ANALOGIES

1 Lefevre 5 July 1974, lot 22.
2 Spuhler, König and Volkmann, *Old
Eastern Carpets*, vol. 1, pl. 52.
3 Herrmann, *SOT* IV, pl. 39.
4 Nagel 13 Oct. 1990, lot 333.
5 Nagel 10 May 1996, lot 40.
6 *Hali* 70, p. 49, ad. for Daniele Sevi,
Milan.
7 Skinner 19 Sept. 1992, lot 275.
8 SNY 22 Sept. 1993, lot 107.

TECHNICAL ANALYSIS

Warp ivory wool; z2s; 15 threads
per inch (58 per dm)

Weft red wool; z2s; 3 shoots;
6 knots per inch (25 per dm)

Pile wool; symmetrical knot;
45 knots per sq. inch
(725 per sq.dm)

Ends not original

Sides 2 cords, each of 3 threads,
overcast with red wool
(restored)

Colours dark red, red, gold, dark
green, green, blue, brown,
ivory (8)

Exner Collection
Photograph: Herbert J. Exner

18 KAZAK

mid-19th century
1.19 × 1.30m (3′11″ × 4′3″)

NOTES

1 The price paid for this rug at Rippon
in 1992 (DM81,200 = $49,015) is one of
the highest auction prices on record
for a nineteenth-century Caucasian
prayer rug, eclipsing the $33,492 paid
at Phillips, London for a Fachralo
prayer rug (13 Feb. 1990, lot 25; *Hali*
50, p. 166, 'Auction Price Guide').
2 Rippon 28 March 1992, lot 34.
3 Variations in colour tonality,
generally in the ground colour
of the field, which result from the
weaver's use of wool dyed in small
batches with minor differences
in colour depth.
4 See Bennett, *Caucasian*, pl. 4;
Herrmann, *SOT* VIII, pl. 21.

PREVIOUS PUBLICATION

1 Eiland, *Pacific Collections*, p. 177.
2 Rippon 28 March 1992, lot 34.

Ex-collection Viola Dominguez,
California
Photograph: courtesy Rippon Boswell
& Co., Wiesbaden

19 KAZAK

dated AH 1221 (1806/7)
0.74 × 1.30m (2′5″ × 4′3″)

NOTES

1 A group of prayer rugs, represented
by pl. 31 below, bear early dates and
have previously been attributed to
Kazak. This group has subsequently
been attributed to Armenian
weavings from Karabagh (see
Herrmann, *ATT* 2, pl. 31; *Hali* 31,
p. 95, 'Marketplace').
2 See McMullan, *Islamic Carpets*,
pl. 49, dated AH 1212 (1797).
McMullan points to the similaries
between this Kazak and certain
Turkish rugs, a comparison which
is also relevant to our example.

PREVIOUS PUBLICATION

Hali 26, p. 63.

ANALOGIES

Skinner 2 Dec. 1989, lot 51. The only
known parallel piece (excluding late
nineteenth-century double-niche
emulations), with a virtually identical
field and border. Dimensions:
0.96 × 1.78m (3′2″ × 5′10″).

TECHNICAL ANALYSIS

Warp ivory wool; 30 threads per
inch (120 per dm)

Weft red wool; 9 knots per inch
(36 per dm)

Pile symmetrical knot; 135 knots
per sq. inch (2160 per sq.dm)

Burns Collection
Photograph: Don Tuttle

20 KAZAK

1st quarter 19th century
1.12 × 1.60m (3′8″ × 5′3″)

ANALOGIES

1 The closest analogy is published in
SNY 5 Nov. 1985, lot 34, from the Carl
Milde Collection, with a serrated
leaf-and-calyx border.

Other related examples are:

2 A rug with similar rosettes in the
mihrab, from the H. McCoy Jones
collection, was published on the
cover of *Prayer Rugs from the Near
East and Central Asia* (McCoy Jones
Collection pamplet, M.H. De
Young Memorial Museum, San
Francisco, Nov. 1984). That rug,
however, has the reciprocal trefoil
border associated wth Borchalo
prayer rugs, and the mihrab is
surrounded by a second mihrab
of diagonal polychrome stripes
(see pl. 11 above).
3 Skinner 4 June 1989, lot 60.
4 CNY 6 Dec. 1988, lot 19, similar to the
McCoy Jones rug in note 1 above.
5 Herrmann, *SOT* VII, pl. 29; sold CNY 7
April 1990, lot 33. Possibly a prayer
rug because of the gabled shape of
the date cartouche in the upper
border. (Dated AH 1278 = 1861.)

TECHNICAL ANALYSIS

Warp ivory wool; z2s; 14 threads
per inch (56 per dm)

Weft red wool; z2s; 7 knots per inch
(28 per dm)

Pile wool; symmetrical knot;
49 knots per sq. inch
(784 per sq.dm)

Ends lower: evidence of
plainweave with ivory weft;
upper: missing

Sides 2 cords, each of 2 threads,
overcast with a variety of
coloured wool

Colours red, yellow, green, blue-
green, indigo, mid-blue,
brown, ivory (8)

Dixon Collection
Photograph: Don Tuttle

21 KAZAK

c.1875
0.90 × 1.33m (2′11″ × 4′4″)

NOTES

1 Published in Thompson, *Carpet
Magic*, p. 126.

PREVIOUS PUBLICATION

Rippon 10 Nov. 1990, lot 179 (attributed
to Kuba, end nineteenth century).

ANALOGIES

1 Lefevre 17 July 1981, lot 37.
2 Skinner 1 July 1991, lot 174.
3 Dodds, *Collection of Dr & Mrs Robert
A. Fisher*, pl. 54.
4 Thompson, *Carpet Magic*, p.126 =
Hali 5/3, p. 33, ad. for Montafian and
Co. Ltd (modern Turkish copy).

TECHNICAL ANALYSIS

Warp undyed wool

Weft red wool; z2s; 3 shoots

Pile wool; symmetrical knot

Ends not original

Sides 3 cords, each of 2 threads,
overcast with red wool

Colours red, yellow, green, blue,
aubergine, brown, ivory (7)

Exner Collection
Photograph: Herbert J. Exner

22 KAZAK

c.1880
1.14 × 2.08m (3′9″ × 6′10″)

NOTES

1 Skinner 3 June 1986, lot 36.
2 Rippon 16 Nov. 1996, lot 100.
3 For example lot 2169 in catalogue
for Rudolf Mangisch, Zurich,
18 March 1989 (Shirvan), and pl. 39
in Cootner, *Oriental Rugs, An
Introduction: Prayer Rugs* (Shirvan).

ANALOGIES

See notes 1–3 above.

TECHNICAL ANALYSIS

Warp red wool; z2s; 12 threads
per inch (48 per dm)

Weft ivory wool; z2s; shoots;
9 knots per inch (36 per dm)

Pile wool; symmetrical knot;
54 knots per sq. inch
(864 per sq.dm)

Ends plainweave with red weft

Sides 4 cords overcast with wool

Colours dark red, light red, gold, yellow, dark green, indigo, mid-blue, sky blue, light blue, dark brown, mid-brown, ivory (12)

Kaffel Collection
Photograph: Don Tuttle

---

23   K A Z A K

dated AH 1278 (1861)
1.12 × 1.63m (3′8″ × 5′4″)

N O T E S

1   It is also sometimes found on Turkish prayer rugs. Examples are the single panel Makri rugs; two rugs assigned to Elazig (see *Turkish Handwoven Carpets*, vol. 3 [Ministry of State and Ministry of Culture and Tourism of Turkey], pl. 0232; ibid. vol. 4, pl. 380); and a vertical saff rug assigned to Kars (ibid. vol 5, pl. 0557).

2   O'Bannon, *Oriental Rugs: The Collector's Guide*, p. 33.

3   Rippon 5 May 1990, lot 124.

4   See Straka and Mackie, *The Oriental Rug Collection of Jerome and Mary Jane Straka*, pl. 113.

P R E V I O U S   P U B L I C A T I O N

Rippon, 5 May 1990, lot 124.

A N A L O G I E S
Analogous borders

1   O'Bannon, *Oriental Rugs: The Collector's Guide*, p. 33.

2   Benardout 1978, no. 8.

3   Rippon 17 Nov. 1977, lot 96.

4   Nagel 5 Nov. 1983, lot 207.

5   Doyle NYC 20 May 1996, code no. N29.

6   Christie's East NY 26 April 1983, lot 43 = SLO 12 April 1989, lot 423.

A number of parallel examples with different borders also exist.

T E C H N I C A L   A N A L Y S I S

Warp ivory wool; z3s; 14 threads per inch (56 per dm)
Weft ivory wool; z2s; 3 or 4 shoots; 7 knots per inch (28 per dm)
Pile wool; symmetrical knot; 49 knots per sq. inch (784 per sq.dm)
Ends lower: complete, 1cm plainweave with red weft; upper: complete, plainweave with red weft, folded
Sides 2 cords, each of 2 threads, overcast with red and green wool
Colours dark red, red, yellow, green, dark blue, light blue, violet, brown, ivory (9)

Exner Collection
Photograph: Herbert J. Exner

---

24   S O U T H W E S T E R N
                 C A U C A S I A N

mid-19th century
1.12 × 1.42m (3′8″ × 4′8″)

N O T E S

1   For the best example of this type see pl. 14 in Bailey and Hopkins, *Through the Collector's Eye: Oriental Rugs from New England Private Collections*, dated AH 1243 (1827).

A N A L O G I E S

1   Lefevre 9 July 1976, lot 35, dated AH 1249 (1833).

2   Skinner 23 April 1994, lot 6, illegibly dated.

3   *Oriental Rug Review* 10/1, dated AH 1222 (1807); in the Columbus Museum of Art, Columbus, Ohio.

4   *Antique Rugs from the Caucasus Region of Russia*, Birdshake's Antique Oriental Rug Gallery, San Francisco, pl. 2 (with a dragon 's' border).

T E C H N I C A L   A N A L Y S I S

Warp undyed wool; z3s; threads per inch (76 per dm)
Weft red wool; z2s; shoots; 11 knots per inch (43 per dm)
Pile wool; symmetrical knot; 104 knots per sq. inch (1634 per sq.dm)
Ends not original
Sides 4 cords, each of 2 threads, overcast with blue wool
Colours bright red, gold-yellow, light green, light blue, aubergine, mid-brown, ivory (7)

Exner Collection
Photograph: Herbert J. Exner

---

25   K A R A B A G H

late 19th century
0.83 × 1.22m (2′8″ × 4′0″)

N O T E S

1   Featured in *Hali* 54, pp. 104–5, 'Connoisseur's Choice'.

2   *Hali* 4/2, pp. 208, 210, 'Rugs on the Market', fig. 7.

3   *Hali* 61, p. 162: 'In both structure and design this very unusual rug is closely related to the example (dated AD 1879) discussed by Gérard Boëly in *Hali* 54 [pp. 104–5] and tentatively attributed to the southeastern Caucasus. The principal difference is the very archaic-looking main border on the Boëly rug which is flanked by two major guard stripes bearing a similar pattern to that on the narrow main border of the Sotheby's rug. Aesthetically there is not much to choose between them, although the Boëly rug is the more impressive and may be slightly older.'

P R E V I O U S   P U B L I C A T I O N

1   SNY 11 Dec. 1991, lot 138.

2   SLO 27 April 1994, lot 16.

A N A L O G I E S

1   See note 1 above.

2   CLO 16 April 1984, lot 39.

T E C H N I C A L   A N A L Y S I S

Warp ivory wool; z2s; 16 threads per inch (64 per dm)
Weft auburn wool; z2s; between 2 and 4 shoots; 8 knots per inch (32 per dm)
Pile wool; symmetrical knot; 64 knots per sq. inch (1024 per sq.dm)
Sides 2 cords, each of 2 threads, overcast with auburn wool

Colours mid- to deep paprika, mid- to deep teal, ivory, china blue, wedgewood, willow, persimmon, chamois, amber, light to mid-auburn, golden oak, taupe (12)

Private Collection
Photograph: courtesy Sotheby's, London

---

26   S O U T H   C A U C A S I A N
             [K A R A B A G H]

c.1875
1.17 × 1.70m (3′10″ × 5′7″)

N O T E S

1   *Hali* 54, pp. 104–5.

2   Similar (though more geometric) border motifs, between similar minor guard stripes, appear in a Genje prayer rug published in Fokker, *Caucasian Rugs of Yesterday*, p. 67. Another similar example is CLO 25 April 1991, lot 212, attributed to Kazak.

T E C H N I C A L   A N A L Y S I S

Warp undyed wool; z3s; 13 threads per inch (50 per dm)
Weft red wool; z2s; 3 or 4 shoots; 7 knots per inch (29 per dm)
Pile wool; symmetrical knot; 45 knots per sq. inch (725 per sq.dm)
Ends not original
Sides 3 cords, each of 2 threads, overcast with a variety of coloured wool
Colours red, yellow, blue-green, mid-blue, light blue, mid-brown, ivory (7)

Exner Collection
Photograph: Herbert J. Exner

---

27   K A R A B A G H

2nd half 19th century
0.84 × 1.30m (2′9″ × 4′3″)

N O T E S

1   See Bennett, *Caucasian*, pl. 108; Herrmann, *Kaukasische Teppichkunst*, pl. 17; Lefevre 29 May 1981, lot 37; Bausback 1980, p. 59.

2   An analogous example was published in *Turkish Handwoven Carpets*, vol. 4 (Ministry of State and Ministry of Culture and Tourism of Turkey), pl. 0436, rather improbably attributed to Melas, eighteenth century.

3   SNY 19 May 1984, lot 13.

A N A L O G I E S

1   Jacobsen, *Oriental Rugs, A Complete Guide*, pl. 165 = Dodds, *Collection of Dr and Mrs Robert A. Fisher*, pl. 37 = Hali 1/2, p. 155 (dated 1814 or 1834).

2   *Hali* 1/3, p. 311, 'Rugs on the Market', no. 6, J. Fairman Carpets.

3   Nagel 25 May 1979, lot 150 = Nagel 13 Oct. 1990, lot 315.

4   Hasson, *Caucasian Rugs* (Hebrew edition), pl. 23.

T E C H N I C A L   A N A L Y S I S

Warp beige wool; z3s; 22 threads per inch (88 per dm)
Weft undyed cotton; between 2 and 4 shoots; 9 knots per inch (36 per m)

Pile wool; symmetrical knot; 99 knots per sq. inch (1584 per sq.dm)
Sides 2 cords, each of 2 threads, overcast
Colours red, green, blue, aubergine (4)

Tschebull Collection
Photograph: Don Tuttle

---

28   K A R A B A G H

dated AH 1312 (1894)
0.84 × 1.17m (2′9″ × 3′10″)

N O T E S

1   For ethnographic maps see Eiland, *Oriental Rugs, A New Comprehensive Guide*, p. 250 and Mehrdad R. Izady, *The Kurds: A Concise Handbook* (Crane Russak, Taylor & Francis International Publishers, Washington DC, Philadelphia and London 1992), pp. 4 and 6, 90 and 97. For further information see William Eagleton, *An Introduction to Kurdish Rugs and Other Weavings* (Interlink Publishing Group, Brooklyn, NY, 1988), p. 9, 'The Kurdish Caucasians'.

2   See Eagleton, *An Introduction to Kurdish Rugs*, pl. 114.

3   For two similar depictions on an mid-nineteenth century Karabagh, see Lefevre 23 Nov. 1984, lot 46.

4   SNY 13 Sept. 1989, lot 29, depicting the Hagia Sophia mosque.

T E C H N I C A L   A N A L Y S I S

Warp brown and white wool, mixed together; z2s; 18 threads per inch (72 per dm)
Weft brown wool; z2s; 12 knots per inch (48 per dm)
Pile symmetrical knot; 108 knots per sq. inch (1728 per sq.dm)
Ends plainweave with shades of ivory and brown weft
Sides 2 cords overcast
Colours dark red, cadmium red, gold, yellow, dark green, blue-green, indigo, periwinkle blue, salmon, peach, dark brown, mid-brown, tan, light brown, black, ivory (16)

Kaffel Collection
Photograph: Don Tuttle

---

29   K A R A B A G H

late 19th century
0.89 × 1.58m (2′11″ × 5′2″)

N O T E S

1   Published in Cootner, *Oriental Rugs, An Introduction: Prayer Rugs*, a (now scarce) exhibition catalogue from the Palo Alto Cultural Center, California, where it was grouped with Persian examples and assigned to Karadagh. Also published (fig. 24A) in *Collector's Choice*, an equally rare catalogue of an exhibition held at Samarkand (rug shop), San Francisco, March 21–31, 1973, assigned to the Caucasus.

2   Rippon 11 May 1991, lot 27.

3   Skinner 7 Dec. 1991, lot 132.

4   The exhibiton was mounted by Michael Craycraft, owner of Adraskand Inc., an antique rug shop in San Anselmo, CA.

ANALOGIES

1 Nagel 9 Dec. 1982, lot 3097 (a virtually identical piece, assigned to Karabagh).
2 A related group of Karabagh rugs has similar features but diamond-shaped central medallions. Examples are Rippon 18 Nov. 1989, lot 42; SLO 6 Oct. 1979, lot 112.
3 A large group of Kazak rugs of similar conception (other than the Fachralos) feature a large, square central medallion containing a quatrefoil element. See Hawley, *Oriental Rugs Antique and Modern*, pl. 50; Hasson, *Caucasian Rugs*, pl. 10.

TECHNICAL ANALYSIS

Warp wool; z3s; 14 threads per inch (56 per dm)
Weft rose wool; z3s; 2 shoots; 7 knots per inch (28 per dm)
Pile symmetrical knot; 49 knots per sq. inch (784 per sq.dm)
Sides 3 cords, each of 2 threads, overcast with rose wool

Dixon Collection
Photograph: Don Tuttle

---
30   [probably] K A R A B A G H
dated AH 1257 (1841)
1.09 × 1.50m (3′7″ × 4′11″)

NOTES

1 *Prayer Rugs from the Near East and Central Asia*. The accompanying pamphlet does not contain specific references to the rugs exhibited (McCoy Jones Collection pamphlet, M.H. De Young Memorial Museum, San Francisco, Nov. 1984).
2 *Hali* 6/4, p. 69, ad. for Konzett Teppichekunst, Graz, Austria (dated 1845).
3 Assigned to Karabagh: Herrmann, *ATT* 2, pl. 31. Assigned to eastern Turkey or southwest Caucasus: pl. 31 below = *Hali* 27, p. 96, 'Marketplace', Gustave Tasch = Rippon 18 Nov. 1989, lot 115; Eskenazi, *L'arte del tappeto orientale*, pl. 155 = Rippon 14 Nov. 1992, lot 140 = Lefevre 16 May 1975, lot 7. Lefevre proposed a relationship to the Talish group, while *Hali*, reviewing the rug in issue 67 ('Auction Price Guide,' p. 31), also suggested Karabagh.

TECHNICAL ANALYSIS

Warp white and white plied with brown wool; z3s; 20 threads per inch (80 per dm)
Weft white cotton; 2 shoots, but occasionally 1 or 3; 11 knots per inch (44 per dm)
Pile wool; symmetrical knot; 110 knots per sq. inch (1760 per sq.dm)
Ends one not original; the other has ⅜″ (1 cm) plainweave with white cotton weft decorated with weft twining in red and aubergine wool
Sides 4 cords, each of 2 threads, overcast with a variety of coloured wool

Colours red, 2 yellows, green, blue-green, dark blue, mid-blue, aubergine, brown, white (10)

Klein Collection
Photograph: Wells C. Klein

---
31   K A R A B A G H
dated AH 1222 (1807)
1.0 × 1.40m (3′3″ × 4′7″)

NOTES

1 See *Hali* 29, p. 2, 'Letters', from Peter Trimbacher, Schloss Plankenstein, Austria.
2 The 'Holbein' rugs are so called after the paintings of Hans Holbein the Younger (1497/8–1543) whose paintings often feature rugs with an octagonal medallion with corner panels. This design is seen in Turkish rugs of the sixteenth and seventeenth centuries. For an example see Mills, *Carpets in Paintings*, pl. 13 (a two-medallion rug in the Museum of Islamic Arts, Istanbul).
3 Lefevre 16 May 1975, lot 7. The rug sold for £3,800 / $8,740 and 17 years later for DM 60,000 / $44,000. The Karabagh attribution was made by Eberhart Hermann (in *Asiatische Teppich und Textilekunst 2*) and is currently the generally accepted provenance for this group.

PREVIOUS PUBLICATION

1 Lefevre 16 May 1975, lot 7.
2 Rippon 14 Nov. 1992, lot 140.
3 *Hali* 67, p. 131, 'Auction Price Guide'.
4 Eskenazi, *L'arte del tappeto orientale*, pl. 156.
5 Black, *The Macmillan Atlas of Rugs and Carpets*, p. 11.

ANALOGIES

Other carpets in this group, chronologically by inscribed date, are as follows:

1 CLO 23 April 1981, lot 50 = *Hali* 4/1, p. 87, 'Auction Report', dated AH 1190 (1776) (1.04 × 1.30m / 3′5″ × 4′3″).
2 *Hali* 27, p. 96, 'Marketplace', ad. for Gustave Tasch = Rippon 18 Nov. 1989, lot 115; dated AH 1215 (1800) (1.12 × 1.47m / 3′8″ × 4′10″).
3 Fiske, *Prayer Rugs from Private Collections*, pl. 26 = King, *Prayer Rugs*, cover = *Hali* 5/2, p. 55, ad. for Andonian = *Hali* 71, p. 152, ad. for George Gilmore; dated AH 1222 (1807).(1.12 × 1.50 m / 3′8″ × 4′11″).
4 Herrmann, *ATT* 2, pl. 31; dated AH 1222 (1807).
5 *Hali* 31, p. 95, 'Marketplace', Sailer exhibition; dated AH 1230 (1815). (1.02 × 1.19m / 3′4″ × 3′11″).
6 *Hali* 70, p. 128, ad. for The Nomad's Loom (fragment); undated.
7 Skinner 1 June 1991, lot 174; dated AH 1282 (1865); the only late example to employ this characteristic border.

TECHNICAL ANALYSIS

Warp white cotton and undyed silk; z3s, one thread of silk plied with 2 of cotton; 30 threads per inch (120 per dm)
Weft pink silk; 2 shoots; 14/15 knots per inch (58 per dm)
Pile wool; symmetrical knot; 217 knots per sq. inch (3480 per sq.dm)

Ends not original
Sides 2 cords, each of 2 threads, overcast with blue cotton
Colours red, yellow, olive green, green, blue-green, dark blue, light blue, aubergine, brown, beige, ivory (11)

Exner Collection
Photograph: Herbert J. Exner

---
32   C H A N - K A R A B A G H
2nd half 19th century
0.85 × 1.44m (2′9″ × 4′9″)

NOTES

1 See Schürmann, *Caucasian Rugs*, pl. 37. This example has a silky wool and fine weave, which led Schürmann to speculate a Saliani origin. (Saliani is in the Moghan steppe and a long way from Karabagh.)
2 For examples see Keshishian, *The Treasure of the Caucasus*, pl. 17 (latchhooked diamonds); Eshkenazi, *L'arte del tappeto orientale*, pl. 98 (linked arrowheads); CLO 24 Oct. 1984, lot 111 ('s' figures); SNY 12 June 1981, lot 5 and Bausback 1978, p. 213 (stepped flowerheads).
3 Lefevre 31 Oct. 1980, lot 18.
4 Rippon 5 May 1990, lot 167.

PREVIOUS PUBLICATION

1 Lefevre 31 Oct. 1980, lot 18.
2 Rippon 5 May 1990, lot 167.

ANALOGIES

1 Bausback 1973, p. 72.
2 SNY 5 March 1982, lot 82.
3 Macey, *Oriental Prayer Rugs*, pl. 33.

TECHNICAL ANALYSIS

Warp ivory wool; z3s; 18 threads per inch (72 per dm)
Weft ivory wool; z2s; 2 shoots; 9 knots per inch (36 per dm)
Pile wool; symmetrical knot; 81 knots per sq. inch (1368 per sq.dm)
Sides 3 cords overcast with blue cotton
Colours red, cochineal red, yellow, dark green, light green, dark blue, mid-blue, light blue, aubergine, dark brown, ivory (11)

Exner Collection
Photograph: Herbert J. Exner

---
33   G E N J E
dated AH 1244 (1828)
0.96 × 1.52m (3′2″ × 5′0″)

NOTES

1 Inv. 378-1923, published in *Hali* 3/2, p. 109, fig. 42.

TECHNICAL ANALYSIS

Warp tan wool; 30 threads per inch (120 per dm)
Weft tan wool; 13 knots per inch (52 per dm)
Pile symmetrical knot; 195 knots per sq. inch (3120 per sq.dm)

Burns Collection
Photograph: Don Tuttle

---
34   G E N J E
c.1800
0.76 × 1.60m (2′6″ × 5′3″)

NOTES

1 One other rug with a mihrab of vertical bare stripes was published in *Hali* 88, p. 48 in an ad. for Iwan Maktabi of Beirut.
2 Bennett, *Caucasian*, pls 161 and 172.
3 For example Nagel June 1984, lot 3457; Eiland, *Oriental Rugs, A New Comprehensive Guide*, fig. 246.
4 Herrmann, *Kaukasische Teppichkunst*, pl. 35b.

ANALOGIES

Schürmann, *Caucasian Rugs*, pl. 74.

TECHNICAL ANALYSIS

Warp ivory wool; 24 threads per inch (96 per dm)
Weft tan wool; 8 knots per inch (32 per dm)
Pile symmetrical knot; 96 knots per sq. inch (1536 per sq.dm)

Burns Collection
Photograph: Don Tuttle

---
35   G E N J E
late 19th century
0.91 × 1.68m (3′0″ × 5′6″)

TECHNICAL ANALYSIS

Warp ivory wool; z2s; 16 threads per inch (64 per dm)
Weft red wool; z2s; 8 knots per inch (32 per dm)
Pile wool; symmetrical knot; 64 knots per sq. inch (1024 per sq.dm)
Ends plainweave with red weft
Sides 2 cords, each of 2 threads, overcast
Colours red, yellow, green, indigo, mid-blue, purple, brown, ivory (8)

Private Collection; courtesy James Blackmon Galleries, San Francisco
Photograph: Don Tuttle

---
36   M O G H A N
2nd half 19th century
1.13 × 1.83m (3′8½″ × 6′0″)

NOTES

1 The reciprocal guard borders, particularly those closest to the field, are imprecisely rendered while in other places the pattern is handled with sureness and skill. No parallel pieces are known.

TECHNICAL ANALYSIS

Warp white and brown wool, mixed together; z3s; 20 threads per inch (80 per dm)
Weft white wool; z3s; 2 shoots; 10 knots per inch (40 per dm)
Pile symmetrical knot; 100 knots per sq. inch (1600 per sq.dm)
Ends not original
Sides not original

Dixon Collection
Photograph: Don Tuttle

37   MOGHAN
1st half 19th century
1.14 × 1.87m (3′9″ × 6′2″)

NOTES
1   Lefevre auction catalogue,
     1 October 1982.
2   The second example appeared in
     Butterweck et al., *Austrian Collec-
     tions*, assigned to Shirvan and dated
     to the first half of the nineteenth
     century. (It was published opposite
     pl. 66, a soumak bag with octagons
     of identical design in the field and a
     border of identical triangles with
     arrowhead motifs. The commen-
     tary relating to the rug read, in part,
     'The overall design was previously
     only known from three soumak
     khordjins [ibid. pl. 66; Bausback,
     Kelim, fig. 113; Reinisch, *Sattletaschen*,
     fig. 24] but this piece is older than the
     three bags.') The third example was
     sold at Skinner's (1 June 1991, lot 172),
     assigned to Shirvan; it was pur-
     chased by a New England dealer and
     re-sold to Eberhart Herrmann, who
     published it in his catalogue ATT 4
     (1992), pl. 49, assigned to Moghan.
     (Herrmann pointed to a relation-
     ship between his rug and another
     that he had previously published in
     SOT IV, pl. 36 which, although it
     employed a different and very rare
     'anchor' design [also used in soumak
     bags] featured identical octagons as
     subsidiary motifs and had a very
     similar colour palette, as well as a
     large 'kochanak' cross under the
     prayer arch.) The fourth example
     appeared at a single-owner sale at
     SNY, 9 March 1994 (lot 3), assigned
     to Shirvan.
3   This also occurs in the *Austrian
     Collections* example cited in note 2
     above.
4   Skinner 7 Dec. 1991, lot 137.

PREVIOUS PUBLICATION
1   Lefevre 1 Oct. 1982, lot 29.
2   *Hali Decorative: A Buyer's Guide to the
     Best of Decorative Carpets* (London
     1988), p. 36.

ANALOGIES
1   Butterweck et al., *Austrian
     Collections*, opposite pl. 66.
2   Skinner 1 June 1991, lot 172.
3   SNY 9 March 1994, lot 3.

Private Collection
Photograph: Lefevre & Partners,
London; courtesy The Hali Archive

38   BAKU-SHIRVAN
3rd quarter 19th century
1.25 × 1.76m (4′1″ × 5′8″)

PREVIOUS PUBLICATION
Rippon 7 May 1988, lot 138.

ANALOGIES
1   Achdjian, *The Rug*, pp. 69–7.
     A related blue-ground rug, with a
     'barber's pole'-striped prayer arch,
     attributed to Chirvan Koubah.
     (The design is described as 'a porch
     with a bishop's throne'.)
2   SNY 24 Sept. 1991, lot 125 = SNY
     22 Sept. 1993, lot 77. A related rug,
     this time with a 'barber's pole'-
     striped border.

TECHNICAL ANALYSIS
Warp   ivory and brown wool; z3s,
           one ivory and 2 brown;
           16 threads per inch (64 per dm)
Weft   ivory wool; z2s; 2 shoots;
           9 knots per inch (38 per dm)
Pile   wool; symmetrical knot;
           average 76 knots per sq. inch
           (1216 per sq.dm)
Ends   complete, ⅜″–¾″ (1–2 cm)
           plainweave
Sides 2 cords, each of 2 threads,
           overcast with ivory wool
Colours red, gold, light yellow, green,
             blue, brown, ivory (7)

Exner Collection
Photograph: Herbert J. Exner

39   BAKU
last quarter 19th century
1.21 × 1.40m (4′0″ × 4′7″)

NOTES
1   Eskenazi, *L'Arte del tappeto orientale*,
     pl. 136
2   Bausback 1976, pp. 96–7; also
     published in Bausback, *Antike
     Orientteppiche*, p. 233.

PREVIOUS PUBLICATION
See note 1.

Private Collection, Florence
Photograph: courtesy John Eskenazi

40   KUBA
2nd half 19th century
1.12 × 1.41m (3′8″ × 4′8″)

NOTES
1   Illustrated in Rippon 13 Nov. 1993,
     lot 16.
2   Bailey and Hopkins, *Through the
     Collector's Eye*. The exhibition was
     held at Rhodes Island School of
     Design, 22 Nov. 1991–9 Feb. 1992,
     coinciding with the first American
     Conference on Oriental Rugs
     (ACOR), held in Boston. The
     exhibition then travelled to the
     Textile Museum in Washington, DC
     (20 March 1992–3 May 1992).
3   Published in Butterweck et al.,
     Austrian Collections, pl. 49.

PREVIOUS PUBLICATION
Bailey and Hopkins, *Through the
Collector's Eye*, pl. 23.

TECHNICAL ANALYSIS
Warp   light brown wool; z2s;
           18 threads per inch (72 per dm)
Weft   white wool; z3s; 2 shoots;
           10 knots per inch (40 per dm)
Pile   wool; symmetrical knot;
           90 knots per sq. inch
           (1440 per sq.dm)
Ends   lower: cut with modern
           fringe; upper: plainweave
           with ivory weft
Sides not original
Colours red, brown-red, gold, dark
             green, green, dark blue, blue,
             light blue, dark brown, tan,
             ivory (11)

Rudnick Collection
Photograph: courtesy Mitchell and
Rosalie Rudnick

41   KUBA
mid-19th century
1.07 × 1.35m (3′6″ × 4′5″)

NOTES
1   See *Hali* 2/1, p. 77 for an example
     of these flowers.

TECHNICAL ANALYSIS
Warp   undyed wool; depressed
Weft   undyed wool; 2 shoots
Pile   wool; symmetrical knot;
           110 knots per sq. inch
           (1760 per sq.dm)
Ends   fringe of warp threads with
           bands of off-set knotting
Sides not original
Colours red, yellow, green, indigo,
             mid-blue, dark brown, tan,
             white (8)

Winter Collection
Photograph: Vincenzo Pietropaolo

42   KUBA
early 19th century
1.02 × 1.32m (3′4″ × 4′0″)

NOTES
1   For further discussion see *Hali* 1,
     p. 77, 'Rugs on the Market'.
2   Kirchheim et al., *Orient Stars*.
     Also published in *Hali* 46, p. 67,
     ad. for Galerie Ostler.
3   *Hali* 67, pp. 130–31, 'Auction Price
     Guide'.

ANALOGIES (pls 42 and 43)
1   Pl. 42 below.
2   Schürmann, *Caucasian Rugs*, pl. 97
     = Erdmann et al., *Kaukasische
     Teppiche*, pl. 52.
3   Burns, *Caucasus: Traditions in
     Weaving*, pl. 28 = Black, *Macmillan
     Atlas*, p. 128 = Bennett, *Rugs and
     Carpets of the World*, p. 157.
4   Bacharach and Bierman, *The Warp
     and Weft of Islam*, pl. 15.
5   Bennett, *Caucasian*, pl. 329 = Nagel
     23 April 1977, lot 170.
6   Lefevre 17 May 1974, lot 54.
7   Hermann, *Kaukasishe Teppichkunst*,
     pl.16
8   Rippon 10 Nov. 1990, lot 136.
9   Rippon 10 Nov. 1979, lot 57.
10 Bausback 1983, p. 69.

PREVIOUS PUBLICATION
SNY 10 Dec 1992.

TECHNICAL ANALYSIS
Warp   ivory wool; z3s; 18–20 threads
           per inch (72–80 per dm)
Weft   ivory cotton; z3s; 3 shoots;
           16–20 knots per inch
           (64–80 per dm)
Pile   wool; symmetrical knot;
           average 172 knots per sq. inch
           (average 2752 per sq.dm)
Sides 3 cords, each of 2 threads,
           overcast with blue cotton
Colours lapis, parsley, tumeric,
             cerulean blue, persimmon,
             teal, strawberry, seal brown,
             ginger, shrimp (11)

Private Collection
Photograph: courtesy Sotheby's

43   KUBA
early 19th century
1.06 × 1.36m (3′6″ × 4′5″)

NOTES
See pl. 42.

ANALOGIES
See pl. 42.

PREVIOUS PUBLICATION
Eskenazi, *L'arte del tappeto orientale*,
pl. 141.

Private Collection
Photograph: courtesy John Eskenazi

44   KUBA
late 18th / early 19th century
0.74 × 1.45m (2′5″ × 4′9″)

NOTES
1   Ellis, *Early Caucasian Rugs*, pls 28,
     29; see also Yetkin, *Early Caucasian
     Carpets in Turkey*, vol. 1, pls 63–78.
2   For examples see Achdjian, *The
     Rug*, p. 69; SNY 22 Sept. 1993, lot 77,
     and pl. 38 above.
3   An example is the Karabagh
     published as pl. 46 in Herrmann,
     SOT VIII.
4   Yetkin, *Early Caucasian Carpets in
     Turkey*, vol. 1, pl. 76.

TECHNICAL ANALYSIS
Warp   white and brown wool,
           mixed together; z3s;
           22 threads per inch (88 per dm)
Weft   white cotton; z3s; 2 shoots;
           11 knots per inch (44 per dm)
Pile   symmetrical knot; 121 knots
           per sq. inch (1936 per sq.dm)
Ends   not original
Sides not original

Dixon Collection
Photograph: Don Tuttle

45   KONAGHEND
mid-19th century or earlier
0.91 × 1.50m (3′0″ × 4′11″)

NOTES
1   Bennett, *Caucasian*, pls 340–46, 349.
     Bennett also references a secular
     example published in Grote-
     Hasenbalg's *Der Orientteppich*,
     vol. 2, pl. 34, dated AH 1274 (1831),
     which shows the artistry and
     spaciousness of the earlier pieces.
     This piece is contemporaneous
     with the examples shown here.

ANALOGIES
With red fields
1   SNY 31 Oct. 1980, lot 82 = Skinner
     31 May 1987, lot 112.
2   Herrmann, SOT VIII, pl. 48 (dated
     AH 1232 = 1817).
3   Berdj Andonian, NYC, Dec. 1986.
     (Unpublished, very similar to
     above.)
4   *Hali* 77, p. 32, ad. for Rascid Rahaim,
     Venice. (Double-niche example.)
5   Nagel 25 May 1979, lot 156.
     (Assigned to Genje [?], with an
     inverted 'v'-shaped prayer arch.)

TECHNICAL ANALYSIS
Warp   white wool; z3s; 22 threads
           per inch (88 per dm)

Weft white cotton; z2s; between
3 and 5 shoots; 10 knots per
inch (40 per dm)
Pile symmetrical knot; 110 knots
per sq. inch (1760 per sq.dm)
Ends not original
Sides not original

Dixon Collection
Photograph: Don Tuttle

---
46   KONAGHEND
mid-19th century or earlier
1.04 × 1.80m (3′5″ × 5′11″)

NOTES
See pl. 45.

ANALOGIES
See pl. 45.

TECHNICAL ANALYSIS
Warp white wool; z4s; 18 threads
per inch (72 per dm)
Weft white cotton; z3s; between
2 and 4 shoots; 11 knots per
inch (44 per dm)
Pile symmetrical knot; 99 knots
per sq. inch (1584 per sq.dm)
Ends ⅜″ (1 cm) plainweave with
ivory wool weft
Sides 2 cords, each of 2 threads,
overcast with white cotton;
white wool used in places

Dixon Collection
Photograph: Don Tuttle

---
47   PEREPEDIL
dated AH 1281 (1864)
1.22 × 1.42m (4′0″ × 4′8″)

NOTES
1 Klose, 'The Perepedil Enigma',
Hali 55, pp. 110–17.
2 A northwest Persian carpet
illustrated in Klose's article (ibid.,
fig. 7) has obvious floral motifs in
the field as well as some of the same
's'-shaped 'blossom' variants, as in
our rug.
3 See figs 8, 9 and 10 ibid.
4 Rather similar to the pattern of
fig. 10 ibid., from the Wilfried
Stanzer collection (dated to mid-
nineteenth century).
5 Interestingly, this variant is most
often found on two types of rug:
Perepedil prayer rugs with ivory
fields, as here, and Mattese cross
Sewan Kazaks. (See Herrmann,
SOT V, pl. 37 for a very similar
border.) The shared use of this
unusual border design in too
greatly dissimilar types from
opposite ends of the Caucasus
is an intriguing sidelight.

PREVIOUS PUBLICATION
1 Lefevre 26 May 1978, lot 3.
2 Lefevre 27 April 1979, lot 35.
3 Lefevre 17 July 1981, lot 38.
4 *Hali* 4/2, p. 199, 'Auction Reports'.

ANALOGIES
*With white fields unless otherwise
indicated (excluding long rugs)*
1 Lefevre, *Caucasian Carpets*, pl. 25.
2 Gombos, *Old Prayer Rugs*, pl. 91.

3 Keshishian, *Treasure of the Caucasus*,
pl. 32 = Pickering et al., *Divine
Images and Magic Carpets from the
Asian Art Collection of Dr and Mrs
William T. Price*, pl. 26.
4 *Hali* 1/4, p. 369.
5 Rippon 6 Nov. 1976, lot 156.
6 Douglass and Peters, *The Lost
Language*, vol. 2, pl. 44 (yellow field).
7 *Oriental Rug Review* 8/5, p. 45,
Huntington Museum of Art.
8 Douglass and Peters, *The Lost
Language*, vol. 2, pl. 51.
9 SNY 13 Dec. 1986, lot 45.
10 Lefevre 16 May 1975, lot 37 =
Lefevre 28 Nov. 1975, lot 51.
11 Herrmann, *SOT* IX, pl. 36.
12 Lefevre 15 April 1981, lot 48.
13 *Hali* 55 cover = Herrmann, *SOT* VI,
pl. 39 = PB 84, 25 June 1980, lot 71.
14 Lefevre 9 July 1976 lot 15 = Eskenazi,
L'arte del tappeto orientale, pl. 146.
15 *Hali* 4, p. 68, 'Gallery', ad. for RASA =
Skinner 4 June 1989, lot 200.
16 Lefevre 28 Sept. 1973, lot 31 = Black,
Macmillan Atlas, p. 21.

TECHNICAL ANALYSIS
Warp brown/beige wool; z3s;
24 threads per inch (96 per dm)
Weft white cotton; z2s; 2 shoots;
11 knots per inch (44 per dm)
Pile symmetrical knot; 132 knots
per sq. inch (2112 per sq.dm)
Sides 2 cords, each of 2 threads,
overcast with mid-blue wool

Tschebull Collection
Photograph: Don Tuttle

---
48   PEREPEDIL *or* SHIRVAN
c.1870
1.19 × 2.57m (3′11″ × 8′5″)

NOTES
1 Rippon 23 May 1987, lot 55 and
catalogue cover illustration.

PREVIOUS PUBLICATION
1 SNY 31 Oct. 1980, lot 43 (dated c.1870).
2 Eiland, *Pacific Collections*, pl. 180.

ANALOGIES
See pl. 47.

TECHNICAL ANALYSIS
Warp wool; z3s; 18 threads per inch
(72 per dm)
Weft white cotton; z2s; shoots;
9 knots per inch (36 per dm)
Pile symmetrical knot; 81 knots
per sq. inch (1296 per sq.dm)
Ends evidence of plainweave
Sides 1 cord oversewn with white
cotton
Colours brick red, light green, dark
blue, mid-blue, mauve,
brown-black, ivory (7)

Kaffel Collection
Photograph: Dennis Anderson

---
49   PEREPEDIL
early 19th century
1.07 × 2.31m (3′6″ × 7′7″)

NOTES
1 Another yellow-ground double-
niche rug assigned to Perepedil is
illustrated in Rippon 7 May 1988,
lot 99. Its Perepedil attribution is
tenuous, however. This rug has a
floral design radiating from the
centre but lacks any of the
characteristic Perepedil elements.
The catalogue dates the rug to the
first half of the nineteenth century.
If the date and attribution are
accurate, this piece would be one
of the earliest known Perepedil
prayer rugs.
2 *Hali* 61, p. 162, 'Auction Price
Guide'.

PREVIOUS PUBLICATION
SNY 11 Dec. 1991, lot 11.

ANALOGIES
Pl. 50 below.

TECHNICAL ANALYSIS
Warp ivory and brown wool; z3s;
14–20 threads per inch
(56–80 per dm)
Weft white cotton; z3s; 2 shoots;
8–9 knots per inch
(32–36 per dm)
Pile wool; symmetrical knot;
average 73 knots per sq. inch
(average 1168 per sq.dm)
Ends incomplete
Sides 2 cords, each of 2 threads,
overcast with white (cotton?)
Colours parchment, lapis, cornflower
blue, paprika, chamois,
spruce, med- to deep teal,
sand, seafoam green, seal
brown, black (11)

Judy Smith Collection
Photograph: courtesy Judith Alper
Smith

---
50   PEREPEDIL
c.1870
0.98 × 2.22m (3′2″ × 7′4″)

NOTES
1 Fokker, *Caucasian Rugs of Yesterday*,
pp. 116–17.
2 See discussion of this rug in *Hali* 58,
p. 79.
3 Burns, *Caucasus: Traditions in
Weaving*, pl. 20
4 Klose, 'The Perepedil Enigma',
Hali 55, pp. 110–17.

PREVIOUS PUBLICATION
Hali 58, p. 79.

ANALOGIES
Pl. 49 above.

TECHNICAL ANALYSIS
Warp ivory and brown wool; z3s;
16 threads per inch (64 per dm)
Weft ivory wool; z2s; 2 shoots;
8 knots per inch (32 per dm)
Pile wool; symmetrical knot; 64
knots per sq. inch (1024 per
sq.dm)
Ends evidence of plainweave

Sides 2 cords, each of 2 threads,
overcast with white cotton
Colours dark red, gold, yellow, green,
light blue, violet, dark brown,
ivory (9)

Exner Collection
Photograph: Herbert J. Exner

---
51   CHICHI
dated AH 1298 (1881)
1.22 × 1.52m (4′0″ × 5′0″)

NOTES
1 See Thompson, *Carpet Magic*, p. 123,
for a similar example with a most
generous spacing of motifs: only
five rows of ornamentation
beneath the arch in contrast to the
more usual ten or more rows (our
example has nine), and just seven
slanted bars in the vertical borders
(our example has ten).
2 See pls 44 and 48 for examples
of the Kufic border.
3 See Keane, *Asia*, p. 388.

PREVIOUS PUBLICATION
1 SNY 30 May 1987, lot 84.
2 Denny, *Sotheby's Guide to Oriental
Carpets*, pl. 9.

ANALOGIES
1 Herrmann, *SOT* VII, pl. 35.
2 Wright, *Rugs and Flatweaves of the
Transcaucasus*, pl. 45 = Skinner 24
May 1984, lot 86A = Rippon 15 Nov.
1986, lot 82.
3 Denny, *Oriental Rugs*, pl. 41.
4 Lefevre, *Caucasian Carpets*, pl. 49.
5 Ettinghausen et al., *Prayer Rugs*,
pl. XXXII.
6 Bausback 1981, p. 49 = SNY 10 April
1981, lot 182.
7 O'Bannon, *Oriental Rugs: The
Collector's Guide*, p. 34.
8 CNY (Franklin & Marshall College,
Lancaster, PA) 10 June 1994, lot 98.
9 *Hali* 32, p. 16, ad. for Kailash Gallery,
Antwerp.
10 Thompson, *Carpet Magic*, p. 123.
11 SNY 11 Dec. 1981, lot 50.

TECHNICAL ANALYSIS
Warp white and dark brown wool,
mixed together; z3s;
18 threads per inch (72 per dm)
Weft white cotton; z2s; 2 shoots;
11–14 knots per inch
(44–56 per dm)
Pile symmetrical knot; average
112 knots per sq. inch (average
1800 per sq.dm)
Ends ½ (1 cm) plainweave with
white cotton and a fringe
with bands of off-set knotting
Sides 1 cord of 2 threads oversewn
with white (cotton?)
Colours magenta red, red, blue-green,
indigo, blue, light blue, dark
brown, tan, ivory (9)

Private Collection
Photograph: courtesy Sotheby's

---

52   KARAGASHLI
early 19th century
1.12 × 1.73m (3′8″ × 5′8″)

NOTES
1 Only five of the 2,045 Caucasian prayer rugs in the research database are assigned to Karagashli. Here, the characteristic Karagashli bracket motifs form two unmistakeable, stepped prayer niches, while in other pieces the motifs are employed primarily as non-directional decorative elements (see *Hali* 78, p. 40, ad. for James F. Connell).
2 The rugs were purchased from the leading London carpet dealer, Vincent Robinson of Wigmore Street. For further discussion see King, 'Caucasian Carpets in the Victoria and Albert Museum: The History of the Collection', *Hali* 3/2, p. 95.
3 Michael Frances and Robert Pinner, 'The Caucasian Collection', *Hali* 3/2, p. 108.
4 An example is a group of prayer rugs from central Anatolia, attributed to Konya or Karapinar, which feature multiple stepped arch-like motifs in a vertical arrangement. See SNY 16 Dec. 1996, lot 54; Dodds and Eiland, *Atlantic Collections*, pls 50 and 52; Brüggeman and Bohmer, *Rugs of the Peasants and Nomads of Anatolia* (Kunst & Antiquitaten, Munich 1983) pl. 46.

PREVIOUS PUBLICATION
Hali 3/2, p. 108., fig.35.

ANALOGIES
Examples of brackets used in the same manner
1 SNY 11 Dec. 1991, lot 22.
2 Skinner 1 Dec. 1991, lot 233.
3 *Hali* 85, p. 121, ad. for Bendas Oriental Carpets.
4 Lefevre 26 May 1978, lot 1.

TECHNICAL ANALYSIS
Warp brown and white wool; z3s, 2 brown threads and one white; 14 threads per inch (55 per dm)
Weft white cotton; z4s; 2 shoots; average 11 knots per inch (average 41 per dm)
Pile wool; symmetrical knot; average 154 knots per sq. inch (average 1128 per sq.dm)
Ends lower; incomplete, ½″ (1.5 cm) plainweave with white cotton weft; evidence of a fringe with bands of off-set knotting; upper: incomplete, 1″ (2 cm) plainweave with white cotton followed by a narrow band with blue wool weft; evidence of a fringe with bands of off-set knotting. Some restoration.
Sides 2 cords overcast with blue wool; white cotton has been used at the lower end
Colours red, yellow, dark green, green, dark blue, blue, dark brown, cream (8)

Victoria & Albert Museum, London
Photograph: V&A Picture Library

---

53   ZEIKHUR
2nd half 19th century
1.14 × 1.43m (3′9″ × 4′8″)

NOTES
1 See also Kirchheim et al., *Orient Stars*, pl. 25.
2 For further discussion of Zeikhur characteristics see Tschebull, 'Zeikhur', *Hali* 62, p. 85.

PREVIOUS PUBLICATION
Lefevre 26 Feb. 1982, lot 2.

Private Collection
Photograph: Lefevre & Partners, London; courtesy The Hali Archive

---

54   ALPAN-KUBA
dated AH 1312 (1895)
0.71 × 1.19m (2′4″ × 3′11″)

NOTES
1 For an embroidered example of this design see Kirchheim et al., *Orient Stars*, pl. 50. For piled examples see Keshishian, *Treasure of the Caucasus*, pl. 30; Spuhler, König and Volkmann, *Old Eastern Carpets*, vol. 1, pl. 71; Tschebull, 'Zeikhur', *Hali* 62, pp. 84–95, pls 16 and 17.
2 Rippon 28 March 1992, lot 62.

PREVIOUS PUBLICATION
Rippon 28 March 1992, lot 62.

Private Collection
Photograph: courtesy Rippon Boswell & Co., Wiesbaden

---

55   DAGHESTAN
1st quarter 19th century
0.97 × 1.38m (3′2″ × 4′6″)

NOTES
1 Meyer-Pünter, *Der Orient-Teppich*, no. 5601.

PREVIOUS PUBLICATION
CNY 11 Sept. 1990, lot 121.

ANALOGIES
1 Erdmann et al., *Kaukasische Teppiche*, pl. 92.
2 Lefevre 20 Feb. 1981, lot 43.
3 SNY 5 March 1982, lot 32 (lacking prayer arch).
4 *Hali* 68, p. 11, ad. for Pietsch.

TECHNICAL ANALYSIS
Warp white and brown wool, mixed together; z3s; 22 threads per inch (88 per dm)
Weft ivory wool; z2s; 12 knots per inch (48 per dm)
Pile wool; symmetrical knot; 132 knots per sq. inch (2112 per sq.dm)
Ends evidence of plainweave with ivory weft and a fringe with bands of off-set knotting
Sides missing
Colours maroon, dark red, yellow, light green, green-blue, indigo, blue, light blue, brown, beige, black, ivory (12)

Kaffel Collection
Photograph: Don Tuttle

---

56   DAGHESTAN
1st quarter 19th century
1.04 × 1.32m (3′5″ × 4′4″)

ANALOGIES
See pl. 55.

TECHNICAL ANALYSIS
Warp white and brown wool, mixed together; z3s; 28 threads per inch (112 per dm)
Weft white wool; z2s; 2 shoots; 11 knots per inch (44 per dm)
Pile symmetrical knot; 154 knots per sq. inch (2464 per sq.dm)
Sides not original

Dixon Collection
Photograph: Don Tuttle

---

57   DAGHESTAN
3rd quarter 19th century
1.12 × 1.32m (3′3″ × 4′4″)

NOTES
1 Also published Bausback 1977, p. 58.

PREVIOUS PUBLICATION
1 SNY 11 Feb. 1984, lot 74.
2 Grogan and Co., Boston 26 Oct. 1996, lot 254.

TECHNICAL ANALYSIS
Warp wool; z2s; 20 threads per inch (80 per dm)
Weft wool; z2s; 9 knots per inch (36 per dm)
Pile wool; symmetrical knot; 90 knots per sq. inch (1440 per sq.dm)
Ends plainweave with ivory weft
Sides ? cord(s) overcast with cotton
Colours cadmium red, gold, yellow, dark green, light green, peacock blue, azure blue, indigo, mid-blue, light blue, peach, walnut, ochre, black, ivory (15)

Kaffel Collection
Photograph: Don Tuttle

---

58   DAGHESTAN
late 19th century
0.81 × 1.80m (2′8″ × 5′11″)

PREVIOUS PUBLICATION
SNY 3 Dec. 1988, lot 89.

ANALOGIES
1 SNY 1 Oct. 1977, lot 9 = Rippon 1 July 1978, lot 99, attributed to Marasali; reviewed in *Hali* 1/2, p. 199, 'Auction Reports'. This is a similar rug to ours, but without the boteh.
2 Hasson, *Caucasian Rugs*, pl. 27; also published *Town and Tribal Carpets* (exhib. cat., Boston, Feb. 1984), fig. 2. From the collection of Vojtech Blau, this is another Marasali, but with boteh.
3 Skinner 11 Sept 1993, lot 114. *Other examples, with vertical bands but otherwise quite different in concept, include*
4 Edelmann 23 Oct. 1982, lot 443 = SNY 12 Feb. 1983, lot 5.
5 Edelmann 14 March 1981, lot 208.
6 Burns, *Caucasus: Traditions in Weaving*, p. 29.

TECHNICAL ANALYSIS
Warp ivory and brown wool, mixed together; z3s; 16–18 threads per inch (64–72 per dm)
Weft ivory wool; z2s; 2 shoots; 11–12 knots per inch (44–48 per dm)
Pile wool; symmetrical knot; average 98 knots per sq. inch (average 1568 per sq.dm)
Ends ⅜″ (1 cm) plainweave with blue cotton weft and a fringe with bands of off-set knotting
Sides 2 cords, each of 2 threads, overcast with light blue
Colours Venetian red, deep indigo, cerulean blue, ivory, maize, ochre, forest green, aubergine, mauve, camel, beaver brown, pale teal, cochineal, black (14)

Private Collection
Photograph: courtesy Sotheby's

---

59   DAGHESTAN
3rd quarter 19th century
0.94 × 1.37m (3′1″ × 4′6″)

NOTES
1 CLO 11 Oct. 1990, lot 33 (see *Hali* 54, p. 169, 'Auction Price Guide').
2 See Herrmann, *SOT* IV, pl. 26.

ANALOGIES
1 Herrmann, *SOT* IV, pl. 26 = CNY 16 March 1982, lot 27 (dated 1879).
2 O'Bannon, *Oriental Rugs from Western Pennsylvania Collections*, pl. 18.
3 Skinner 3 Dec. 1995, lot 165.
4 SNY Arcade 16 Sept. 1987, lot 2.
5 *Hali* 54, p. 59, ad. for Klasic Collection (modern Turkish copy).
6 Skinner 24 April 1993, lot 108.
7 Herrmann, *Kaukasische Teppichkunst*, pl. 18.
8 CLO 11 Oct. 1990, lot 33 (dated 1877).
9 Lefevre 17 Feb. 1984, lot 12.
10 Lefevre 17 Feb. 1984, lot 17 (dated 1880).
11 Edelmann 10 Nov. 1979, lot 60.
12 Rudolf Mangisch, Zurich 6 Nov. 1993, lot 226.
13 Nagel 7 June 1980, lot 264.

TECHNICAL ANALYSIS
Warp white wool; z3s; 18 threads per inch (72 per dm)
Weft white wool; z2s; 2 shoots; 13 knots per inch (52 per dm)
Pile symmetrical knot; 117 knots per sq. inch (1872 per sq.dm)
Sides not original

Dixon Collection
Photograph: Don Tuttle

---

60   DAGHESTAN
c.1800 or earlier
0.71 × 1.35m (2′4″ × 4′5″)

ANALOGIES
1 Lefevre 17 Feb. 1984, lot 14 (gold field).
2 Rippon 14 May 1994, lot 88 (gold field).
3 *Pars: Carpets in the Persian Style* (exhib. cat., Zadeh Gallery, London 1983), fig. 7 = SLO 1 Feb. 1984, lot 150.

TECHNICAL ANALYSIS
Warp ivory wool; 36 threads per inch (144 per dm)
Weft ivory cotton; 10 knots per inch (40 per dm)
Pile symmetrical knot; 180 knots per sq. inch (2880 per sq.dm)

Burns Collection
Photograph: Don Tuttle

61 DAGHESTAN
1st quarter 19th century
0.86 × 1.07m (2′10″ × 3′6″)

NOTES
1 This arch-to-field relationship occurs in other contemporaneous rugs, such as the two Kubas published in Schürmann, *Caucasian Rugs* (pl. 97, eighteenth century) and Bausback 1983 (p. 69, *c*.1800) as well as on later pieces, such as a mid-nineteenth century Shirvan (Lefevre 17 Feb. 1984, lot 12) and a small group of rugs represented by pl. 62.
2 Both *Hali* (no. 52, p. 172, 'Auction Reports',) and *Oriental Rug Review* (10/6, p. 58) concurred regarding the early dating of this rug.

PREVIOUS PUBLICATION
Skinner 10 June 1990, lot 143.

TECHNICAL ANALYSIS
Warp ivory wool; z2s; 20 threads per inch (80 per dm)
Weft ivory wool; z2s; 2 shoots; 13 knots per inch (52 per dm)
Pile wool; symmetrical knot; 130 knots per sq. inch (2080 per sq.dm)
Sides not original
Colours maroon, red, yellow, green, mid-blue, light blue, brown, ivory (8)

Rothberg Collection
Photograph: Don Tuttle

62 DAGHESTAN
late 19th century
1.04 × 1.22m (3′5″ × 4′0″)

PREVIOUS PUBLICATION
SNY 11 Dec. 1991, lot 8.

ANALOGIES
1 Herrmann, *Kaukasische Teppichkunst*, pl. 12.
2 Skinner 1 Dec. 1990, lot 3.
3 Skinner 24 April 1993, lot 100.

TECHNICAL ANALYSIS
Warp ivory and dark brown wool, plied together; z3s; 20–22 threads per inch (80–88 per dm)
Weft white cotton; z3s; 2 shoots; 13–16 knots per inch (52–64 per dm)
Pile wool; symmetrical knot; average 153 knots per sq. inch (average 2448 per sq.dm)
Ends ¾″ (2 cm) plainweave with white cotton weft, ¾″ (2 cm) bands of warp twining and a fringe with bands of off-set knotting
Sides 1 cord of 4 threads oversewn with white

Colours cinnabar, ivory, sapphire, ochre, teal, cinnamon, wheat, celery, port, mahogany, brown (11)

Private Collection
Photograph: courtesy Sotheby's

63 DAGHESTAN
2nd half 19th century
1.14 × 1.44m (3′9″ × 4′9″)

NOTES
1 See Burns, *Caucasus: Traditions in Weaving*.

PREVIOUS PUBLICATION
SLO 7 Jan. 1981, lot 137 = Lefevre 16 Oct. 1981, lot 26.

ANALOGIES
Ettinghausen and Robert, *Bulletin, Allen Memorial Art Museum*, pl. 47. Very close analogy with a golden field.

Private Collection
Photograph: Lefevre & Partners, London; courtesy The Hali Archive

64 DAGHESTAN
mid-19th century
0.55 × 1.20m (1′8″ × 3′4″)

NOTES
1 Jonas Hanway, a British merchant, referred to 'an act of parliament of 1749' allowing the importation of raw silk into Britain (in his *Travels* of 1753). Jean Lefevre, quoting the 1824 writings of Major Keppel, cited the mysterious 'Laurijaumee tribe … near Karabagh … winding raw silk' (Lefevre, *Caucasian Carpets*, p. 37).

Achdjian Collection
Photograph: courtesy Berdj Achidjian, Paris

65 SOUTH CAUCASIAN KILIM
early 19th century
0.88 × 1.62m (2′1″ × 5′4″)

NOTES
1 Landreau and Pickering, *From the Bosporus to Samarkand*, pl. 33; later published as pl. 48 in Cootner, *The Arthur D. Jenkins Collection, vol. 1: Flat-Woven Textiles* (attributed to Shusha by Cootner).
2 Lefevre 25 Nov. 1977, lot 44.
3 Edelmann 30 May 1981, lot 205.
4 Similarities include the blue and red medachyl guard borders and the ewers, combs and scissors in the spandrels. Edelmann's kilim has the more crowded field.
5 SNY 30 Oct. 1982, lot 10.

PREVIOUS PUBLICATION
1 Vok, *Caucasus Persia: Gilim and Other Flatweaves*, pl. 1.
2 Yanni Petsopoulos, *Kilims: Flatwoven Tapestry Rugs* (Rizzoli, New York 1979), fig. 293.
3 Herrmann, *Von Lotto bis Tekke*, pl. 30.
4 Lefevre 25 Nov. 1977, lot 4.

ANALOGIES
Kilims
1 Edelmann 30 May 1981, lot 205 = Herrmann, SOT IV, pl. 18.
2 SNY 30 Oct. 1982, lot 10 = Volkmann, *Old Eastern Carpets*, vol. 2, pl. 46.
3 *Hali* 55, p. 33, ad. for Kelimhaus Johannik.
4 Nagel 26 Sept. 1987, lot 3992 = Nagel 7 June 1988, lot 4086.
5 *Hali* 93, p. 59, 'Fragments'.

Vernehs
6 Herrmann, SOT VII, pl. 17 (mixed technique).
7 Nagel 28 Sept. 1985, lot 4339.
8 SLO 29 April 1981, lot 18.
9 Nagel 14 Nov. 1981, lot 229.

Sumakhs
10 Landreau and Pickering: *From the Bosporus to Samarkand*, p. 33 = Cootner, *Arthur D. Jenkins Collection*, pl. 48.
11 Spuhler, König and Volkmann, *Old Eastern Carpets*, vol. 1, pl. 70.

NOTE Vok also published a prayer kilim that he attributed to northwest Persia / West Azerbaijan (Kurdish work), while Herrmann attributed the piece to west Persia. The geographical origin is sufficiently ambiguous to justify the inclusion of this piece in the list of analogies here. Vok, *Caucasus Persia*, pl. 2 = Herrmann, SOT VII, pl. 51. A comparable piece, attributed to north Persia[?] is published in Volkmann, *Old Eastern Carpets*, vol. 2, pl. 49.

TECHNICAL ANALYSIS
Warp brown wool; z2s
Weft (1) slit-tapestry: 7 colours: red, yellow, 2 blues, brown, black, white wool; z-spun, unplied; (2) brocading: 5 colours: red, yellow, blue, ochre, white; z4s
Ends twisted warp fringe
Sides returned weft over 2 cords

Vok Collection
Photograph: courtesy Ignazio Vok

66 DAGHESTAN
1st half 19th century
0.89 × 1.51m (2′1″ × 5′0″)

NOTES
1 Some exceptions are Bausback 1975, p. 166 ('x' border); SNY 23 Nov. 1985, lot 7 (zigzag chevrons), and Skinner 20 April 1996, lot 173 = SNY 15 Dec. 1994, lot 154 (blue rosette border).
2 CNY 22 Jan 1991, lot 107. A similar example was sold at Skinner 24 April 1993, lot 97.

TECHNICAL ANALYSIS
Warp white wool; z3s
Weft white cotton; 2 shoots
Pile symmetrical knot
Sides not original
Colours dark red, gold, yellow, green, blue, brown, camel, black, white (11)

Klein Collection
Photograph: courtesy Wells C. Klein

67 DAGHESTAN
2nd half 19th century
0.97 × 1.47m (3′2″ × 4′10″)

NOTES
1 Jonas Hanway referred to 'the Lesgees having plundered Shemakee' in his *Travels* of 1753, and Moritz Von Kotzebue wrote in 1819 that 'one could not even leave the great gates of Tiflis wihout falling into the hands of the Lesginers' (*Narrative of a Journey into Persia*). Jean Lefevre, in *Caucasian Carpets from the 17th to the 19th Century* (p. 20) quotes Major Keppel's 1824 narrative: 'Lezguistan … inhabited by the most warlike tribe of Mount Caucasus, and which till within these few years was considered invincible.'
2 A similar rug was assigned to Daghestan by Eberhart Herrmann, SOT II, pl. 39.
3 Another similar rug was assigned to Kuba in *Hali* 1/2, p. 205, 'Rugs on the Market' no. 15 (Benardout and Benardout).
4 Schürmann, *Caucasian Rugs*, pl. 129, with a floral lattice design on a brilliant yellow field; ibid. pl. 30 illustrates another yellow-ground rug with a latticed palmette field topped by a blue parabolic prayer arch. This piece and another very similar example were published as pls 80 and 81 in Erdmann et al., *Kaukasische Teppiche* (pl. 81 also published as pl. 32 in Macey, *Prayer Rugs*). Surprisingly, no similar examples are known to have emerged since.

PREVIOUS PUBLICATION
1 Lefevre 30 Oct. 1980, lot 16
2 *Magazine Antiques*, New York, March 1983, p. 485, ad. for Fred Moheban.

ANALOGIES
1 SNY 22 Sept. 1993, lot 61 (unillustrated).
2 Herrmann, SOT III, pl. 39.
3 *Hali* 1/2, p. 205, 'Rugs on the Market', no. 15.
4 SLO 1 Jan. 1981, lot 33.
5 Skinner 3 Dec. 1993, lot 33.
6 Skinner 15 Feb. 1991, lot 109.
7 Dodds, *Collection of Dr & Mrs Robert A. Fisher*, pl. 38.
8 SNY 5 Oct. 1973, lot 113.
9 Skinner 23 April 1994, lot 47.
10 Straka and Mackie, *Collection of Jerome and Mary Jane Straka*, pl. 107.

Private Collection
Photograph: Lefevre & Partners, London; courtesy The Hali Archive

68   S H I R V A N
2nd half 19th century
1.23 × 1.35m (4′0″ × 4′5″)

N O T E S
1 See Aslanapa, *One Thousand Years of Turkish Carpets*, ill. 46, p. 147.
2 See CNY 9 April 1988, lot 76, Konya runner.
3 See Schürmann, *Caucasian Rugs*, pl. 105.
4 *Oriental Rug Review* 8/5, p. 17.
5 Straka and Mackie, *Collection of Jerome and Mary Jane Straka*, pl. 112.
6 *Trefoil: Guls, Stars and Gardens*, a thematic exhibition organized and produced by California collectors Gil and Hillary Dumas, Jim Dixon and John Webb Hill, held at the Mills College Art Gallery, 28 Jan.–11 March 1990. This rug was exhibited as no. 6 but not pictured in the catalogue of the exhibition, though the technical analysis was published and is reprinted below.

A N A L O G I E S
Crab border
1 CLO 8 July 1982, lot 41.
2 Edelmann 14 March 1981, lot 274.
3 Dodds, *Collection of Dr & Mrs Robert A. Fisher*, pl. 39.
4 Lefevre 5 July 1974, lot 38.
5 *Hali* 48, p. 77, ad. for Giacomo Manoukian Noseda, Como.
6 *Hali* 45, p. 58, 'Gallery', ad. for E. Gulesserian, Madison, Wis.

T E C H N I C A L   A N A L Y S I S
Warp   ivory and brown wool, mixed together; z2s; 23 threads per inch (90 per dm)
Weft   ivory cotton; z2s; 2 shoots; 13 knots per inch (53 per dm)
Pile   wool; symmetrical knot; 149 knots per sq. inch (2385 per sq.dm)
Ends   ⅜″ (1 cm) plainweave with ivory cotton weft followed by 6 rows of braiding
Sides   1 cord of 4 threads oversewn
Colours   dark red, light red, dark yellow, light yellow, dark blue, blue, light blue, rose, brown, ivory (10)

Levi Collection
Photograph: Fabrizio Catalano

69   D A G H E S T A N
2nd half 19th century
1.23 × 1.45m (4′1″ × 4′9″)

N O T E S
See pl. 68.

P R E V I O U S   P U B L I C A T I O N
Eiland 1973, colour pl. XXXI.

A N A L O G I E S
See pl. 68.

T E C H N I C A L   A N A L Y S I S
Warp   brown and ivory wool; z3s, 2 threads of brown and 1 ivory; 22 threads per inch (88 per dm); depressed
Weft   ivory wool; z2s; 2 shoots; 17 knots per inch (68 per dm)
Pile   wool; symmetrical knot; 187 knots per sq. inch (2992 per sq.dm)

Ends   lower: plainweave with wool weft and 3 cord plaited brown and white wool braid; upper: plainweave with cotton weft and 3 cord plaited brown and white wool braid.
Sides   2 cords overcast with white cotton and, in places, white wool

Gil and Hillary Dumas Collection
Photograph: courtesy Hillary Dumas

70   S H I R V A N
dated AH 1233 (1820)
1.23 × 1.42m (4′1″ × 4′8″)

N O T E S
1 This attribution was first proposed by Herrmann (ATT 2, pl. 31). For further discussion see *Hali* 27, p. 96; *Hali* 31, p. 95; Fiske, *Prayer Rugs from Private Collections*, pl. 26.
2 Lefevre 9 Feb. 1979, lot 43.
3 The rug is illustrated and discussed in *Hali* 29, p. 2, 'Letters'.
4 Skinner 4 June 1989, lot 155.
5 *Hali* 29, p. 2, 'Letters'.
6 See *Hali* 2/1, p. 70 for a rug dated 1916 and Kerimov, *The Russian Collections*, p. 27, for a rug dated 1925; see also Douglass and Peters, *The Lost Language*, vol. 2, pl. 18, for an example with the dragon 's' border.

T E C H N I C A L   A N A L Y S I S
Warp   ivory wool; z3s; 18 threads per inch (72 per dm)
Weft   coral wool; z2s; 2 shoots; 8–9 knots per inch (134 per dm)
Pile   wool; symmetrical knot; 76 knots per sq. inch (1224 per sq.dm)
Ends   missing
Sides   not original
Colours   dark red, light red, light yellow, light green, dark blue, light blue, aubergine, black, ivory (9)

Levi Collection
Photograph: Fabrizio Catalano

71   S H I R V A N
2nd half 19th century
1.24 × 1.80m (4′11″ × 5′7″)

N O T E S
1 Schürmann, *Caucasian Rugs*, pl. 71.
2 Other examples are published in Eiland 1973, pl. XXVIII (colour) = Eiland 1981, pl. 25a (black & white); and *Hali* 61, p. 84, ad. for Abraham Moheban.
3 See Schürmann, *Teppiche aus dem Orient*, p. 79 and Lefevre 26 Feb 1982, lot 3.
4 For examples see *Tapetes Orientais*, Colecção Calouste Gulbenkian (exhib. pamphlet, Museu Calouste Gulbenkian, Lisbon 1985), pl. 5 (Mosul); SNY 13 Oct. 1979, lot 8 (Malayer); and Nagel 6 May 1978, lot 80 (Feraghan).

P R E V I O U S   P U B L I C A T I O N
Herrmann, SOT II, plate 38.

Herrmann Collection
Photograph: courtesy Eberhart Herrmann

72   S H I R V A N
2nd half 19th century
0.96 × 1.32m (3′2″ × 4′4″)

N O T E S
1 A Shirvan of that configuration is illustrated in Macey, *Oriental Prayer Rugs*, pl. 29.

P R E V I O U S   P U B L I C A T I O N
Rippon 14 May 1994, lot 101.

Private Collection
Photograph: courtesy Rippon Boswell & Co., Wiesbaden

73   S H I R V A N
last quarter 19th century
0.89 × 1.31m (2′11″ × 4′6″)

N O T E S
1 A typical example was published as pl. XXXIII in Ettinghausen et al., *Prayer Rugs*.
2 See Bausback 1980, p. 45; Rippon 6 Nov. 1976, lot 169.
3 See pl. 72 above; Schürmann, *Caucasian Rugs*, pl. 74; Macey, *Oriental Prayer Rugs*, pl. 29.

A N A L O G I E S
Analogies include
1 Lefevre 26 Nov. 1976, lot 9.
2 *Hali* 5/3, 'Gallery', ad. for Peter Pap = O'Bannon, *Oriental Rugs, The Collector's Guide*, p. 33.
3 Gardiner, *Oriental Rugs from Canadian Collections*, pl. 37.
4 Skinner 8 April 1995, lot 109.
5 Black, *Macmillan Atlas*, p. 115.
6 *Hali* 54, p. 54, ad. for Samarkand Galleries.
7 *Weltkunst*, Munich, 15 July 1991, p. 2,016, ad. for Bernard Voloder.
8 SLO 24 May 1982, lot 19.
9 Rippon 13 Nov. 1993, lot 6.
10 Rippon (Basel) 2 Oct. 1976, lot 78.

P R E V I O U S   P U B L I C A T I O N
1 *Oriental Rug Review* 3/9, p. 32, ad. for Transcaspia.
2 *Hali* 6/1, p. 11, ad. for Transcaspia.
3 SNY 13 Sept. 1989, lot 106.

Private Collection
Photograph: courtesy Sotheby's

74   S H I R V A N
2nd half 19th century
1.0 × 1.41m (3′3″ × 4′7″)

N O T E S
1 Published in SLO 1 June 1981, lot 64; Edelmann 12 Dec. 1981, lot 26; Christie's East 22 May 1984, lot 28; *Hali* 6/4, p. 6, 'Gallery', ad. for Bausback. Herrmann published a yellow-ground Kuba prayer rug with an ivory floral border in SOT V, pl. 25, and referred to a connection between this field pattern and a group of related eighteenth-century Caucasian floral carpets (see Yetkin, *Early Caucasian Carpets in Turkey*, vol. 1, pls 40, 53, 58, 61). Two other examples, very similar to each other, have pale yellow grounds and unusual geometric prayer arches of inverted 'v' shapes. The first of these was offered at CLO on 9 July 1981, lot 36; the second, formerly from the Rudnick Collection, was sold at Grogan and Co., Boston on 23 June 1993, lot 3074.

P R E V I O U S   P U B L I C A T I O N
1 Rippon 30 May 1992, lot 54.
2 *Hali* 53, p. 186, ad. for George Gilmore.

A N A L O G I E S
1 Nagel 23 June 1993, lot 3074. (A white-ground Shirvan example, very similar to ours.)

Secular Kuba rugs
2 Volkmann, *Old Eastern Carpets*, vol. 2, pl. 64 = Herrmann, *Von Lotto Bis Tekke*, pl. 37 = Kirchheim et al., *Orient Stars*, pl. 27 = Purdon et al., *Shirvan and Related Weavings from the North Caucasus*, pl. 5.
3 *Hali* 1/3, p. 2, ad. for Galerie Sailer = Butterweck et al., *Austrian Collections*, pl. 58.
4 Bennett, *Caucasian*, pl. 328 = Nagel 18 Nov. 1978, lot 467, colour pl. 213.
5 Herrmann, ATT 4, pl. 46 = Skinner 3 Nov. 1983, lot 76 = *Hali* 46, p. 70, 'Gallery', ad. for George Gilmore = Rippon 28 March 1992, lot 146 = *Hali* 63, p. 134, 'Auction Price Guide'.
6 Herrmann, SOT IX, pl. 34.
7 *Hali* 63, p. 67, ad. for Uwe Werner (with dragon 's' border).
8 Rippon 15 May 1993, lot 60 (with dragon 's' border).

Private Collection
Photograph: courtesy Rippon Boswell & Co., Wiesbaden

75   S H I R V A N
2nd half 19th century
1.14 × 1.22m (3′9″ × 4′0″)

N O T E S
1 See L. Beresneva, *The Decorative and Applied Art of Turkmenia*, (Aurora Art Publishers, Leningrad 1976), pl. 105.
2 Rippon 30 May 1992, lot 141.
3 *Oriental Rug Review* 10/1, p. 26, ill. 1 (Joseph Galton Collection).
4 Straka and Mackie, *Collection of Jerome and Mary Jane Straka*, pl. 112, gift to Textile Museum 1977 (no. 36.51).

TECHNICAL ANALYSIS

Warp brown and white wool plied together
Weft white wool; 2 shoots
Pile wool; symmetrical knot; 68 knots per sq. inch (1088 per sq.dm)
Ends missing
Sides overcast or oversewn with white wool
Colours dark yellow, light yellow, yellow-green, dark turquoise, indigo, mid-blue, dark brown, mid-brown, beige, white (10)

Winter Collection
Photograph: Vincenzo Pietropaolo

76   SHIRVAN
c.1875
0.96 × 1.90m (3′2″ × 6′3″)

NOTES

1 Vok, *Caucasus Persia*; a spectacular example is illustrated in pl. 11.
2 Yanni Petsopoulos, *Kilims: Flatwoven Tapestry Rugs* (Rizzoli, New York 1979). The book illustrates 13 examples (pls 279–291), with pls 281, 285, 286, 287 and 288 having borders similar to our rug.

PREVIOUS PUBLICATION

1 *Hali* 53, p. 65, ad. for Krausse Teppichantiquitaten (published next to a page depicting a Kuba kilim of similar design).
2 *Frühe Teppichkunst*, exhib. cat., Hans-Jürgen Krausse, Munich 1990, no. 8.
3 SLO 16 April 1985, lot 736 (assigned to Kuba).

ANALOGIES

Secular piled analogies include
1 *Hali* 2/4, p. 26, ad. for Templeton, Toronto = SNY 31 Oct. 1980, lot 218.
2 Lefevre 14 April 1978, lot 17.
3 Bennett, *Caucasian*, pl. 248.
4 Gardiner, *Oriental Rugs from Canadian Collections*, pl. 22.
5 Sotheby's, Geneva 15 May 1984, lot 123.
6 *A Rich Inheritance*, Josyln Art Museum (Omaha, Nebraska 1974), p. 47 = Denny, *Oriental Rugs*, pl. 43.
7 Lefevre 30 Nov. 1979, lot 38 (a large and very beautiful example with wonderful colours).
8 *Hali* 4/1 p. 64, ad. for Ewaldsen, Medford, Oregon.

Private Collection
Photograph: courtesy Hans-Jürgen Krausse, Munich

77   SHIRVAN
c.1865
1.14 × 1.63m (3′9″ × 5′4″)

PREVIOUS PUBLICATION

Skinner 29 Nov. 1984, lot 76 = Eiland, *Pacific Collections*, pl. 179.

ANALOGIES

1 Herrmann, *SOT* V, pl. 23 = *Hali* 5/4, pp. 506, 508 (fig. 3) = SNY 30 Oct. 1982, lot 27. (Dotted ivory field with burnt yellow 'bird' border. Dated AH 1252 / 1836.)

2 Gombos, *Régi Keleti Imaszönyegek*, pl. 107; exhibited at Damjanich Janos Museum, Szolnok, 1 April–28 May 1978 and Iparmüveszeti Museum, Budapest, 28 June–30 Oct. 1978. Exhibition reviewed and rug published in *Hali* 1/4, pp. 368–70, fig. 7. (Probably the best-known analogous example, and very similar to Herrmann's rug discussed above.)
3 *Hali* 41, p. 22, ad. for Mischioff, Zurich. (A blue-ground example dated *c*.1870, with an ivory and blue border very similar to our example.)
4 Nagel 23 June 1993, lot 3100.
5 Edelmann 15 Feb. 1984, lot 220; offered by Peter Pap in *Hali* 5/1, p. 81, 'Rugs on the Market', no. 15.
6 Skinner 1 Dec. 1990, lot 112.

There are many other latchhook diamond examples but they either have extremely crowded designs (of more recent date) or have latticed fields, and are therefore not considered here.

TECHNICAL ANALYSIS

Warp dark and light brown wool; z2s; 20 threads per inch (80 per dm)
Weft white cotton; z3s; 2 shoots; 11 knots per inch (44 per dm)
Pile wool; symmetrical knot; 110 knots per sq. inch (1760 per sq.dm)
Sides 2 cords overcast with white cotton
Colours dark brick red, dark yellow, green, dark blue, light blue, brown-black, ivory (7)

Kaffel Collection
Photograph: Dennis Anderson

78   SHIRVAN
c.1875
1.12 × 1.55m (3′8″ × 5′1″)

NOTES

1 Bonham's, London 22 July 1993, lot 84. *Hali*, describing the main border of this rug in issue 71, p. 156 ('Auction Price Guide'), wrote: 'Although we are used to seeing variations of a "Kufic" design in main borders of Caucasian prayer rugs, the version here, which might be described as a reprise of the oldest version found on Anatolian rugs, the Kufic "box" border, is very unusual.'

ANALOGIES

1 Skinner 24 May 1984, lot 29.
2 Rippon 15 Nov. 1980, lot 380.
3 Keshishian, *Treasure of the Caucasus*, pl. 24.
4 Herrmann, *SOT* VIII, pl. 4 (assigned to Kuba).
5 SLO 7 June 1995, lot 3 (Toms Collection).
6 Rudolf Mangisch, Zurich 6 Nov. 1993, lot 221.
7 Bausback 1973, p. 115.
8 PB 84 13 June 1979, lot 51.
9 Nagel 14 Nov. 1981, lot 260.
10 SLO 16 April 1986, lot 500.
11 Bonham's, London 22 July 1993, lot 84.

TECHNICAL ANALYSIS

Warp ivory ?; z2s; 24 threads per inch (96 per dm)
Weft ivory ?; z2s; 10 knots per inch (40 per dm)
Pile wool; symmetrical knot; 120 knots per sq. inch (1920 per sq.dm)
Ends plainweave with ivory weft and a red band; evidence of a knotted fringe
Sides 2 cords
Colours dark red, red, yellow, dark green, light green, indigo, mid-blue, light blue, rose, ecru, black, ivory (12)

Kaffel Collection
Photograph: Don Tuttle

79   SHIRVAN
late 19th century
1.02 × 1.65m (3′4″ × 5′5″)

PREVIOUS PUBLICATION

Hali 2/1, p. 26, ad. for J.P.J. Homer.

ANALOGIES

Denny, *Looms of Splendor: Oriental Rugs from Columbus Collections*, pl. 34 (an example with a similar field of 'x' forms and a dragon border).

TECHNICAL ANALYSIS

Warp ivory and brown wool; z2s; 18 threads per inch (72 per dm)
Weft white wool; z2s; 2 shoots; 11 knots per inch (44 per dm)
Pile wool; symmetrical knot; 99 knots per sq. inch (1584 per sq.dm)
Ends missing
Sides 2 cords overcast with white wool
Colours maroon, red, yellow, green, light green, dark blue, mid-blue, light blue, black, ivory (10)

Kaffel Collection
Photograph: Don Tuttle

80   SHIRVAN
early 19th century
1.17 × 1.32m (3′10″ × 4′4″)

ANALOGIES

Lefevre 6 Feb. 1976, lot 3, attributed to Shirvan, early nineteenth century. (A very close parallel to this rug.) While similar later rugs exist (see Bennett, *Caucasian*, pl. 327; Rippon 18 Nov. 1989, lot 74; Skinner 10 June 1990, lot 88), there are no known early analogies.

TECHNICAL ANALYSIS

Warp wool; z3s; 28 threads per inch (112 per dm)
Weft white wool; z2s; 2 shoots; 11 knots per inch (44 per dm)
Pile symmetrical knot; 154 knots per sq. inch (2464 per sq.dm)
Ends incomplete, plainweave with white cotton weft
Sides 2 cords, each of 2 threads, overcast with white cotton

Dixon Collection
Photograph: Don Tuttle

81   SHIRVAN
c.1860
0.81 × 1.68m (2′8″ × 5′6″)

NOTES

1 Bennett, *Caucasian*, p. 187, pls 226, 225.
2 See *Hali* 75, p. 59.

ANALOGIES

With dragon borders unless otherwise indicated
1 Herrmann, ATT 2, pl. 28 = SNY 12 Sept. 1989, lot 137.
2 CNY 11 Sept. 1990, lot 92.
3 Grogan and Co., Boston 25 Sept. 1990, lot 533.
4 *Hali* 39, p. 76, 'Gallery', ad. for Maqam, Dennis Dodds.
5 Skinner 14 Feb. 1992, lot 9.
6 Rippon 14 Nov. 1992, lot 68.
7 Rippon 11 May 1996, lot 15.
8 Schürmann, *Caucasian Rugs*, pl. 125 ('x' border).
9 Bausback 1977, p. 85 (latchhook border).
10 Nagel 19 Nov. 1994, lot 1121 (latchhook border).
11 Skinner 23 April 1995, lot 68 (leaf-and-calyx border).
12 Robert C. Eldred, East Dennis, MA, *The Andrew Rollins Dole Collection*, vol. IV, 13 June 1978, lot 58 (bird border).
13 Wright, *Rugs and Flatweaves of the Transcaucasus*, pl. 36 (bird border).
14 SNY 1 Dec. 1985, lot 5 (linked hook border).
15 Bennett, *Caucasian*, pl. 225.

TECHNICAL ANALYSIS

Warp white wool; z2s; 18 threads per inch (72 per dm)
Weft white wool; between 2 and 4 shoots; 9 knots per inch (36 per dm)
Pile wool and camel hair; symmetrical knot; 81 knots per sq. inch (1296 per sq.dm)
Colours madder red, cochineal red, yellow, green, dark blue, light blue, dark brown, light brown, undyed camel, white (10)

Klein Collection
Photograph: courtesy Wells C. Klein

82   SHIRVAN
1st quarter 19th century
0.96 × 1.35m (3′2″ × 4′5″)

NOTES

1 Pl. 41 in Ittig, *Woven Dreams: Oriental Carpets from the Collection of the Montreal Museum of Fine Arts*; pl. 2 in Herrmann, *Kaukasische Teppichkunst*.

ANALOGIES

In addition to the two rugs cited above, the following white-lattice examples are known
1 Lefevre 26 Nov. 1976, lot 11.
2 Lefevre 1 Oct. 1982, lot 37 = Bausback 1983, p. 67.
3 Bausback 1982, p. 65.
4 *Hali* 2/2, p. 163.
5 Skinner 31 May 1987, lot 110.
6 Rippon 14 Nov. 1987, lot 51.

TECHNICAL ANALYSIS

Warp white wool; z4s; 28 threads per inch (112 per dm)

Weft white cotton; z2s; 3, sometimes 4, shoots; 12 knots per inch (48 per dm)

Pile symmetrical knot; 168 knots per sq. inch (2688 per sq.dm)

Ends missing

Sides missing

Dixon Collection
Photograph: Don Tuttle

---
83   SHIRVAN
dated AH 1310 (1892)
1.19 × 1.27m (3′11″ × 4′2″)

PREVIOUS PUBLICATION
Skinner 20 Nov. 1985, lot 109 (assigned to Konaghend).

TECHNICAL ANALYSIS

Warp ivory and brown wool, mixed together; z2s; 18 threads per inch (72 per dm)

Weft ivory wool; ?-spun, unplied; 10 knots per inch (40 per dm)

Pile symmetrical knot; 90 knots per sq. inch (1440 per sq.dm)

Sides not original

Colours dark red, yellow, light green, blue-green, indigo, mid-blue, light blue, salmon, dark brown, ivory (10)

Kaffel Collection
Photograph: Don Tuttle

---
84   SHIRVAN
2nd half 19th century
1.07 × 1.25m (3′6″ × 4′1″)

NOTES
1   SNY 11 Dec. 1991, lot 27.
2   *Hali* 61, p. 163, 'Auction Price Guide'.
3   SLO 28 April 1981, lot 198.

PREVIOUS PUBLICATION
1   SNY 11 Dec. 1991, lot 27.
2   *Hali* 68, p. 57, ad. for Robert Müller.

ANALOGIES
1   CLO 8 July 1982, lot 47 = Herrmann, *Kaukasische Teppichkunst*, pl. 27. (An ivory-ground Marasali with a very similar boteh field but with a typical yellow and red bird border.)
2   Rippon 30 May 1992, lot 161. (With dragon 's' border.)

TECHNICAL ANALYSIS

Warp ivory wool; z3s; 18–20 threads per inch (72–80 per dm)

Weft white cotton; z2s; 2 shoots; 13–17 knots per inch (52–68 per dm)

Pile wool; symmetrical knot; average 144 knots per sq. inch (average 2296 per sq.dm)

Ends ½″ (1 cm) plainweave with white cotton weft, ¾″ (2 cm) braiding and a remains of a knotted fringe

Sides 2 cords, each of 2 threads, overcast with white cotton

Colours cardamom, midnight blue, pale to deep azure, tea rose, cayenne, caramel, cinnamon, pale to deep chocolate, saddle brown, khaki, black, walnut (12)

Private Collection
Photograph: courtesy Sotheby's

---
85   SHIRVAN AKSTAFA
2nd half 19th century
0.94 × 1.85m (3′1″ × 6′1″)

NOTES
1   See Erdmann et al., *Kaukasische Teppiche*, pl. 77; SNY 10 Dec. 1992, lot 89.
2   A related white-ground boteh rug with a square arch and a variant of a bird border was published in *Hali* 2/4, p.67 (stolen from Galerie Ostler, Munich, in 1979.)

TECHNICAL ANALYSIS

Warp ivory wool; z3s; 18 threads per inch (72 per dm)

Weft white cotton; 10 knots per inch (40 per dm)

Pile symmetrical knot; 90 knots per sq. inch (1440 per sq.dm)

Ends missing

Sides 2 cords overcast with blue cotton

Colours brick red, cherry red, light yellow, indigo, mid-blue, sky blue, salmon, brown-black, beige, ivory (10)

Mull Collection
Photograph: Don Tuttle

---
86   AKSTAFA
3rd quarter 19th century
0.91 × 1.68m (3′0″ × 5′6″)

NOTES
1   Hawley, *Oriental Rugs Antique and Modern*, p. 291.
2   For an example of 'latchhook and dice' borders see Rippon, London 4 Dec. 1976, lot 59; for a border with latchhooked lozenges see Lefevre 31 Oct. 1980, lot 17 and 5 Oct. 1979, lot 32.

ANALOGIES
1   SNY 9 March 1994, lot 48.
2   Lefevre 31 Oct. 1980, lot 17 = Rippon 15 Nov. 1986, lot 62.
3   Lefevre 5 Oct. 1979, lot 32.
4   SLO 12 Oct 1988, lot 447.
5   Douglass, *The Lost Language,* vol. 2, pl. 46.
6   Nagel 5 Nov. 1983, lot 290.
7   SNY 31 May 1986, lot 33.

TECHNICAL ANALYSIS

Warp white wool; z3s; 22 threads per inch (88 per dm)

Weft white cotton; z2s; 2 shoots; 8 knots per inch (32 per dm)

Pile symmetrical knot; 88 knots per sq. inch (1408 per sq.dm)

Ends missing

Sides 2 cords overcast with blue cotton

Dixon Collection
Photograph: Don Tuttle

---
87   AKSTAFA
1st half 19th century
1.01 × 1.61m (3′4″ × 5′3″)

NOTES
1   Herrmann, *SOT* X, pl. 32 = *Hali* 3, p. 32, ad. for Thornborough Galleries.
2   The arch has a triangular cartouche enclosing the date beneath it. An example related to Herrmann's, also with a striped field and boteh, was offered at Skinner's, 5 Dec. 1988, lot 155.

PREVIOUS PUBLICATION
Rippon 15 Nov. 1986, lot 49.

Private Collection
Photograph: courtesy Rippon Boswell & Co., Wiesbaden

---
88   AKSTAFA
3rd quarter 19th century
0.84 × 1.40m (2′9″ × 4′7″)

NOTES
1   Rippon 28 March 1992, lot 140. This example has a lattice field.
2   Examples include one with a diagonally striped field at SLO 6 Oct. 1979, lot 115 and a similar unillustrated example at CNY 15 Dec. 1995, lot 140.

ANALOGIES
Analogies with linked-medallion fields
1   Bennett, *Caucasian*, pl. 221.
2   SNY 30 Oct. 1982, lot 17.
3   SLO 28 April 1982, lot 151.
4   *Hali* 5/2. p. 167, ad. for Kunsthaus Pollman, Munich.
5   Nagel 2 Oct. 1982, lot 4535.
6   *Oriental Rug Review* 10/6, p. 9, ad. for John Murray, Williamsburg, VA.
7   Denny and Walker, *The Markarian Album*, pl. 52.
8   SNY 9 March 1994, lot 73.

TECHNICAL ANALYSIS

Warp ivory wool; z2s; 18 threads per inch (72 per dm)

Weft ivory and light brown wool; z2s; 2 shoots; 12 knots per inch (48 per dm)

Pile wool; symmetrical knot; 108 knots per sq. inch (1728 per sq.dm)

Sides 2 cords, each of 2 threads, overcast with light blue cotton

Colours mid-red, light red, saffron, yellow, olive green, blue-green, indigo, mid-blue, purple (9)

Mazzie Collection
Photograph: Don Tuttle

---
89   MARASALI
early 19th century
1.06 × 1.38m (3′6″ × 4′6″)

NOTES
1   See James Opie, *Tribal Rugs of Southern Persia* (James Opie Oriental Rugs, Portland, Oregon 1981), p. 20.
2   David R. Milberg, 'A History for the Buta', *Oriental Rug Review* 9/6, pp. 24–26.

---
3   Kerimov, in *Azerbaijanski Kovjer*, *vol. 1*, illustrates 30 variants of the boteh in Azerbaijan alone. David Milberg has suggested that the presence of boteh in a rug signifies that it was woven in a region influenced by Persia. (The boteh motif is virtually non-existent in Turkish weavings.)

ANALOGIES
See pl. 90.

Achdjian Collection
Photograph: Berdj Achdjian, Paris

---
90   MARASALI
early 19th century
1.06 × 1.40m (3′5½″ × 4′7″)

NOTES
1   Dixon's description of this rug is quoted in Elizabeth Callison, 'Unorthodox Conservation of a Marasali Prayer Carpet', in *Oriental Rug Review* 6/11, p. 4.

PREVIOUS PUBLICATION
See note 1.

ANALOGIES
Other black Marasalis in the 'curved arch' group include
1   Pl. 89 above.
2   Pl. 91 below.
3   The 'Ballard' rug, dated 1808/9, assigned to Baku by Dimand in *Peasant and Nomad Rugs of Asia*, p. 59 = Dimand and Mailey, *Oriental Rugs in the Metropolitan Museum of Art*, p. 71, pl. 237.
4   The 'Perez' rug, ex-collection Shell Co., London and Professor Giuliani, *Hali* 26, p. 2/3, ad. for Davide Halevim = Michele Campana, *Il tappeto orientale* (Libre Artistici Alfiere, Milan 1962), pl. XXVI = Reed, *Oriental Rugs and Carpets*, p. 33 = Herrmann, *ATT* 4, pl. 48.
5   The 'Kalmann' rug, exhibited Château Ramezay, Montreal, *Hali* 6/3, p. 344 = *Oriental Rug Review* 10/5, p. 48 = Rippon 15 May 1993, lot 159.
6   Butterweck et al., *Austrian Collections*, pl. 56.

TECHNICAL ANALYSIS

Warp white wool; z3s; 16 threads per inch (64 per dm)

Weft white wool; z2s; 2 shoots; 16 knots per inch (64 per dm)

Pile symmetrical knot; 128 knots per sq. inch (2048 per sq.dm)

Ends incomplete, plainweave with white cotton weft and knotted fringe

Sides 2 cords, each of 2 threads, overcast with white cotton

Dixon Collection
Photograph: Don Tuttle

---

91 MARASALI
early 19th century
0.89 × 1.14m (2′11″ × 3′9″)

NOTES
1 *Oriental Rug Review* 6/11, p. 23, 'Auction Review'.
2 Eiland, *Pacific Collections*, p. 183.
3 Ettinghausen et al., *Prayer Rugs*, p. 94.
4 They had first seen it at an exhibition in Krakow in 1934, published as no. 38, ill. 41 in *Katalog Wystawy Kobiercow Mahometanskich Ceramiki Azjatyckiej I Europejkiej*, identified as a Persian prayer rug, 17th/18th century. The Strakas tried to buy it from the owner, Dr Kazimierz Iwanicki, but he would not sell. They were finally were able to acquire it three years later.
5 The letter was dated 13 February 1987. I quote in part: 'I suppose it is unusual to want to keep in touch with a rug but this isn't just any rug; it has been a special part of our family … We saw "our" rug (yours and ours) at an exhibition in Krakow and wanted to buy it. It belonged to a veterinary surgeon with the Polish Cavalry. He did not want to sell. Three years later we had a postcard [saying] "You may have your rug." Since then it has been our prized possession.'

PREVIOUS PUBLICATION
The rug has been published and referenced numerous times. This is a summary list.
1 *Katalog Wystawy Kobiercow Mahometanskich Ceramiki Azjatyckiej I Europejkiej* (Krakow 1934), cat. 38, ill. 41.
2 *Fortune* magazine, May 1968, p. 65.
3 Ettinghausen et al., *Prayer Rugs*, pl. xxix.
4 Straka and Mackie, *The Oriental Rug Collection of Jerome and Mary Jane Straka*, 1978, cover and pl. 102.
5 *Sotheby's Newsletter*, Dec. 1986, p. 5.
6 SNY 13 Dec. 1986, lot 49.
7 *Sotheby's Art at Auction 1986–87*, p. 420.
8 *Hali* 34, p. 84, 'Auction Price Guide'.
9 *Oriental Rug Review* 6/11, p. 23, 'Auction Review'.
10 Eiland, *Pacific Collections*, pl. 181a.
11 Frank Ames, *The Kashmir Shawl* (Antique Collectors' Club, Woodbridge, Suffolk 1986), pl. 220.

TECHNICAL ANALYSIS
Warp ivory wool; z4s; 25 threads per inch (100 per dm)
Weft wool; 2 shoots; 23 knots per inch (92 per dm)
Pile wool; symmetrical knot; 287 knots per sq. inch (4600 per sq.dm)
Ends not original
Sides not original
Colours maroon, brown-red, mustard, blue-green, dark blue, mid-blue, brown, green-tan, ivory (9)

Kaffel Collection
Photograph: Don Tuttle

---

92 MARASALI
3rd quarter 19th century
1.12 × 1.52m (3′8″ × 5′0″)

NOTES
1 See Buchanan et al., *Antique Rugs from the Caucasus*, pl. 12; Sotheby's Geneva 13 Nov 1984, lot 76; SLO 28 April 1993, lot 28.

PREVIOUS PUBLICATION
1 SLO 15 June 1983, lot 76.
2 Eiland, *Pacific Collections*, pl. 181.

ANALOGIES
1 Skinner 9 Dec. 1995, lot 91.
2 SLO 28 April 1993, lot 23.
3 Bausback 1978, p. 239.
4 Edelmann 12 April 1979, lot 5.
5 Bausback 1987/88, p. 84.
6 CLO 16 Oct. 1997, lot 43.

TECHNICAL ANALYSIS
Warp wool; z3s; 22 threads per inch (88 per dm)
Weft cotton; z3s; 10 knots per inch (40 per dm)
Pile symmetrical knot; 110 knots per sq. inch (1760 per sq.dm)
Ends plainweave, with a fringe of warp loops at the lower end
Sides overcast or oversewn with white cotton
Colours dark red, brick red, yellow, light green, dark blue, mid-blue, light blue, dark violet, peach, brown-black, ivory (11)

Kaffel Collection
Photograph: Dennis Anderson

---

93 MARASALI
1st quarter 19th century
0.86 × 1.12m (2′10″ × 3′8″)

NOTES
1 Lefevre 25 May 1984, lot 32. Published in Herrmann, *SOT* VI, pl. 40.
2 The history of these rugs is more fully explored in an article by Steven Price in *Oriental Rug Review* 15/1, pp. 36–7.
3 Offered by Lefevre in its pre-restored condition (cut and reduced in length and width with the remaining sections sewn together), it was assigned to Daghestan, dated AH 1232 (1817) and sold for little money in 1979 (Lefevre, 10 May 1979, lot 30); after which it was restored. It was then purchased by a leading London dealer who made the decision to remove the restored portions and mount the rug as we now see it. Although the restoration was excellent, it could not compare with the original portions of the piece.

PREVIOUS PUBLICATION
1 Burns, *Caucasus: Traditions in Weaving*, pl. 8.
2 Lefevre 10 May 1979, lot 30.

TECHNICAL ANALYSIS
Warp ivory wool; z2s; 42 threads per inch (168 per dm)
Weft ivory silk; 25 knots per inch (100 per dm)
Pile symmetrical knot; 525 knots per sq. inch (8400 per sq.dm)

Burns Collection
Photograph: Don Tuttle

---

94 MARASALI
early 19th century
1.02 × 1.30m (3′4″ × 4′3″)

NOTES
1 Bennett, *Caucasian*, p. 194 lists the knot count of the 'Straka' Marasali (pl. 89 above) at 287.5 psi, and that of the 'Ballard' rug at 210 psi. Bausback in his 1978 catalogue illustrates a rug with 258 knots psi.
2 Burns, *Caucasus: Traditions in Weaving*, pl. 7 = SNY 31 May 1986, lot 7.
3 Robert C. Eldred, East Dennis, MA, 24 June 1976, lot 38.
4 Hermann, *SOT* IX, pl. 37.

TECHNICAL ANALYSIS
Warp white wool; z3s; 32 threads per inch (128 per dm)
Weft white cotton; z2s; 2 shoots; 13 knots per inch (52 per dm)
Pile symmetrical knot; 208 knots per sq. inch (3328 per sq.dm)
Ends not original
Sides not original
Colours magenta, wine, red, pearl, yellow (5)

Dixon Collection
Photograph: Don Tuttle

---

95 MARASALI
dated AH 1274 (1858)
0.92 × 1.20m (3′0″ × 3′11″)

NOTES
1 The exhibition was held from 17 Nov. 1962 to 16 Dec. 1962. The rug is illustrated as pl. 108 in the exhibition catalogue (Erdmann et al., *Kaukasische Teppiche*).

PREVIOUS PUBLICATION
1 Erdmann et al., *Kaukasische Teppiche*, pl. 108.
2 Rippon 12 Nov. 1994, lot 159.

TECHNICAL ANALYSIS
Warp white wool; z3s; 42 threads per inch (168 per dm)
Weft white cotton; z2s; 2 shoots; 12–13 knots per inch (51 per dm)
Pile wool; symmetrical knot; 273 knots per sq. inch (4284 per sq.dm)
Ends plainweave with white cotton weft
Sides 2 cords overcast with white cotton

Private Collection
Photograph: courtesy Rippon Boswell & Co., Wiesbaden

---

96 MARASALI
c.1800
1.24 × 1.45m (4′1″ × 4′9″)

NOTES
1 *Hali* 5/4, p. 27, ad. for Robert Müller.
2 See also *Hali* 3/1, pl. 13, ad. for Fred Moheban, and Rippon 16 Nov. 199, lot 73 (lacking a prayer arch).
3 Peter Bausback (Bausback 1982) refers to one published in Bennett, *Rugs and Carpets of the World*, p. 155. Other similar examples include Herrmann, *Asiatische Teppich und Textilekunst* 4, pl. 50; Curatola, *The Simon & Schuster Book of Oriental Carpets*, p.173; *Hali* 73, ad. for Kelimhaus Johannik. A wonderful, early Shirvan example with similar horses on a golden field, without a prayer arch, was published in Bausback 1982, pp. 46–7.

PREVIOUS PUBLICATION
1 Bausback 1982, pp. 54–5.
2 Skinner 25 June 1982, lot 498.
3 *Hali* 5/1, p. 71, 'Auction Price Guide'.

TECHNICAL ANALYSIS
Warp beige cotton; 20 threads per inch (80 per dm)
Weft beige cotton; 12–13 knots per inch (50 per dm)
Pile wool; symmetrical knot; 120–125 knots per sq. inch (2000 per sq.dm)
Ends not original
Sides 2 cords overcast with white wool

Bausback Collection, Mannheim
Photograph: courtesy Peter Bausback

---

97 MARASALI
mid-19th century
1.17 × 1.52m (3′10″ × 5′0″)

NOTES
1 *Oriental Rug Review* 2/1, p. 21, ad. for Nicky Eltz.
2 Skinner 2 Dec. 1989, lot 220.
3 Volkmann, *Old Eastern Carpets*, vol. 2, pl. 66.

ANALOGIES
In addition to the analogies cited in notes 1–3 above, the following have similar borders:
1 *Hali* 3/2, p. 68, ad. for Daniele Sevi.
2 Skinner 31 May 1987, lot 123.
3 Nagel 9 Dec. 1982, lot 3087.
4 Bausback 1983, p. 73.
5 Buchanan, *Antique Rugs from the Caucasus*, pl. 11.
6 Skinner 8 Jan. 1982, lot 3.
7 Sotheby's Geneva 29 Nov. 1982, lot 42.
8 SLO 11 March 1982, lot 31.

TECHNICAL ANALYSIS
Warp light and dark undyed cotton and brown wool, mixed together; z-spun, unplied; 22 threads per inch (88 per dm)
Weft white cotton; z2s; 2 shoots; 8 knots per inch (32 per dm)
Pile symmetrical knot; 88 knots per sq. inch (1408 per sq.dm)

Dixon Collection
Photograph: Don Tuttle

ABRASH Variations in colour tonality, generally in the ground colour of the field, which result from the weaver's use of wool dyed in small batches with minor differences in colour depth.

AKSTAFA BIRD A peacock with a large tail of geometric diagonal lines, depicted as a subsidiary motif on a group of Shirvan rugs, usually of runner format, called Akstafa.

ALPAN KUBA An 'endless repeat' design in the field of certain rugs from the Kuba region, which consists of star-like medallions surrounded by elongated, crab-like hexagons.

AVSHAN PATTERN An all-over floral design of right-angled calyxes interspersed with rosettes and other floral forms. This pattern, used in eastern Caucasian rugs in the eighteenth and nineteenth centuries, developed from earlier Persian and Indian sources.

BOTEH (BUTA) 'Cluster of leaves' in Farsi. A pear-shaped motif which descended from the seventeenth- and eighteenth-century 'paisley' shawls of Kashmir (and later Kerman). It has been variously interpreted as representative of a pine cone, a cluster of flowers, the Sacred Flame of Zoroaster, an almond, a pear, and even a closed fist.

BOXFLOWER BORDER Trade term for a border of stepped stylized flowerheads framed by small triangles.

'CHAFER' PALMETTE Geometric palmette design so-called by Ulrich Schürmann because of its resemblance to a beetle called chafer (also related to the scarab and rose bug).

ELEM A 'skirt' or supplementary border. Usually the end panels in Turkoman main carpets and the bottom panels in Turkoman bags.

GUL (GÖL) 'Flower'. A medallion-like emblem used in a variety of (primarily) Turkoman rugs and bags. Elena Tsareva calls it a 'tribal emblem pattern, a kind of coat-of-arms'.

'HEAD AND SHOULDERS' MIHRAB In prayer rugs, a turret-like, geometric design of two or three compartments surmounted by an octagon, resembling a keyhole. Also known as a 'keyhole' mihrab.

KEYHOLE MIHRAB See 'Head and Shoulders' mihrab.

KILIM A tapestry-woven, pileless textile.

KOTCHAK (KOCHANAK, GOTCHAK) 'Horn' or 'ram's horn'. A subsidiary motif, often used in Turkoman rugs and as a border or (more rarely) field motif in Caucasian rugs.

'KUFIC' BORDER Type of ornate border design which developed from the ancient calligraphic Kufic script used in Islamic manuscripts, tiles, metalwork, carpets and textiles.

LEAF-AND-CALYX BORDER Type of border design, most often used in Kazak rugs, which combines diagonal, serrated leaves with geometric calyxes. Also known as leaf-and-winecup or leaf-and-chalice (the calyxes resemble winecups or chalices).

MEDACHYL BORDER A reciprocal diamond and triangle border which derived from the more ornate reciprocating trefoil motif.

MEMLING GUL Stepped, hooked floral motif named after Hans Memling, a fifteenth-century painter whose works often included rugs with this design.

MET-HANE Design featuring an empty field, often abrashed.

PINWHEEL Kazak design patterned after the ancient swastika motif.

RAM'S HORN See Kotchak.

SAFF (SAPH) Multiple-niche, horizontally aligned prayer rug, sometimes called a 'family prayer rug'.

'SOLOMON' STAR Eight-pointed star.

TREE OF LIFE Geometric or naturalistic motif appearing in many oriental rugs, most frequently in Baluch rugs. Among Caucasian rugs, it is most often seen in Kazaks. The meaning of the Tree of Life (also sometimes referred to as the Tree of Knowledge) has been the subject of varied theories, none of which has won general acceptance.

GLOSSARY

ACHDJIAN Albert. *Le Tapis /
The Rug*. Paris: Editions Self, 1949.

—. *Tapis d'orient anciens* (exhibition
catalogue). Paris: Achdjian & Fils, 1979.

ALEXANDER Christopher.
A Foreshadowing of 21st Century Art.
Oxford: Oxford University Press, 1973.

AMPE Patrick, and Rie Ampe. *Textile
Art: A Personal Choice.* Antwerp:
Kailash Gallery, 1994.

Antichi tappeti dell'Anatolia e del Caucaso
(exhibition catalogue). Turin: Museo
Nazionale della Montagna, 1986.

ASLANAPA Oktay. *One Thousand
Years of Turkish Carpets.* Istanbul: Eren
Yayinlari Ltd, 1988.

Association libanaise des amateurs
du tapis ancien (ALATA), *Antique and
Ancient Prayer Rugs dating from the
Sixteenth to the Nineteenth Century.*
(exhibition catatalogue). Beirut:
Goethe Institute and ALATA, 1975.

BABAYAN Levon. *The Romance of the
Oriental Rug.* Toronto: Babayan's Ltd,
1925.

BACHARACH Jere L., and Irene A.
Bierman (eds.) *The Warp and Weft of
Islam: Oriental Carpets and Weavings
from Pacific Northwest Collections*
(exhibition catalogue*).* Seattle: Henry
Art Gallery, University of Washington,
1978.

BAILEY Julia, and Mark Hopkins.
*Through the Collector's Eye: Oriental Rugs
from New England Private Collections.*
Providence, Rhode Island: Museum of
Art, Rhode Island School of Design,
1991.

BALPINAR Belkis, and Udo Hirsch.
Carpets of the Vakiflar Museum, Istanbul.
Wesel, Germany: Uta Hülsey, 1988.

BATTILOSSI Maurizio. Dealer's
catalogues:
• *Tappeti d'antiquariato* (Antique
  Carpets). Turin: Battilossi, 1985
• *Tappeti d'antiquariato.* Turin: 1987.
• *Tappeti d'antiquariato.* Turin: 1988.
• *Tappeti d'antiquariato.* Turin: 1989.
• *Tappeti d'antiquariato.* Turin: 1990.

—. *Arte tesseli dell'Azerbadjan, dal 1550 al
1850.* Turin: Battilossi, 1996.

BAUSBACK Peter. Dealer's
catalogues:
• *Alte und Antike Meisterstücke
  Orientalischer Teppichknüpfkunst.*
  Mannheim: 1969.
• *Alte und Antike Meisterstücke
  Orientalischer Teppichknüpfkunst.*
  Mannheim: 1970.
• *Alte und Antike Meisterstücke
  Orientalischer Teppichknüpfkunst.*
  Mannheim: 1971.
• *Alte und Antike Meisterstücke
  Orientalischer Teppichknüpfkunst .*
  Mannheim: 1972.
• *Alte und Antike Meisterstücke
  Orientalischer Teppichknüpfkunst.*
  Mannheim: 1973.

• *Antike Meisterstücke Orientalischer
  Knüpfkunst* (50th Anniversary
  Issue). Mannheim: 1975.
• *Antike Orientalische Knüpfkunst.*
  Mannheim: 1976.
• *Antike Orientalische Knüpfkunst.*
  Mannheim: 1977.
• *Alte und Antike Orientalische
  Knüpfkunst.* Mannheim: 1979.
• *Alte und Antike Orientalische
  Knüpfkunst* Mannheim: 1980.
• *Alte und Antike Orientalische
  Knüpfkunst.* Mannheim: 1981.
• *Alte und Antike Orientalische
  Knüpfkunst.* Mannheim: 1982.
• *Alte und Antike Orientalische
  Knüpfkunst.* Mannheim: 1983.
• *The Old and Antique Oriental Art of
  Weaving* (English edition of 1983
  catalogue). Mannheim: 1983.

—. *Antike Orientteppiche* (Antique
Oriental Carpets). Braunschweig:
Klinkhardt & Biermann, 1978.

—. *Antike Teppiche Sammlung Franz
Bausback* (Franz Bausback Antique
Rugs Collection). Mannheim: Franz
Bausback, 1988.

BEATTIE May H. *The Thyssen-
Bornemisza Collections of Oriental Rugs.*
Castagnola: Villa Favorita, 1972.

BENARDOUT Raymond. *Exhibition
Catalogue, 23 Oct.–4 Nov. 1978.* London:
Raymond Bernardout, 1978.

—. *Antique Rugs.* London: Raymond
Benardout, 1983.

—. *Caucasian Rugs.* London: Raymond
Benardout, 1979.

—. *Woven Stars: Rugs and Textiles from
Southern Californian Collections.*
Newport Beach, California: IPM
Antiques LLC, 1996.

BENET Sula. *Abkhasians: The Long-
Living People of the Caucasus.* New York:
Holt, Rinehart and Winston, Inc., 1974.

BENNETT Ian. *Book of Oriental
Carpets and Rugs.* London: Hamlyn
Publishing Group Ltd, 1972.

—. *Oriental Rugs: Volume 1, Caucasian.*
(N.p.): Oriental Textile Press Ltd, 1981.

—. *Oriental Carpet Identifier.* Secaucus:
Chartwell Books, Inc., 1985.

BENNETT Ian, et al. *Rugs and Carpets
of the World.* New York: A & W
Publishers, 1977.

BENZOOR Nina (ed.). *Mountain
Jews / Urban Moslems* (exhibition
catalogue). Haifa: Music and
Ethnology Museum, 1992.

BLACK David (ed.). *The Macmillan
Atlas of Rugs and Carpets.* New York:
Macmillan Publishing Co., 1985.

BLAIR Sheila S., and Jonathan M.
Bloom (eds). *Images of Paradise in
Islamic Art.* Hanover, New Hampshire:
Hood Museum of Art, Dartmouth
College, 1991.

BODE Wilhelm Von, and Ernst
Kühnel. *Antique Rugs from the Near East.*
London: G. Bell & Sons, 1970.

BUCHANAN Glenn, et al. *Antique
Rugs from the Caucasus* (exhibition
catalogue). Melbourne: Australian
Society for Antique Rugs, 1974.

BURNS James D. *The Caucasus:
Traditions in Weaving.* Seattle,
Washington: Court Street Press, 1987.

BUTTERWECK Georg, et al.
*Antique Oriental Carpets from Austrian
Collections.* Vienna: Society for Textile
Art Research, 1986.

CASSIN Jack. *Kelim, Soumak, Carpet
and Cloth: Tribal Weavings of the
Caucasus.* New York: Jack Cassin, 1990.

COEN Luciano, and Louise Duncan.
The Oriental Rug. New York: Harper
and Row, 1978.

COHEN Maria. *Tappeti Kazak* (Kazak
Rugs). Turin: Umberto Allemandi &
C., 1984.

—. *Shirwan.* Turin: Umberto
Allemandi & C., 1995.

COOTNER Cathryn M. *Oriental Rugs,
An Introduction: Prayer Rugs* (exhibition
catalogue). Palo Alto, California: Palo
Alto Cultural Center, 1974.

—. *The Arthur D. Jenkins Collection,
volume 1: Flat-Woven Textiles.*
Washington, DC: The Textile Museum,
1981.

—. *Prayer Rugs from the Near East and
Central Asia* (exhibition
pamphlet). San Francisco: M.H. De
Young Memorial Museum, 1984.

COXON Herbert. *Oriental Carpets,
How They Are Made and Conveyed to
Europe with a Narrative of a Journey to
the East in Search of Them.* London:
Unwin, 1884.

CROSSELY Louise (ed.). *Unravelling
the Rug Puzzle* (exhibition catalogue).
New South Wales: Trustees of the
Museum of Applied Arts and Sciences,
1983.

CURATOLA Giovanni. *The Simon
& Schuster Book of Oriental Carpets.*
New York: Simon & Schuster, 1982.

DE CALATCHI Robert. *Oriental
Carpets.* Rutland, Vermont and Tokyo,
Japan: Charles E. Tuttle Company, 1970.

DE HELL Xavier Hommaire. *Travels
in the Steppes of the Caspian Sea, The
Crimea, and The Caucasus.* London:
Chapman & Hall, 1847.

DECREDICO A.V., and W.R.
Pickering. *Oriental Rugs from Members of
the Oriental Rug Society of New England*
(exhibition catalogue). Providence,
Rhode Island: Brown University, 1975.

DENNY Walter B. *Oriental Rugs.*
Washington: The Smithsonian
Institution, 1979.

—. *Looms of Splendor: Oriental Rugs from Columbus Collections* (exhibition catalogue). Columbus: Columbus Museum of Art, 1980.

—. *Sotheby's Guide to Oriental Carpets.* New York: Simon & Schuster, 1994.

DENNY Walter B., and Daniel Walker. *The Markarian Album.* Cincinnati: The Markarian Foundation, 1988.

Descriptive catalogue of an Exhibition of Oriental Rugs from the Collection of James Franklin Ballard. San Francisco: San Francisco of Modern Art, 1923.

DILLEY Arthur Urbane (revised by M.S. Dimand). *Oriental Rugs and Carpets, A Comprehensive Study.* New York and Philadelphia: J.B. Lippincott Co., 1959.

DIMAND Maurice S. *The Ballard Collection of Oriental Rugs in the City Art Museum, St Louis.* St Louis, Missouri: City Art Museum of St Louis, 1935.

—. *Peasant and Nomad Rugs of Asia.* New York: Asia House Gallery, 1961.

DIMAND Maurice S., and Jean Mailey. *Oriental Rugs in The Metropolitan Museum of Art.* New York: Metropolitan Museum of Art, 1973.

DODDS Dennis R. *Oriental Rugs: The Collection of Dr & Mrs Robert A. Fisher in the Virginia Museum of Fine Arts.* Richmond, Virginia: Virginia Museum of Fine Arts, 1985.

DODDS Dennis R., and Murray L. Eiland, Jr. *Oriental Rugs from Atlantic Collections.* Philadelphia: Eighth ICOC, Inc. 1996.

DONCHIAN John B. *Threads from the Oriental Loom.* (N.p.): John B. Donchian, 1913.

DOUGLASS J. M., and S. N. Peters. *The Lost Language.* Vols. 1 and 2. Bell Canyon, California: WNL Communications, 1990.

DUMAS Hillary, and Gilbert Dumas. *Trefoil: Güls, Stars and Gardens.* Oakland, California: Mills College Art Gallery, 1990.

EILAND Murray L. *Oriental Rugs, A Comprehensive Guide.* Greenwich, Connecticut: New York Graphic Society, 1973.

—. *Oriental Rugs, A New Comprehensive Guide.* Boston: Little, Brown and Co., 1981. (Revised and updated edition to be published as *Oriental Rugs: A Complete Guide,* with Murray Eiland III. London: Laurence King Publishing, 1998.)

—. *Oriental Rugs from Pacific Collections.* San Francisco: San Francisco Bay Area Rug Society, 1990.

EILAND Murray L., Jr., Robert Pinner and Walter B. Denny (eds). *Oriental Carpet and Textile Studies, IV.* Berkley, California: San Francisco Bay Area Rug Society and OCTS Ltd, 1993.

ELLIS Charles Grant. *Early Caucasian Rugs.* Washington, DC: The Textile Museum, 1975.

—. *Oriental Carpets in the Philadelphia Museum of Art.* Philadelphia: Philadelphia Museum of Art, 1988.

ELLWANGER W.D. *The Oriental Rug.* New York: Dodd, Mead and Co., 1903.

ENGELHARDT Eva. *Teppiche die Bilder des Orients* (Carpets, Pictures of the Orient). Heidelberg: Carl Winter Universitäts Verlag, 1977.

—. *Teppiche die Bilder des Orients* (Carpets, Pictures of the Orient), vol. 2. Trans. Jim Ford. Heidelberg: Carl Winter Universitäts Verlag, 1978.

ENGELHARDT Horst, and Eva Engelhardt. *Orientteppiche der Sonderklasse* (Exceptional Oriental Carpets). Heidelberg: Carl Winter Universitäts Verlag, 1980, 1982, 1990.

ERDMANN Kurt. *Seven Hundred Years of Oriental Carpets.* London: Faber and Faber, 1970.

—. *Oriental Carpets, An Account of their History.* Fishguard, Wales: The Crosby Press, 1976.

ERDMANN Kurt, et al. *Kaukasische Teppiche* (Caucasian Rugs) (exhibition catalogue). Frankfurt: Museum für Kunsthandwerk, 1961.

ESKENAZI John J. *L'arte del tappeto orientale.* Milan: Giorgio Mondadori e Associati, 1983.

ETTINGHAUSEN Richard. *Ancient Carpets in the L.A. Mayer Memorial Institute.* Jerusalem: L.A. Mayer Memorial Institute for Islamic Art, 1977.

ETTINGHAUSEN Richard, M.S. Dimand, Louise W. Mackie, Charles Grant Ellis. *Prayer Rugs* (exhibition catalogue). Washington, DC: The Textile Museum, 1974.

ETTINGHAUSEN Richard, and Ernest H. Robert. *Bulletin, Allen Memorial Art Museum,* Oberlin, Ohio: Oberlin College, 1978.

EVANS Bill. *Caspian Gallery Brochure.* Paddington, New South Wales: Caspian Gallery, 1989.

—. *Caspian Gallery Brochure: Woven Art of the Caucasus.* Paddington, New South Wales: Caspian Gallery, 1992.

FENLON Sharon. *Oriental Rugs: An Exhibit from Area Collections* (exhibition catalogue). Neenah, Wisconsin: John Nelson Bergstom Art Center and Museum, 1979.

FISKE Patricia L. *Prayer Rugs from Private Collections* (exhibition catalogue). Washington, DC: The Textile Museum, 1975.

—. *Caucasian Rugs from Private Collections* (exhibition catatalogue). Washington, DC: The Textile Museum, 1976.

FOKKER Nicolas. *Caucasian Rugs of Yesterday.* London: George Allen and Unwin Ltd, 1979.

FORMENTON Fabio. *Oriental Rugs and Carpets.* London: Hamlyn, 1972.

FRANSES Michael. *The World of Rugs* (exhibition catalogue). London: Hugh M. Moss Ltd, 1973.

FRESHWELD Douglas W. *The Exploration of the Caucasus* (2 vols). London and New York: Edward Arnold, 1896.

GANS-RUEDIN Erwin. *Caucasian Carpets.* New York: Rizzoli, 1986.

—. *Antique Oriental Carpets.* Tokyo and New York: Kodansha International, 1975.

GANTZHORN Volkmar. *The Christian Oriental Carpet.* Cologne: Benedikt Taschen Verlag, 1991.

GARDINER Roger F. *Oriental Rugs from Canadian Collections* (exhibition catalogue). Ontario: Oriental Rug Society, Inc., 1975.

GOMBOS Károly. *Régi Keleti Imaszönyegek / Old Prayer Rugs* (exhibition booklet). Szolnok, Hungary: Damjanich János Museum, n.d.

—. *Régi Keleti Imaszönyegek / Old Prayer Rugs* (exhibition pamphlet). Budapest: Castle Museum of Nagytétény, 1979.

—. *Aszkéták, Dervisek, Imaszönyegek* (Ascetics, Dervishes and Prayer Rugs). Budapest: Museum of Applied Arts, 1984.

GREGORIAN Arthur T., and Joyce Gregorian Hampshire. *Armenian Rugs from the Gregorian Collection* (exhibition catalogue). Newton, Massachusetts: 1987.

GROGAN Michael B. *Town and Tribal Carpets* (exhibition catalogue). Newton, Massachusetts: Barry Fine Art Pavilion, Boston College, 1984.

GROTE-HASENBALG Werner. *Der Orientteppich, Seine Geschichte und Seine Kultur* (3 vols). Berlin: Scarabaeus, 1922.

Guide to the Collection of Carpets. London: Victoria and Albert Museum Dept of Textiles, The Board of Education, 1931.

HAACK Hermann. *Oriental Rugs, An Illustrated Guide.* London: Faber and Faber, 1972.

Hali: The International Magazine of Antique Carpet and Textile Art. London: Hali Publications Ltd, 1978 (vol. 1 / 1) to March 1997 (vol. 91), particularly the following:

- Amirian, Lemyel. 'The Origin of the Dragon and Phoenix Rug in Berlin.' *Hali* 4 / 1, p. 31.
- Bier, Carol. 'Weavings from the Caucasus, Tradition and Technology.' *Hali* 48, pp. 17–25.
- Boëly, Gérard. 'A Tree of Life Rug' (Connoisseur's Choice). *Hali* 54, pp. 104–105.
- Franke, Jerome. 'Carpets of the Caucasus: Dramatic designs from before the Russian Revolution.' *Hali* 34, p. 95.
- Franses, Michael, and Robert Pinner. 'Star Kazaks.' *Hali* 3 / 1, pp. 17–26.
- Gombos, Károly. 'Old Caucasian Rugs' (exhibition review). *Hali* 1 / 4. pp. 368–70.
- Houston, Robert G. 'The Pittsburgh Rug Society Caucasian Rug Exhibition.' *Hali* 2 / 4, pp. 339–40.
- Kerimov, Liatif. Classification of the rugs of Azerbaijan. *Hali* 3 / 1, pp. 27–30.
- King, Donald, Michael Franses and Robert Pinner. 'Caucasian Rugs in the Victoria and Albert Museum.' *Hali* 3 / 2, pp. 95–115.
- Klose, Christine. 'The Perepedil Enigma.' *Hali* 55, pp. 110–17.
- Lefevre, Jean. 'Unidentified Caucasian Rugs.' *Hali* 2 / 3, pp. 216–18.
- Schürmann, Ulrich. 'The Age and Artistic Value of Caucasian Carpets.' *Hali* 2 / 3, pp. 214–15.
- Shaffer, Daniel. 'The Boston Rug Party.' *Hali* 62, pp. 96–99.
- Shelley, Louise, and Richard E. Wright. 'Caucasian Rugs in the late Nineteenth Century.' *Hali* 3 / 1, pp. 3–7.
- 'Three Caucasian Rugs photographed in 1885.' *Hali* 3 / 1, p. 47.
- Tschebull, Raoul. 'The Development of Four Kazak Designs.' *Hali* 1 / 3, pp. 257–61.
- —. 'Methods of Dating Caucasian Village and Nomad Rugs.' *Hali* 2 / 3, pp. 218–21.
- —. 'Zeikhur.' *Hali* 62, pp. 84–95.

HANWAY Jonas. *An Historical Account of the British Trade over the Caspian Sea with a Journal of Travels* (4 vols). London: 1753.

HARRIS Nathaniel. *Rugs and Carpets of the Orient.* London: Hamlyn Publishing Group Ltd, 1977.

HARRIS Walter B., F.R.G.S. *From Batum to Baghdad via Tiflis, Tabriz and Persian Kurdistan.* Edinburgh and London: William Blackwood and Sons, 1896 (first published 1846).

HASSON Rachel. *Caucasian Rugs.* Jerusalem: L.A. Mayer Memorial Institute for Islamic Art, 1986.

—. *Caucasian Rugs* (Hebrew edition). Jerusalem: L.A. Mayer Memorial Institute for Islamic Art. Jerusalem, 1986.

HAWLEY Walter A. *Oriental Rugs Antique and Modern*. New York: Dover Publications, 1970 (reprint; orig. pub. 1921).

HERMANN Fritz. *Teppiche Aus dem Orient* (Rugs of the Orient) (exhibition catalogue). Zurich: Museum Rietberg, 1986.

HERRMANN Eberhart. Exhibition catalogues:
• *Von Lotto bis Tekke* (*Seltene Orientteppiche aus Vier Jahrhunderten*). Munich: 1978.
• *Von Uschak bis Yarkand* (*Seltene Orientteppiche aus Vier Jahrhunderten*). Munich: 1979.
• *Von Konya bis Kokand* (*Seltene Orientteppiche/Rare Oriental Carpets*). Munich: 1980.
• *Seltene Orientteppiche/Rare Oriental Carpets*, vol. IV. Munich, 1982.
• *Seltene Orientteppiche*, vol. V. Munich: 1983.
• *Seltene Orientteppiche*, vol. VI. Munich: 1984.
• *Seltene Orientteppiche*, vol. VII. Munich: 1985.
• *Seltene Orientteppiche*, vol. VIII. Munich: 1986.
• *Seltene Orientteppiche*, vol. IX. Munich: 1987.
• *Seltene Orientteppiche*, vol. X. Munich: 1988.
• *Asiatische Teppich und Textilekunst*. Band 1. Munich: 1989. (English Supplement: *Asian Carpet and Textile Art*, vol. 1.)
• *Asiatische Teppich und Textilekunst*. Band 2. Munich: 1990.
• *Asiatische Teppich und Textilekunst*. Band 3. Munich: 1991.
• *Asiatische Teppich und Textilekunst*. Band 4. Munich: 1992.

—. *Kaukasische Teppichkunst im 19. Jahrhundert: Ein Bilderbuch*. Munich: Eberhart Herrmann, 1993.

HOLT Rosa Belle. *Oriental and Occidental Rugs, Antique and Modern*. Chicago: A.C. McClurg Co., 1901.

HOPF Albrecht. *Tapis d'orient*. Paris: Morance, 1962.

HUBEL Reinhard. *Alte Orientteppiche und Nomadadenknüpfarbeiten*. Munich: Staatliches Museum für Volkerkunde, 1978.

—. *The Book of Carpets*. Accokeek, Maryland: Washington International Associates, 1979.

ITTIG Annette. *Woven Dreams: Oriental Carpets from the Collection of the Montreal Museum of Fine Arts*. Montreal: 1994.

JACKSON A.V. Williams. *From Constantinople to the Home of Omar Khayyam*. New York: The Macmillan Company, 1911.

JACOBSEN Charles W. *Oriental Rugs, A Complete Guide*. Rutland, Vermont and Tokyo: Charles E. Tuttle Company, 1962.

JACOBY Heinrich. *En Samling Orientaliska Mattor* (A Collection of Oriental Rugs). Stockholm: Tryckeri Artiebolaget Thule, 1935.

—. *Meisterstücke Orientalischer Knüpfkunst* (exhibition catalogue). Wiesbaden: Im Städt Museum, 1966.

JAJCZAY Janos. *Acta Historiae Artium: Symbology of the Oriental Carpet*. Budapest: Académiai Kiadó, 1975.

JENSEN Inge Lise. *Kaukasiske Taepper en Dansk Privatsamling* (Caucasian Rugs: A Private Danish Collection). Køge, Denmark, 1974.

Katalog (exhibition catalogue). Cracow: Wystawy Kobierców Museum Narodowem, 1934.

KEANE Augustus H., M.A.I. *Asia, with Ethnological Appendix*. London: Edward Stanford, 1882.

KELL Thomas R., and R. Jay Friedmann. *Oriental Rug Price Guide*. Carpinteria, California: Tom Kell and Jay Friedman, 1977.

KENDRICK A.F., and C.E.C. Tattersall. *Handwoven Carpets: Oriental and European*. London: Benn Brothers Ltd, 1922.

—. *Fine Carpets in the Victoria and Albert Museum*. London: Ernest Benn Ltd, 1924.

KERIMOV Liatif, et al. *Rugs and Carpets from the Caucasus: The Russian Collections*. London and Leningrad: Aurora Art Publishers, 1984.

—. *Azerbaijansky Kovjer* (Azerbaijan Carpets). Baku: Ministry of Culture, 1961.

KESHISHIAN Harold M. *The Treasure of the Caucasus* (exhibition catalogue). Washington, DC: Near Eastern Art and Research Center, 1992.

KESHISHIAN James Mark. *Inscribed Armenian Rugs of Yesteryear*. Washington, DC: Near Eastern Art Research Center, 1994.

KEVORKIAN R.H., and Berdj Achdjian. *Tapis et textiles arméniens*. Marseilles: La Maison Arménienne, 1991.

KING Donald, and David Sylvester. *The Eastern Carpet in the Western World from the 15th to the 17th Century*. London: Arts Council of Great Britain, 1983.

KING Steven. *Prayer Rugs* (exhibition catalogue). Concord, MA: The Steven King Gallery, 1983.

KIRCHHEIM E. Heinrich, et al. *Orient Stars: A Carpet Collection*. Stuttgart: E. Heinrich Kirchheim and London: Hali Publications Ltd, 1993.

KRAUSSE Hans-Jurgen. *Frühe Teppichkunst* (Early Carpet Art). Munich: 1990.

KREIDER Lois Sommer, and John Sommer. *Anatolian Carpets: A Family Connection* (exhibition catalogue). North Newton, Kansas: Kauffman Museum, 1986.

KYBURZ Gustav, et al. *Alte Teppich Aus dem Orient* (Old Oriental Rugs) (exhibition catalogue). Basel: Gewerbemuseum, 1980.

LANDREAU Anthony N., and W.R. Pickering. *From the Bosporus to Samarkand: Flat-Woven Rugs*. Washington, DC: The Textile Museum, 1969.

LANGLANDS Ross and Irene. *Rare Oriental Rugs, Nomadic Rug Traders*. Pyrmont, Australia: 1993.

LEDERMAN A.J., Daniel Walker and Marilyn Wolf. *A Skein Through Time* (exhibition catalogue). New York: The Hajji Baba Club, 1996.

LEFEVRE Jean, and Jon Thompson. *Caucasian Carpets from the 17th to the 19th Century*. London: Lefevre and Partners, 1977.

LERCH Max. *Teppichhaus Lerch* (dealer's catalogue). Munich: Max Lerch, 1991.

LEWIS George Griffin. *The Practical Book of Oriental Rugs*. Philadelphia: J.B. Lippincott Company, 1920.

MACEY R.E.G. *Oriental Prayer Rugs*. Leigh-on-Sea: F. Lewis Publishers Ltd, 1971 (reprint).

MACLEAN Fitzroy. *To Caucasus, the End of all the Earth (An Illustrated Companion to the Caucasus and Transcaucasia)*. Boston and Toronto: Little, Brown and Co., 1976.

MANUELIAN Lucy Der, and Murray L. Eiland. *Weavers, Merchants and Kings: The Inscribed Rugs of Armenia* (exhibition catalogue). Fort Worth, Texas: Kimbell Art Museum, 1984.

MARTIN F.R. *A History of Oriental Carpets before 1800*. Vienna: Imperial and Royal State and Printing Office, 1908.

MCGONAGLE William A., and Ruth H. Cloudman. *A Rich Inheritance* (exhibition catalogue). Omaha, Nebraska: Joslyn Art Museum, 1975.

MCMULLAN Joseph V. *Islamic Carpets*. New York: Near Eastern Art Research Center, 1965.

MCMULLAN Joseph V., and Donald O. Reichert. *The George W. Vincent and Belle Townsley Smith Collection of Islamic Rugs*. Springfield, Massachusetts: G.W.V. Smith Art Museum, (n.d.).

MCQUADE Walter. 'Flying High on Magic Carpets.' *Fortune* magazine, May 1968, pp. 162–67.

MESCHOULAM Eber. *Mostra del tappeto d'arte*. Genoa: 1984.

MEYER-PÜNTER Carl. *Der Orient-Teppich in Geschichte Kunstgewerb und Handel* (The Oriental Rug in Art History and Trade). Zurich: Carl Meyer-Pünter, 1917.

MIDDLETON Andrew. *Rugs and Carpets: Techniques, Traditions and Designs*. London: Mitchell Beazley, 1996.

MILHOFER Stefan A. *The Colour Treasury of Oriental Rugs*. Oxford: Phaidon Press Ltd, 1976.

MILLS John. *Carpets in Paintings*. London: National Gallery, 1983.

MOSTAFA Dr Mohamed. *Turkish Prayer Rugs: Collections of the Museum of Islamic Art, I*. Cairo: Education Press, 1953.

MOUNSEY Augustus H., F.R.G.S. *A Journey Through the Caucasus and the Interior of Persia*. London: Smith, Elder & Co., 1872.

MUMFORD John K. *Oriental Rugs*. New York: Charles Scribner's Sons, 1900.

NEFF Ivan C., and Carol V. Maggs. *Dictionary of Oriental Rugs*. Johannesburg and London: A.D. Donker Ltd., 1977.

NEMATI Parviz. *Rugs as an Investment*. New York: Agate Press, 1980.

NEUGEBAUER R., and Julius Orendi. *Handbuch der Orientalischen Teppichkunde* (Handbook of Oriental Rug Art). Leipzig: Hiersemann, 1909.

NEUGEBAUER R., and Siegfried Troll. *Handbuch der Orientalischen Teppichkunde* (Handbook of Oriental Rug Art). Leipzig: Hiersemann, 1930.

OAKLEY Penny. *Oriental Carpets and Textiles*. London: Bernheimer Fine Arts Ltd, 1987.

O'BANNON George. *Oriental Rugs from Western Pennsylvania Collections* (exhibition catalogue). Greensburg, Pennsylvania: The Westmoreland County Museum of Art, 1975.

—. *Woven Treasure* (exhibition catalogue). Princeton, New Jersey: The Squibb Gallery, 1986.

—. *Oriental Rugs: The Collector's Guide to Selecting, Identifying and Enjoying New and Antique Oriental Rugs*. London: Courage Books, Quintet Publishing Ltd, 1995.

ÖLÇER Nazan, et al. *Turkish Carpets from the 13th to the 18th Centuries*. Istanbul: Ahmet Ertug, 1996.

OPIE James. *Tribal Rugs: Nomadic and Village Weavings from the Near East and Central Asia*. Portland, Oregon: The Tolstoy Press, 1992.

Oriental Rug Review. Meredith, New Hampshire, March 1981 (vol. 1/1) to Dec. 1995/Jan. 1996 (vol. 16), particularly the following:
- Amirian, Lemyel. 'The Pazyryk Rug, Another View.' *ORR* 1/8, pp. 7–8.
- —. 'The Village of Khondzores.' *ORR* 4/2, pp. 56–57.
- Bloom, Joseph. 'Collecting according to Burns.' *ORR* 8/1, p. 24.
- Boxdorfer, Loretta. 'A review of "Eastern Armenia in the Last Decades of the Persian Rule 1807–1923" by George A. Bermontian.' *ORR* 3/5, pp. 10–11.
- Callison, Elizabeth. 'Unorthodox Conservation of a Marasali Prayer Carpet.' *ORR* 6/11, p. 4.
- Davis, Michael. 'Prayer Rugs' (exhibition review). *ORR* 4/10, p. 25.
- Fling, Russell S. 'Armenia, Ancient Republic Survives.' *ORR* 3/9, pp. 367–68.
- Gombos, Károly. 'Prayer Rugs.' *ORR* 2/6, pp. 2–3.
- Houston, Robert G. 'Islamic Prayer Rugs' (exhibition review). *ORR* 2/12, pp. 23–24.
- Long, Joan C. 'Passages: Art in the BART' (exhibition review). *ORR* 11/3.
- Milberg, David R. 'A History for the Buta.' *ORR* 9/6, pp. 24–26.
- Musak, Paul, and George O'Bannon. 'An Unusual Shirvan of the Commercial Period.' *ORR* 3/2, pp. 16–19.
- O'Bannon, George. 'A Group of rugs attributed to Shusha.' *ORR* 3/4, pp. 2–5.
- —. 'The Rugs of Glencairn.' *ORR* 9/5, cover and pp. 14–18.
- —. 'Caucasian Rug Nomenclature and Structure.' *ORR* 10/4, pp. 40–41.
- *ORR* staff. 'A Caucasian Rug Book Bibliography.' *ORR* 10/4, p. 54.
- —. 'A Price Guide to Five Caucasian Rug Types from 1983 to 1990.' *ORR* 10/4, pp. 30–34.
- Price, Steven. 'Dyes and Dating Caucasian Weavings.' *ORR* 15/4, pp. 52–53.
- Scheller, William. 'In the Caucasus in 1889–90.' *ORR* 2/8, pp. 18–19.
- Sella, Vittorio. 'In the Caucasus in 1889–90: a portfolio of photographs.' *ORR* 2/8, pp. 1–3, 18, 19, 36.
- Stone, Peter F. 'Daghestan, Derbend and Lesghistan.' *ORR* 4/8, pp. 26–29.
- Van Mierlo. 'A Group of Kars Rugs and their Relations to Transcaucasian Rugs.' *ORR* 11/3, pp. 22–25.
- Wright, Richard E. 'On the Origins of Caucasian Village Rugs.' *ORR* 10/4, pp. 44–48.
- —. 'The Prayer Rug Observed.' *ORR* 8/5, pp. 15–19.

PICKERING William Russell, et al. *Divine Images and Magic Carpets from the Asian Art Collection of Dr and Mrs William T. Price* (exhibition catalogue). Amarillo, Texas: Amarillo Art Center, 1987.

PINNER Robert, and Walter B. Denny (eds). *Oriental Carpet & Textile Studies I.* London: Hali Magazine and OCTS Ltd, 1985.

—. *Oriental Carpet & Textile Studies II: Carpets of the Mediterranean Countries 1400–1600.* London: Hali Magazine and OCTS Ltd, 1986.

—. *Oriental Carpet & Textile Studies III, part 1.* London: Hali Magazine and OCTS Ltd, 1987.
—. *Oriental Carpet & Textile Studies III, part 2.* London: Sotheby's and OCTS Ltd, 1989.

POPE Arthur Upham. *Catalogue of a Loan Exhibition of Early Oriental Carpets.* Chicago: The Art Club of Chicago, 1926.

PURDON Richard, et al. *Shirvan and Related Weavings from the North Caucasus.* Cirencester, England: Thornborough Galleries, 1978.

PUSHMAN Garabed T. *Art Panels from the Handlooms of the Far Orient as Seen by a Native Rug Weaver.* Chicago: Pushman Bros, 1911 (orig. pub. 1902).

REED Stanley. *Oriental Rugs and Carpets.* New York: Putnams, 1967.

RIEGL Alois. *Altorientalische Teppiche* (Old Oriental Rugs). Leipzig: T.O. Weigel Nachfolger, 1891.

ROALFE W. Robert. *Collectors' Choice* (exhibition catalogue). San Francisco: Samarkand Gallery, 1973.

ROBERTS Ernest H. *Treasures from Near Eastern Looms* (exhibition catalogue). Brunswick, Maine: Ernest H. Roberts, 1981.

ROLL Christian. 'Prayer Rugs of the East.' *Arts of Asia* July/Aug. 1974, pp. 47–57.

ROPERS Hinrich. *Morgenländische Teppiche* (Eastern Carpets). Berlin: Schmidt and Co., 1922.

SARRE Friedrich, and Hermann Trenkwald. *Alt-Orientalische Teppiche* (Old Oriental Carpets) (2 vols). Trans. A.F. Kendrick. Vienna: Anton Schroll and Co., 1926.

SASSOUNI Viken, et al. *Calendar of Armenian Rugs, 1982.* Chevy Chase, Maryland: Armenian Rug Society, 1981.

SAUNDERS Peter E. *Tribal Visions* (exhibition catalogue). Novato, California: Marin Cultural Center, 1981.

SCHLOSSER Ignaz. *The Book of Rugs, Oriental and European.* New York: Crown Publishers, 1963.

SCHÜRMANN Ulrich. *Caucasian Rugs.* Accokeek, Maryland: Washington International Associates, 1974.

—. *Oriental Carpets.* London: Octopus Books, 1979.

—. *The Pazyryk, Its Use and Origin.* New York: Armenian Rug Society, 1984.

SCHWARTZ Hans-Günther. *Carpets from the Orient* (exhibition catalogue). Halifax, Nova Scotia: Dalhousie Art Gallery, Dalhousie University, 1977.

SEVI Daniele. *Tappeti caucasici del XVIII XIX secolo* (Caucasian Rugs of the 18th and 19th Centuries). Milan: Daniele Sevi, 1982.

SEWELL Jack V., and Donald Jenkins. *Near Eastern Art in Chicago Collections* (exhibition catalogue). Chicago: The Art Institute of Chicago, 1973.

SPUHLER Friedrich. *Islamic Carpets and Textiles in the Keir Collection.* London: Faber and Faber, 1978.

—. *Oriental Carpets in the Museum of Islamic Art, Berlin.* Washington, DC: Smithsonian Institution Press, 1987.

SPUHLER Friedrich, Hans König and Martin Volkmann. *Old Eastern Carpets, Masterpieces in German Private Collections.* Vol 1. Munich: Verlag Callwey, 1978.

STONE Peter F. *Rugs of the Caucasus: Structure and Design.* Chicago: Greenleaf Co., 1984.

—. *The Oriental Rug Lexicon,* Seattle: University of Washington Press, 1997.

— (ed.). *Mideast Meets Midwest: Ethnographic Rugs from Midwest Collections.* Chicago: The Chicago Rug Society, 1993.

STRAKA Jerome A., and Louise W. Mackie. *The Oriental Rug Collection of Jerome and Mary Jane Straka.* Washington, DC: The Textile Museum, 1978.

SYLVESTER David, Joseph McMullan, and May H. Beattie. *Islamic Carpets from the Collection of Joseph V. McMullan* (exhibition catalogue). London: The Arts Council of Great Britain, 1972.

TATTERSALL C.E.C. *Notes on Carpet Knotting and Weaving.* London: Victoria and Albert Museum, 1969.

THOMPSON Jon. *Carpet Magic: The Art of Carpets from the Tents, Cottages and Workshops of Asia.* London: Barbican Art Gallery, 1983.

The Tiffany Studios Collection of Notable Antique Oriental Rugs. New York: Tiffany Studios, 1906.

TSCHEBULL Raoul. *Kazak.* New York: Near Eastern Art Research Center and the New York Rug Society, 1971.

—. 'Kazak Rugs.' *The Textile Museum Journal* II/2, 1971, pp. 2–5.

VEGH Gyula, and Károly Layer. *Turkish Rugs in Transylvania* (new edition by Marino and Clara Dall'Oglio). Fishguard, Wales: The Crosby Press, 1977.

VOK Ignazio. *Caucasus Persia: Gilim and Other Flatweaves.* Munich: Edition Vok, 1996.

VOLKMANN Martin. *Old Eastern Carpets: Masterpieces in German Private Collections.* Vol. 2. Munich: Verlag Georg D.W. Callwey, 1985.

VON KOTZEBUE Moritz. *Narrative of a Journey into Persia, in the suite of the Imperial Russian Embassy, in the year 1817.* London: Longman, Hurst, Rees, Ormé and Brown, 1819.

WALKER Daniel S. *Oriental Rugs of the Hajji Babas.* New York: The Asia Society and Harry N. Abrams, Inc., 1982.

—. *Oriental Rugs in Cincinnati Collections* (exhibition catalogue). Cincinnati: Cincinnati Art Museum, 1976.

WARE Joyce C. *Official Price Guide: Oriental Rugs.* New York: House of Collectables, 1992.

WHEELER Pamela. *Antique Rugs from the Caucasus Region of Russia* (exhibition catalogue). San Francisco: Pamela Wheeler, 1974.

WILLBORG Peter. *Textile Treasures from Five Centuries* (exhibition catalogue). Stockholm: J.P. Willborg Antique Rugs, 1995.

WOLFE ffrida, and A.T. Wolfe. *How to Identify Oriental Rugs.* London: Ernest Benn Ltd, and New York: Harper & Brothers Publishers, 1927.

WRIGHT Richard E. *Rugs and Flatweaves of the Transcaucasus.* Pittsburg: Pittsburg Rug Society, 1980.

WRIGHT Richard E., and John T. Wertime. *Caucasian Carpets and Covers: The Weaving Culture.* London: Hali Publications Ltd in association with Laurence King, 1995.

YERKES Charles T. *The Charles T. Yerkes Collection* (auction catalogue). New York: The American Art Association, 1910.

YETKIN Şerare. *Early Caucasian Carpets in Turkey,* vols 1 and 2. London: Oguz Press Ltd, 1978.

ZADEH GALLERY. *Pars: Carpets in the Persian Style* (exhibition catalogue). London: Zadah Persian Carpets, 1983.

ZAVITUKHINA M.P., et al. *Frozen Tombs: The Culture and Art of the Ancient Tribes of Siberia.* London: British Museum Publications Ltd, 1978.